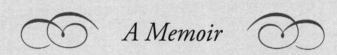

Drinking from the Saucer

A Memoir

Charlene C. Duline

authorHOUSE®

AuthorHouse™
1663 Liberty Drive, Suite 200
Bloomington, IN 47403
www.authorhouse.com
Phone: 1-800-839-8640

First published by AuthorHouse   4/23/2008

ISBN: 978-1-4343-8104-0 (sc)

Library of Congress Control Number: 2008903285

Printed in the United States of America
Bloomington, Indiana

This book is printed on acid-free paper.

Acknowledgments

I am indebted to the following people for their contributions to my life and to this book:

To my "other parents," Mama Gladys Jackson and Daddy Dougie Jackson, for always being there when I needed them and for being the most loving parents a girl could ever have.

To O. Lucille Powell, for having so much faith in me, and pushing and prodding me to finish this book before she "leaves this earth."

To my "sisters," Joyce Poindexter, Bernie Easton, and Queen Johnson, who have always been loving, caring and understanding; blood sisters couldn't be thicker or more loving.

To another sister and brother of mine who have made a spiritual difference in my life – Nona and Gene Dottery.

To my "brothers," Michael E. Weider, my heart's own; Christopher Beakey, writer extraordinaire, and Kenton Draigh, a Peace Corps brother since 1962.

To my Foreign Service sistahs, Sallybeth Bumbrey, Millie McCoo, the late Pat Byrd, Joan V. Smith, Lucille Thomas Lea, Vivian Harvey, Dorothy Anderson, Rosemary Crockett, Dorothy Whitehead and Mattie Sharpless, among others.

To all my children: Sweetmeat, Amy, Happy, Sheba, Sugarfoot, Missy, Tweetie-Pie, Ebony and her favorite kitties, Samantha, Lou, Darwin and Boomer.

To my former secondary school teachers who always inspired me, visited me in Paris, put me in the School #87 Hall of Fame, Mrs. Blanche Butts and Mrs. Katherine Mayes.

To all of my incarcerated fallen angels who are prayed for daily: may God's choicest blessings be yours in abundance. Thank you for your love and trust. God loves you and so do I.

To the widow of Fr. John Crowley, Dolores Crowley, my Alaskan sister, who reaches out to me and to our fallen angels, even in her deep grief over the devastating loss of her beloved husband.

To all of the fantastic women who have been a part of my life: my grandmother, Gertrude Small; my mother, Bertha M. Small; my aunts, Bessie Johnson, Alma Greene, Annie Jackson, and Johnnie Barry. Until we meet again.

Drinking from the Saucer

I've never made a fortune and I'll never make one now,
But it doesn't matter 'cause I'm happy anyhow.
As I go along my journey I've reaped more than I've sowed.
I'm drinking from the saucer 'cause my cup has overflowed.
(Amen)

John Paul Moore
copyright 1970

In the Beginning
Indianapolis — 1937 — 1946

Been in Sorrow's kitchen and licked out all the pots.
- Zora Neal Hurston

A small woman lay in a large bed in another woman's house. She was my grandmother, and she was dying. She reached out to take the cold glass of buttermilk from me. Our hands lightly touched. She seemed to be withering away. She smiled at me, and reached under her pillow where she kept her insurance money and handed me a dime. I managed a small smile and quickly left the room where death hovered. I didn't understand why Mama, as I called her, was in bed all the time these days. I didn't know why we had moved from our cozy one room to Aunt Bess' house, but I had a lot of neighborhood girls to play with and I was having a grand time. My grandmother and my heart, Gertrude Young Small, matriarch of a family of seven, lay in the wretched agony of cancer. At the door, I turned and watched as she sipped the cold buttermilk. I watched as her small hand made an effort to lift the glass that suddenly seemed almost too heavy. I loved taking buttermilk to her. It was our way of seeing each other. It was the only time that I was allowed in her room. Mama never refused my glass of buttermilk. I stopped outside the bedroom door, and thought again about how we came to be in Aunt Bess' house.

I remembered the afternoon in our room when Mama lay in bed, but it was not bedtime. Sitting around the room were my mother, Bertha, Aunt Alma, Uncle Rabbit, and Uncle Charlie. I crawled in bed and curled up beside Mama. She put her arm around me and drew me close. I heard them say that Mama was sick, and they were making plans to move us.

I trembled when Uncle Rabbit said, "Junebug shouldn't be sleeping with Mama anymore."

Nobody said why. Nobody uttered the dreaded word "cancer." They didn't know cancer was not contagious. Neither did they know that by taking us away from each other, it was like severing a limb. Since the day I was born I had always been with my grandmother. My mother was not quite 16 years old when I was born. She knew nothing about taking care of a baby. Mama was the first mama I knew. When they separated us, they took away my lifeline and the one who loved me unconditionally. They didn't know that I would never again know the joys of childhood or ever feel as loved.

Mama and I lived in one room on the second floor of a rooming house. I didn't know we were poor. I thought we had everything we needed. Our large room had a big, pot-bellied stove in the middle of it, a bed, a sofa, a kitchen table with two chairs and a two-burner hotplate. Mama turned out delicious meals on those two burners. We baked sweet potatoes in the hot ashes of the pot-bellied stove and ate them smothered with margarine. We never went hungry.

Two other women also had rooms on our floor. The couple who owned the house lived downstairs with their two children and the wife's father. The two kids, Godfrey and Kenny, were my only playmates after school. One summer afternoon the three of us were playing in the backyard. Their grandfather came out to call them into the house. One of the boys, undoubtedly Godfrey, didn't want to go in and he ran around the yard shouting, "Funky drawers!" at his grandfather. I found it so hilarious that I joined in. Mr. Hughes tried to catch the boys, but they were way too quick for him. We ran around the yard yelling, "Funky drawers!" at their grandfather and laughing. In the midst of my glee something caught my attention. It was my grandmother standing in the yard with a switch in her hand. I immediately stopped running and laughing. She motioned for me to come to her. I then did the worst thing I could have done: I ran from her. She caught me with little effort and I was hauled into the house, up the stairs, and into our room. I knew my legs were about to get the switching of a lifetime, which they did. Mama always had a switch handy for my naughty moments. She definitely did not spare the rod or my legs.

When one of Mama's favorite radio programs was on, I had to be quiet. Sometimes I listened along with Mama to *Portia Faces Life* or *Stella Dallas* and I could not understand how Mama could enjoy listening to somebody else's problems. I came to hate soap operas. On Saturday nights Mama got out the tin tub and heated water for our weekly baths. The rest of the week we washed thoroughly from a wash pan. I remember going to kindergarten at the Flanner House which was across the street from us.

When I began school, it was at St. Bridget's Catholic School at the other end of our block. I thought all children were taught by nuns who wore long, black habits and starched, stiff white bib-like things around their necks, and a veil over their heads. The long rope of beads worn at the waist and almost reaching the floor was what they used to say the Rosary, the prayer that I too learned. The nuns seemed to glide rather than walk. Most of them spoke softly and were gentle. My favorite teacher was Sister Mary Terrence. There was one, Sr. Agnella, who was positively mean and often had to sit on a doughnut. We thought whatever problems she had with her behind was God punishing her for being mean to us. I loved learning the Latin prayers, and listening to stories of young boys running through the streets of Rome hiding the sacred Host, the body of Christ, out of fear of the pagan Romans. We were required to attend daily Mass before school began. St. Bridget's church, as did all Roman Catholic Churches then, called for silence and prayerful worship. It was dimly lit; tiny candles added a soft glow, and large statues of the Blessed Mother and some saints were sprinkled throughout the church. We knelt with our backs ever so straight, with our little hands pressed together, with fingers under the chin. I felt sorry for Catholics during Lent because they could not eat meat for 40 days. They had to fast every day except Sunday.

Now I thought about all the fun we had as Mama and I enjoyed the antics of Mother, and my aunts and uncles. It was 1945 and Mother and Aunt Alma worked in Chicago, and came home to Indianapolis on weekends. My uncles came over, the bourbon flowed, and there was a lot of joking and laughing. We had so much fun together in the room which only seemed larger when the family gathered.

When the uncles made Mama a drink with a little bourbon, sugar and water, Mama said I had to have one too. They protested every time.

Mama would say, as she always did, "If you don't want her to have it, don't bring it in here. If you bring it in, she's going to have some. I want her to know what it is."

Then one of my uncles would fix me a tiny glass with a drop of whiskey, and a lot of sugar and water. Mama sat in her big rocking chair, and I sat in my little rocking chair. We sipped our "cocktails" and laughed at the antics of Mother and my aunts and uncles. I was surrounded with love and happiness. All was right with the world, but that world was about to end.

As I slowly walked away from Mama's room that day I remembered one day when school was over and I started to walk home. I saw a hearse parked in front of our house. There was a funeral home across the street from us, but I had never seen the hearse on our side of the street. To me a hearse meant a dead body. I thought Mama had died, and my little world began crumbling. I was afraid to go home because I didn't want her to be dead. I didn't know what to do, so I sat in the playground until Sr. Mary Terrence saw me and came out to ask why I had not gone home.

"There's a hearse in front of our house," I replied.

She seemed to understand.

She smiled and said, "Your grandmother is fine."

She took my hand to walk me home, but before reaching the house we met Mama on her way to look for me. Mama didn't scold me, she just hugged me tightly.

Now, Mama lay in bed dying. She would not live to see her granddaughter succeed in life, to achieve things none of their family had ever achieved. As I left Mama's door, Aunt Annie, Mama's oldest daughter who had come up from Kentucky to be with her mother, settled herself in the chair beside the bed. I joined the rest of the family in the kitchen, eating hot chili and laughing and talking. I loved being in the midst of them. This was a magical time for me because the family was together daily. I didn't know they were all together these days because they knew death lurked outside Mama's door. I didn't notice the descent of silence when I walked into a room where they were gathered. Someone always grabbed me and hugged me. Now, warmed by the banter, I basked in their love. Suddenly Aunt Annie appeared in the kitchen doorway.

I was the only one who noticed her, and the only one who heard her say softly, "Mama's gone."

What did that mean? Gone where? She was in bed sick. The talk and laughter continued.

Aunt Annie spoke louder, "Y'all, Mama's gone."

Everyone broke for the kitchen door, tore through the dining room and up the stairs. Mother was halfway up the stairs when she looked back and saw me looking up at her.

She said softly, "You can come."

I raced up the stairs and clutched Mother's hand. Outside Mama's closed door I heard Uncle Rabbit ask for pennies for Mama's eyes. The others went into Mama's room, but Mother and I remained outside. Mama was gone. I didn't cry.

I wanted to be strong for Mother who sobbed. As I stood beside my mother, I thought of the day they moved us from our little room on the other side of town to Aunt Bess'.

Mama and I sat side by side, in our rocking chairs watching them pack our few possessions. Mama smoked her pipe. I had my tiny pipe in my mouth. I knew the end of something was near, but I asked no questions as I looked from Mama to the family scurrying about. Uncle Rabbit had my blackboard under his arm; the blackboard that caused me such anguish when I was unable to master printing a letter of the alphabet. I did not understand that that Mama couldn't help me because she didn't know how to read or write. Few members of our family could read or write.

Mama patted my hand that day and said, "We're going to live with Aunt Bess."

Aunt Bess was the third oldest of Mama's children. She was the stable one with a house and a hardworking husband. She seldom visited Mama and me in our little room, and we seldom visited her. I knew that Mama did not want to live with Aunt Bess and neither did I. The good news was that Mother was moving back to Indianapolis from Chicago to help take care of Mama. My eyes were big as I watched the family packing our few belongings, but I never opened my mouth. There was no laughter that day, and there was little talking. They were taking us away from our little heaven. And then it was time to leave our rented room. Mama stood up, and took a look around the room. Mother reached for my hand, but my eyes were on Mama.

Mama smiled down at me, took my hand, and said, "Come on, Junebug. We're going to a big, fine house."

The two of us walked out of that room and neither of us looked back. I knew without knowing how, that from that moment on, nothing would ever be the same. I promised myself I would never forget that moment. I never have.

Mr. Walt

1946-56

It is the heart which carries one to Hell or to Heaven.
Kanuri (Nigeria)

I called him, "Mr. Walt" because I didn't know what else to call him. Nobody ever told me what to call him. His first name was Walter, but I certainly couldn't call him that. Mr. Walt worked with Uncle Frank, Aunt Bess' husband, at the American Paper Stock Company. Uncle Frank had introduced him to Mother. He never spoke to me. It was as if I were invisible. Often I overheard Aunt Bess and Uncle Frank telling Mother that she should marry him, that he could give us a good home, that he had just gotten out of the Army and wanted to settle down. Aunt Bess called him "good-looking." He was tall, muscular, had a thin moustache, and hard, cold eyes that peered from under hooded lids. I didn't think that Mother loved him. Deep inside I felt that Mother loved another man, Willie, who was like a family member. Willie was always there when the family needed him. He drove us to Kentucky to bury Mama. He was cute, funny, and I loved him. I had hoped that Mother would marry Willie because I knew he would be a great father, but Aunt Bess and Uncle Frank convinced Mother that she should marry Mr. Walt.

Nothing was said to me. It seemed that one day I was at Aunt Bess' house, and the next day we moved into a house with Mr. Walt on another side of town.

We moved into a house in a newly integrated neighborhood on the north side of Indianapolis. The house seemed immense to me who had grown up in one room. There were two bedrooms, living room, dining room, one bath, kitchen and a back porch. There was also a half-finished basement with an old furnace that made loud, strange noises, and an attic. The house was on a street lined with huge maple trees, and at night the street shadows seemed like huge monsters lurking everywhere. Mama was gone. Gone was St. Bridget's School, the dimly lit church from which incense and Latin chants flowed, the kind and gentle nuns, and the friends I had begun first grade with. Mother said I was too young to take the trolley and bus across town alone to go to St. Bridget's. I would be going to a neighborhood school.

Mr. and Mrs. Dink Hubble lived next door. They were an elderly couple who owned a smelly cocker spaniel named Beauty. Around the corner lived Mrs. Hubble's sister, Nettie, the wife of Robert Brokenburr. Years later I learned that he had been a prominent black attorney and a Republican state senator for some 20 years. He was the first black to serve in the Indiana State Senate. I sensed that the Hubbles and the Brokenburrs were different from the folks I knew.

I was lonely and isolated, away from family members, and I didn't know any kids in the neighborhood. But I had Sweetmeat, the doggie given to me by Uncle Pete, a great-uncle in Kentucky. He had handed the two-month old puppy to me through the car window as we were preparing to drive back to Indianapolis after burying Mama. Sweetmeat was all black with a white chest. I cuddled that tiny fur ball and declared that his name would be Sweetmeat because he was so sweet. Mother didn't like that name and suggested that Sport might be a better name. Sweetmeat was my doggie and he would always be Sweetmeat to me. It didn't bother me if others called him Sport.

The summer we moved into the house I was alone all day. I used my allowance of 50 cents a week to buy one comic book each day. I loved reading. I spent a lot of time in my bedroom in order to avoid Mr. Walt. He never talked to me, and the way he looked at me made me very uncomfortable. After several months Mother told me to call him either Mr. Parks or Parks. But it was too late by then, and I was unable or unwilling to call him anything except Mr. Walt, which apparently he did not like.

8

Before life with Mr. Walt, Sundays meant Mass at the Catholic Church, and then I accompanied Mama to the Baptist church directly across the street from the Catholic Church. I was accustomed to going to Mass six days a week, and I was absolutely enthralled with the solemnity of the Mass, the smell of the incense, and the Latin songs. I envied my classmates who could receive Holy Communion. I didn't like going to Mama's church, but I had no say in the matter. The preacher hollered, and some of the women got "happy," a euphemism for shouting and jumping around in church, a practice that frightened me. I thought Mother went to church every Sunday, but she didn't and neither did Mr. Walt. I was saddened when I learned this. So much that I was accustomed to had changed drastically. Not going to church was a blow to me. I had no way to get to church unless Mother took me, and I knew better than to ask her to interrupt her Sunday morning breakfasts of steak, gravy, potatoes and biscuits.

I knew what was missing in my life and what I wanted more than anything. Finally, I got up my nerve and asked Mother if I could become a Catholic. I was ten years old.

She looked at me curiously, and then she replied, "When you reach 16 if you still want to become a Catholic, then you can."

That was a long way off, but I never said another word about it. Occasionally I would go to church with a friend. I even joined Joyce's Lutheran church because its rites were closer to Catholicism than the other protestant churches I had attended. But even the Lutheran church was not what I yearned for.

When Mother worked in Chicago and came home on weekends, she always took me to the Automat for dinner and then to a Betty Davis or Joan Crawford movie. The Automat was magical to me. I always carefully made my food selection, put my quarters into the machine, pushed a button and watched wide-eyed as the tiny door opened to reveal the dish I had selected. All week I looked forward to that evening out with my mother. I noticed that after Mother got married, the two of us had no more evenings out.

One day I timidly asked, "Mother, when are we going to the Automat again?"

She responded gruffly, "Automat? I don't have time for no Automat. I'm working, and trying to keep this house together. "

I was crushed. Our weekly ritual was over.

On Sunday afternoons Mother and me usually drove over to visit Aunt Bess and to see Uncle Charlie and Aunt Ree, and Uncle Rabbit and his girlfriend of the moment. This was the highlight of the week. Once one of Uncle Rabbit's girlfriends invited the family to dinner. I looked forward to dessert because I saw she had baked a sweet potato pie. We all ate and laughed and then came dessert. I had a big slice of pie. I bit into it and it was the worst pie I had ever tasted. I wondered if Ms. Mabel had grabbed the washing powder instead of the sugar. I felt a kick under the table. It was Mother or one of my aunts. I heard Ms. Mabel telling the family that she was learning how to cook. I wondered why she hadn't waited until she had learned before inviting the family over. Every time I tried to put my fork down, I got a kick under the table. It took a long time for me to finish that slice. After that I would only eat Aunt Bess's sweet potato pies. It was 30 years before I could bring myself to eat anybody else's. I loved being with my aunts and uncles because they made me feel special. They were so proud of anything I did. I felt love when I was with them. I didn't feel any love at our house. It was never a home to me. Mother barely noticed me, and I tried to keep out of Mr. Walt's way.

The next jolt in my life was being told that I could not attend the public school that was a few blocks from our house. The city of Indianapolis did not allow black children to attend white schools. I remember going to the office of the School Board along with Mother and other black parents and kids. Our parents wanted us to attend the school close to where we lived. City authorities had a bus pick up the few black children in my predominantly white neighborhood.

I never heard anyone in my family or their friends make any disparaging remarks about whites. Some things were just accepted.

I was eleven years old when I got up one morning and saw blood spots in my panties. I woke Mother to tell her. She simply got a sanitary belt and a box of Kotex and showed me how to put the pad on. Nothing more was said. I didn't know what to make of this latest jolt in my life. On the back of the Kotex box was a coupon for a booklet explaining menstruation. When the booklet arrived I devoured it in order to learn what was happening to my body. One day Mr. Walt rubbed his huge hands over my budding breasts and said they were "firm and ripe." I felt filthy. He apparently watched my breasts develop and then he told Mother when he thought it was time for me to begin wearing a brassiere. I was beginning to dislike Mr. Walt more and more, but I kept it to myself.

Mother left her house cleaning job with a white family and took a factory job at RCA that paid more money. The only problem, as I saw it, was that she worked the night shift – from 11 pm – 7 am. I was always asleep when she left for work, but I was painfully aware that I was alone with Mr. Walt who didn't talk to me. I felt his eyes raking my body every time I passed by him, but I never dreamed of what was about to take place. Every morning he got up at 5 am and turned the radio up as loud as it would go. It always awakened me, and I could not go back to sleep until he left for work. I never complained because children didn't complain.

One night I woke up in darkness and confusion. Something stirred beside me. My mind exploded with the realization that someone was in my bed. I moved and tried to cry out, but a hand went over my mouth.

Another hand groped my breasts and moved down over my stomach. I was fully awake now, and scared. I struggled to get out of the tight grip.

A man's voice whispered harshly, "Be still!"

I knew that voice. It was Mr. Walt. I didn't know why he was in my bed, but I sensed something bad was going to happen. As I continued to struggle, he jerked me onto my back and forced my legs apart. I felt something at my head.

He said, "I have a gun and when I finish we're going to the basement and I'm going to kill both of us."

He knew he was doing something terribly wrong to me, and he was going to kill both of us after he raped me. As he forced his penis inside me, the pain was excruciating. I struggled and cried as he hurt me more and more. He yelled at me to be quiet. He cursed me because he had difficulty entering me. In the midst of the searing pain, my mind took me away from the agony. When he finished, he rolled off me and I curled up into a ball. I hurt all over. I knew that my childhood had ended. Now it was time to die. Perhaps death would be my friend. I knew little of death, and certainly was not afraid of it. My only thought was of Mother returning home from work the next morning and finding our bodies in the basement. I would have done anything to spare her that. I promised Mr. Walt that I would never tell anyone what had happened that night. He made me say it over and over until finally he believed me and left my bed. I lay there and allowed the tears to fall silently for fear that he would hear me and return. I cried for Mama in whose arms I had always found love. I cried because I hurt all over. Finally, I cried myself to sleep.

When I awakened, I resolved to myself that never again would Mr. Walt hurt me the way he had. The next time I would be the one with a weapon. Every night after that, I slept with a butcher knife under my pillow.

Mr. Walt tested me again and again. Once he told Mother that he had come home and found me on the sofa having sex with a boy. I didn't know any boys except those urchins at school, and I only saw them at school. My friends and I didn't know anything about sex. We didn't even know enough to talk about it. All I knew about sex was that it was all that boys wanted and it was the one thing that I must not do. I averted my eyes when I saw a pregnant woman, never mind that the woman was probably married. I felt that the woman was announcing to the world by her swollen stomach that she had had sex, and I was embarrassed for her. S-E-X was a four letter word to me.

The month after the rape my period did not start on time. My little body was traumatized by the rape. Every day Mr. Walt took me down to the basement and asked me over and over who I had slept with. The man was evil. I never opened my mouth or uttered a word. I just looked at him with as much hate as I could conjure up in my eyes. He was daring me to name him as my rapist. I knew that revelation would destroy Mother, and I desperately wanted her to be happy. He continued telling Mother that I must be pregnant, and he began demanding to know who the father was. It was a cruel, cruel game he played with me. But my lips remained sealed. I decided that if I were pregnant, I would run away. I didn't know where I would go, but I knew I would have to leave that house. Finally, Mother took me to our family doctor.

After he examined me, he said to Mother, "She's not pregnant, but she has been messing around."

I wanted to yell at the doctor that I had not "been messing around," that I had been raped, but I didn't say anything. After we left the doctor's office Mother cried, and when we got home she screamed at me demanding to know who I had been "messing around" with. Mr. Walt got into the act. He demanded to know who I had been "screwing." I could only glare at him with hate, but I never said a word.

I wanted to scream at him, "It was you! You! You!"

Shortly thereafter Mother was switched to a day job at the factory which meant she was at home at night. Even so, I tried to never be alone in a room with Mr. Walt. I was never disrespectful, but I only spoke directly to him if he asked me a question. He seemed to dislike me more and more. He was the one who had perpetrated a crime against me. I had done nothing to him, and was in effect protecting him by keeping his horrendous act a secret. I had been taught to never show or act in any manner to disrespect an adult. And so I spoke pleasantly when addressed, and tried to shut out the unpleasantness surrounding me.

Mr. Walt became even more mean spirited. He told Mother that I was rebellious, and he continually told lies about me to keep her distressed and argumentative. Once he even told Mother that I was having sex with my dog. When Mother questioned me about this, I was incredulous that anyone could even think such a thing. I even wondered if Mother was losing her mind to believe such a lie.

Mother's behavior during those years had a lasting effect on me.

She probably never knew why as an adult, I was always short tempered with her and always on the verge of an outburst when I was with her. I think I was angry with her for not protecting me from her husband, even though she didn't know.

Mr. Walt hated Sweetmeat and was cruel to him. At night he made Sweetmeat stay in the garage. The dog never bothered him, but he was inclined to whip Sweetmeat for any minor incident, such as barking at a meter reader. He never whipped him when Mother was at home. The brave little mutt never backed down, nor did he ever stop growling when being whipped. He stayed in an attack position. He didn't like Mr. Walt either. I would stand close by, watching and wanting to say something to stop that awful man from hurting my dog, but I was taught that adults were always right, and that children should be seen and not heard. Afterwards, Sweetmeat and I would try to comfort each other. Oh, the tears I shed in his fur. He would climb into my lap in an effort to stop my tears, and he never let me be sad for long. We were both little and vulnerable, and neither of us could protect the other, but we were a great comfort to each other. He was the first animal in my life and what a blessing he was.

Sweetmeat - 1956

No one knew what secrets lay buried in my heart. I was active in high school. I went to proms, dressed up and laughed with friends. But at home I was watchful, and always on my guard. When walked through the living room and Mr. Walt was in there alone, I hurried through but his eyes always feasted on me. I felt that somehow I had brought this misery upon myself. I didn't know that I had joined the ranks of young girls who were abused by their stepfathers or other family members. I felt ashamed and guilty.

At the dinner table, I kept my eyes on my plate and only spoke if Mother asked me something. I didn't like to talk to her in front of Mr. Walt. I ate fast and retreated to my bedroom where I buried myself in books that transported me to places where girls my age had loving parents and were always happy.

I started to wonder if all men were like Mr. Walt. I began to watch Uncle Charlie and Uncle Rabbit very carefully. Mother's two brothers had always been wonderful, loving uncles. Uncle Rabbit gave me my first wristwatch. Uncle Charlie gave me my first pearl bracelet. I loved them with all of my heart, but now I didn't know if I could trust them. Perhaps they were like Mr. Walt. I watched them like a hawk for several months, and then I relaxed, secure in the knowledge that neither of those loving men would ever do anything wrong to me. Only later did I realize that during that watchful period, any imagined incorrect, but innocent, touch would have damned them forever in my eyes. At least now I knew there were two men in the world who could be trusted not to molest me. As I watched them laughing and talking to Mr. Walt, I could only imagine their anger if they ever knew what he had done to me. I knew they would kill him. Both men would happily have forfeited their lives to protect their sister and niece. I was not going to ask such a sacrifice of them.

Not long after the rape, Mother's oldest sister, Aunt Annie, became ill in Covington, Kentucky. For some reason she became mute. She understood whatever was said to her, but she didn't speak. She did whatever she was told, and she could bathe and dress herself, but she remained silent. I was deliriously happy when she came to live with us because we shared my bed.

I no longer had to sleep with a knife under my pillow. I no longer had to worry about Mr. Walt molesting me. Life was getting better.

My best friend at the time was Adrienne Griffin. We met while we were at School #87. Her father was our mailman. She was an only child, as was I, and we had the same interests. When I went to Shortridge High School, it was the second year that it had been integrated. Shortridge had been integrated in the early 1900s, until the Ku Klux Klan took over the state government. The imposing building projected wealth and influence. It had a swimming pool, radio station and a daily newspaper. With the exception of one journalism class, I was always the only black in my classes during the entire four years. The white students were not hostile to black students. They basically ignored us.

A few black students joined in the many activities that Shortridge offered. Of course, the black athletes were wildly popular and fawned over by white females as well as white males. Our white classmates, mostly from wealthy families, drove their own cars to school. I didn't know a single black student who owned a car. The white girls wore cashmere sweaters and Capezio slippers in colors to match their outfits. Bakers, where my family bought my shoes, didn't sell Capezios. Adrienne and I wrote for the Monday edition of our high school daily newspaper, *The Shortridge Daily Echo.* Shortridge was one of three high schools in the entire U.S. that had a daily newspaper. Adrienne and I also had a weekly jazz program on the FM station at Shortridge. We knew all of the disc jockeys in town, and often visited their studios.

We wrote a gossip column for a black weekly, *The Hoosier Herald,* and we had press passes that enabled us to attend jazz concerts free of charge, and go backstage to interview jazz greats such as Duke Ellington, Count Basie, Stan Kenton, George Shearing, among others. These interviews were carried in the *Shortridge Daily Echo.* Mother knew little of my school activities. I never told her much because I wanted Mr. Walt to know as little as possible about my life.

The day after my 16th birthday I reminded Mother of her promise that I could become Catholic at 16 if I still wanted to. She was surprised that I remembered for all of those years. She gave me permission and I was baptized at St. Bridget's Church. I was back at my home church. I was where I belonged. Thereafter, the word in our family was that if anybody promised me anything, they had to do it. I took promises seriously.

Every year at Shortridge the junior class hosted the "Junior Vaudeville." Various groups put together musical acts and several acts were selected to perform for the public in our auditorium. One member of the team had to be a junior. When Adrienne and I were seniors we decided to produce an act for the Junior Vaudeville, along with a junior member. In previous years the only blacks seen during the Vaudeville program were the black ushers. We were never in any of the acts. Our program consisted of a ballerina, a modern dancer, and various musical numbers. Our performers had worked tirelessly and their audition was flawless. We were crushed when our act was not chosen, but we dutifully went to the program and ushered.

In 2005 for the Fiftieth reunion of my graduating class of 1955, attendees were asked to write about our memories of Shortridge, and those memories were included in our program book. I wrote:

"I have some sad thoughts about Shortridge... During Junior Vaudeville shows, the black students were the ushers and white students were the performers...several of us black students worked on, and presented, a terrific show for the Vaudeville, but we were not selected."

One of my former classmates, a white male, wrote the Salutatory for our program book. The title was, "An Exhilarating Journey."

"We were the first class at Shortridge to be fully integrated from start to finish, but very few of us, except our black brothers and sisters, noted that there was no black Junior Vaudeville act or any black cheerleaders. These omissions failed to register so it did not occur to most of us to question why this was so. Our blindness to prejudice and our willingness to tolerate second class citizenship was directed not only toward the black community, but toward all the minority communities, as well as women."

I was amazed that it took 50 years for a classmate to recognize the injustices at our school, and to admit it.

After graduating from high school I went to Indiana University in Bloomington. It was heavenly being away from home and free. Previously my dates had consisted of going to junior and senior proms with guys who were just buddies. In my senior year in high school I went to a few movies with a young man, and even wore his class ring for awhile. It was at the dinner table one evening that Mother noticed the ring and asked about it. I was mortified.

She and Mr. Walt stopped eating and stared at me. I mumbled that it was Jimmy's ring.

Mother asked, "What does that ring mean?"

I said, "Nothing. It's a ring."

"Well, why are you wearing it?"

"I'm just wearing it."

I don't know what she thought, but I was about to choke on air because I could not eat another bite. I wanted to leap up from the table, run to my room, and throw the ring at Jimmy. Anyway, I didn't wear it for long because Jimmy asked for it back and gave it to my best friend, Adrienne.

At Indiana University I dated an older guy. He was an odd ball, just out of the service. He was nice enough, certainly not dashing or exciting, but on weekends we would go to the Elks Club with four other friends and the girls drank mixed drinks while the guys drank beer. I excelled in my Composition class, but I was not a stellar student otherwise. I tended to study the subjects I liked, which weren't many, and the other courses got short shrift. Life was a continuous party. The second semester began and I was thinking of pledging Alpha Kappa Alpha. The AKA women were welcoming, gracious, and had fun. Whereas, the women in the other black sorority, Delta Sigma Theta, seemed to be mainly high-yellow women whose fathers were doctors and lawyers. They were definitely not my cup of tea, and since I was neither high-yellow, nor from a well-to-do family, I felt that their sentiments about me were the same.

Harry Belafonte came to the campus for a concert to be held on a Monday night. I invited my good friend, Joyce Woods, to spend the weekend to be there on Monday to hear Belafonte. She arrived on Saturday. I lived in a dorm, and the housekeeper changed our linen every Monday.

Apparently she noticed Joyce's suitcase and notified the Dorm Counselor that I had a visitor. Nothing was said to me until we arrived back at the dorm from the concert around 10 pm. The dorm counselor telephoned and asked me to come to her office. I was told that my guest would have to leave because it was against dorm rules to have overnight guests during week nights. I had not been aware of that policy. I explained to her that neither of us had enough money for Joyce to stay in a hotel. She replied that she didn't care. I said I knew there was a late bus going to Indianapolis, but that I would have to go with my friend to the bus station so that she would not be standing outside alone.

The counselor said, "You are not to leave this dorm. If you do leave, don't come back."

Furious now, I left her office, slamming the door as hard as I could. I returned to my room and told Joyce and my roommate, Gretta Bridgeforth, the problem. I checked the bus schedule and sure enough there was a bus at 1 a.m. I called the guy I was dating and asked him to take us to the bus station and he agreed. We sneaked out a side door on the second floor and met him. He drove us to the bus station where we waited in his car for several hours until the bus arrived. I prayed that Joyce would be safe after arriving in Indianapolis. The Indy bus station was a favorite hangout of drifters. After seeing Joyce onto the bus I returned to the dorm and Gretta let me in the side door. Early the next morning there was a note under my door ordering me to see the Dean of Women, Virginia Whitehead. This was southern Indiana, Bloomington, in the 1950s, and the Dean of Women was from Texas, and eminently ready to deal with a recalcitrant black girl.

Dean Whitehead greeted me coldly and demanded to know why I had left the dorm after being told not to. I explained why I left the dorm against the counselor's order. I said I could not simply put a friend out on the street with no money and let her stand outside the closed bus station at that late hour. The Dean ignored that and hastened to point out that I was already on probation for being noisy. Oh, I had forgotten that little annoyance. Every evening several girls who had difficulty in their composition classes piled into my room, and while Gretta and I wrote our own compositions, we dictated theirs. We finished around midnight, and at that exact time a favorite song of ours, "Around Midnight" came on the radio, and we began dancing and singing. Apparently we disturbed those who were trying to sleep. We were warned by the counselor to stop the noise. Instead, we put a skull and crossbones on her door and continued being noisy.

The Dean had neither patience nor sympathy, and telephoned Mother to come for me and my belongings. Mother and Aunt Bess arrived within hours. I was ashamed and also very angry. I wrote a letter to the Dean pointing out the differences in the treatment of white students and black students. Two white girls in the dorm had been stealing money from purses in the dorm for months. We never locked our rooms and seldom carried our purses, but most people were

19

honest. The theft went on, and finally one day money was planted. As soon as the money disappeared the dorm doors were locked, and everyone had to line up and place their hands under a light that revealed the dye on the hands of the thieves. Those girls were not thrown out of school, but I was being thrown out for doing something that I knew was right.

Mother had almost convinced the Dean to let me remain at the university when I presented my letter. That was the final nail. I was sent packing.

I always marveled that Mother never scolded or reprimanded me. I felt terrible because she had spent so much money on my one year at college, and I had thrown it all away by misbehaving. I was forced to leave the school one month before final exams which I was not allowed to take. But there was some good news. Mr. Walt had gotten a job with the post office and as the new man, he was often called to work, and was seldom at home.

Harlem, New York City
1956 - 1962

When I discover who I am, I'll be free.
- Ralph Ellison

After being tossed out of Indiana University I returned to Indy with my head hanging. To my mother's everlasting credit, she never scolded me for disobeying the school rules or for insisting on leaving with Joyce to go to the bus station. I moped around the house for a few months, and then Aunt Alma came from New York for a visit. Aunt Alma had always been my favorite aunt. She was two years older than my mother and they had the same sense of humor. I celebrated my 19th birthday while Aunt Alma was in town. When she asked if I would like to visit her in New York, I leaped at the chance. I knew that this was my way out. I knew I would never again live under Mr. Walt's roof.

Aunt Alma was glamorous and she lived in the magical sounding New York City. The idea of living in an apartment was exciting to me. In an apartment there would be people around me and I would no longer have to live in a big, scary house. Off I went for what Mother thought was a short vacation. We arrived in Grand Central Station in New York City and took a taxi to Harlem. As we drove I looked around at men hanging on the street corners and talking loud and laughing.

People hung out of windows as we drove past dilapidated building after dilapidated building. It looked like a war zone.

Young and old men, seemingly drunk, hung on the street corners and on stoops of apartment buildings. Each block looked worse than the previous one. I had never seen such a neighborhood. The streets were filled with the kind of men "nice, young ladies" would never speak to, let along date. So this was New York, a city so nice they named it twice. Yuk!

We arrived at Aunt Alma's apartment building and walked up three flights of stairs and into a two room apartment where she lived with her boyfriend. I knew Mother did not know that Aunt Alma lived with her boyfriend, or she would never have let me come. In fact, had I known she had a live-in boyfriend, I probably would not have come. It never occurred to me that I could go back to Indy. That was never an option for me. I had escaped from hell, and would now make my own way in the world. Before I could ask where the kitchen and bathroom were, Aunt Alma took me down the hall. She used a key to open the door to another apartment where the communal bathroom and kitchen were located. I was horrified. If I had to go to the bathroom in the middle of the night, and I did when I was on my period, I would have to leave our apartment, walk down the hallway, and go into somebody else's apartment. A nice woman and her daughter lived in the other apartment and we became friends. The daughter, Shirley, was my age.

I didn't know that Aunt Alma drank or that she fought when she got drunk. I began to dread the weekends. One Friday night she got drunk and she and her boyfriend were fighting in the hallway. I cowered inside the apartment.

Fighting was new to me, and very scary. Suddenly I heard Shirley's mother in the hallway trying to separate Aunt Alma and Adam.

Adam was trying to throw Aunt Alma over the stairway railing. Shirley's mother wrenched her back trying to get Adam away from Aunt Alma. I knew I had to get out of that situation.

I went to the Urban League and lucked up on a wonderful job. A black woman was there who worked as a receptionist at a Wall St. law firm. She was resigning and the attorneys asked her to recommend somebody just like her. When I walked in the door, the Urban League knew they had found her replacement. I was interviewed for the job and I got it. I worked on the 43rd floor at a Jewish law firm on Wall Street. For several years I was one of two black women there. The other woman was the file clerk. Practically everybody at the firm adopted me because I was young and new to the city. I enjoyed working there. In the winter when night fell early, I loved looking out the windows. From the 43rd floor the city lights below gleamed like sparkling jewels.

After a few months, Shirley and I had enough money to move into our own apartment, also in Harlem. Mother wanted me to come home. She threatened to have the police return me. I told her if she did, she would never see me again. I would have left the city and gone somewhere, anywhere, in order not to return to that house and Mr. Walt. I was not ever going to live under his roof again. I hated causing pain to Mother, but she did not know what I had suffered at the hands of her husband. Shirley and I could barely afford our tiny apartment. The entire apartment was smaller than the one room Mama and I had lived in, but it was ours.

I thought all black people in New York City lived in Harlem. I even wondered if black folks were allowed to live anywhere else.

I never became accustomed to men hanging on the street corners, or bums drinking wine standing around, or men whistling or saying fresh things to me. Sometimes I would take a taxi from the subway to my apartment, a short six blocks away, simply because I could not stomach encountering the types of men who hung on the corners. I shrunk inside myself and tried not to stand out. I was young and attractive, but the remarks and the stares made me want to wear a tent to hide myself.

For Christmas of 1956, Joyce came to visit me. Christmas Day arrived and Mother and I telephoned each other every hour and cried. I missed her and she missed me. That was my first Christmas away from the place I knew as home. I missed the ritual, the preparation, the gifts, the excitement, and most of all, I missed being with Mother and my aunts and uncles. It was Joyce's first visit to the Big Apple and we had a wonderful time. She hated to leave and I hated seeing her leave.

My roommate, Shirley, had a steady boyfriend, Len, who she had been dating for a few years. It was another friend of Shirley's who introduced me to a guy who was older than we were – I was 19 and he was in his 30s. The first time Al took me out, we went to a club in our neighborhood. As we sat sipping our drinks, several guys came over to the table to talk to Al and to ask when he got back, and how long he had been "out."

I listened politely, and finally I asked, "Where have you been?"

He said he had just gotten out of the military service. Al was a sharp dresser and much more sophisticated than other guys I knew.

I eventually learned that Al had been away as a guest of the state, and that's why people kept asking him how long he had been out. He had been in prison for armed robbery. Shortly thereafter, we broke up.

At work I listened to the white secretaries talk about going to Florida. I did not know any black people who went away on vacations. Back in Indianapolis, when people I knew took vacations, they painted the house or went "down south" to visit their families. I didn't know any black people who went to Florida to lay about on the beach and get tanned. On the elevators at the office in the summer I often heard whites boasting about how "black" they were when they returned from vacations with a tan. My "vacations" and Christmases were spent in Indianapolis. I didn't consider it vacation. To me a vacation meant being in a hotel and dining out, for which one needed money.

Every time I left to return to New York, Mother would break down in tears. I knew how unhappy her life had to be with Mr. Walt, but I didn't know how I could make things better for her. I noticed that she was drinking more and I asked Aunt Bess if she thought Mother was an alcoholic. She said she didn't know. We didn't think she was an alcoholic because during the week she never drank liquor, but she began on Friday night and continued drinking until Sunday. I hated it when she was drunk. She slurred her speech, and she threw up in the bathroom. She was somebody I did not like when she was drunk. I knew why she drank, and my heart ached for her. She drank to blot out, even if only briefly, the misery she was now tied to. When she drank, she became somebody I didn't know.

A year or so after I moved to New York, Mother and Mr. Walt moved to a new house on the outskirts of town, near the airport. My bedroom was downstairs in their new house. When I was there every night I pushed a large chest of drawers against my bedroom door to prevent Mr. Walt from coming into my room. Whenever I was alone in the house with Mr. Walt, I stayed in my bedroom with my eyes fixed on the door. The fear of another attack never left me, but this time I would be ready. We never had a conversation, and I could feel his resentment descending into anger and hate.

In the summer of 1961 I decided to go to the Catskill Mountains in upstate New York instead of going home. I noticed that Mother did not protest as she usually did when I didn't go to Indiana. After an enjoyable week at Cab Calloway's vacation center I returned to NYC. I had a letter from Mother the next week telling me that Sweetmeat was getting older and that I should not be surprised if he died.

The same day I had a letter from Aunt Bess which began, "I guess by now your mother has told you she had to have Sweetmeat put to sleep."

I grabbed the phone and called Mother. I was inconsolable. She tried to explain, with pain in her voice, that Sweetmeat could barely walk, he could no longer eat, and there was nothing the vet could do. As much as she loved him, she had to let him go. She said she wanted to prepare me gently. The next day I received her letter telling me she had to put my precious Sweetmeat to sleep. She spoke of my love for him and his love for me. I had him for 15 years. I remember him with much love.

Welcome to the Peace Corps
1962-1964

We can do no great things – only small things with great love.
- Mother Teresa

On October 14th, 1960, an exhausted candidate for president arrived late at the University of Ann Arbor. He spoke to the students and others waiting to greet him at 2 a.m., and he asked if Americans were willing to volunteer to live abroad to work with the poor people of third world countries. That idea gave birth to the Peace Corps, two words soon heard around the world and welcomed in many countries.

Three months later in Washington, DC, John F. Kennedy became the country's 35th President. From the steps of the Capitol he told a rapt audience that the torch of freedom had "been passed to a new generation of Americans – tempered by war, disciplined by a hard and bitter peace, proud of our ancient heritage - unwilling to witness or permit the slow undoing of those human rights to which this nation has always been committed, and to which we are committed today at home and around the world."

Kennedy's words brought hope to the poor of the world. He reached out to those in huts and villages around the world, and he pledged to help the poor to help themselves. To "our sister republics south of our border" he made a special pledge of an alliance for progress to help them throw off the chains of poverty.

President Kennedy ended his inaugural speech with the famous words: "And so, my fellow Americans: ask not what your country can do for you – ask what you can do for your country. My fellow citizens of the world: ask not what America will do for you, but what together we can do for the freedom of man."

On March 1, 1961 President Kennedy signed an executive order establishing the Peace Corps, and a few days later, Sargent Shriver became the first Peace Corps Director. One month later the first Peace Corps group was in Ghana even before Congress had authorized the agency. I was the 132nd person to write to the White House asking for the chance to be a volunteer for peace. I was a young, idealistic woman who wanted to see the world. This was a chance to better my life by enriching it and doing something to help those less fortunate. At that time a college degree was not necessary to become a Peace Corps Volunteer. I took the first Peace Corps exam. Photographers were everywhere, and they were allowed in the examining room before we began. I didn't tell anyone at my office about my desire to join the Peace Corps. One year later, in March, 1962, I received an invitation from Sargent Shriver to participate in a training program for a Peace Corps project in Peru. I was on my way.

A few weeks later everyone who accepted the invitation to participate in the "Peru II – Health and Nutrition Project," met in Baltimore. None of the 47 of us considered ourselves experts in health or nutrition, but we were ready to learn.

Throughout our training we were told that no matter how little we knew about nutrition that we knew more than the people we would be working with.

That was little consolation, but eventually we realized that it was probably true, and that our efforts could only result in better nutrition for the children of Peru. We were mainly in our 20s. There were a few people in their 30s, and there were two women in their late 60s. How we marveled at the "ancient ones." One was a sweet, little woman from California. The other was a slightly-built, tough, chain-smoking, liquor-drinking, journalist from the

Midwest. The youngest in our group was 18 years old. There were five blacks: an accountant from Washington, DC; a mortician and his wife, a beautician, from Michigan; a journalist from Illinois, and me. A college degree was not a Peace Corps requirement during the early years.

The Peruvian government had asked the Peace Corps to work with the schools to institute a program in nutrition to help the children of the poorer classes who suffered from constant hunger. The job of the volunteers was to organize parents and teachers to prepare food donated by the U.S. government for breakfast programs in the schools. We were to supervise the preparation of the food at the schools, and the baking and distribution of breakfast rolls from bakeries. It was emphasized constantly that we would live with frustration, and that we would seldom see the results of our work. We were expected to rely on our own resources in order to thrive in a foreign environment, learn to contend with delays in everything, to get involved in community development projects, and to rise above culture shock. Above all, we were taught over and over to never offend our host country nationals. We were guests in their country, and while we were donating U.S. food, we were Peace Corps volunteers who wanted to be there: act like it.

In order to be successful volunteers we would test our inner and physical resources during a one-month training period in the rain forest of Puerto Rico. That training would include tasks designed to strengthen our self-reliance, improve our self-confidence, survival techniques, and provide an opportunity for us to experience living in another culture. The month at camp would also allow the camp staff to observe how we interacted with each other which would give them some idea of how we would behave in Peru. We could be "selected out" of the program at any time. We were not hammered on the head with that threat, but it sure began to hit home when the deselecting began during our camp training. For now, we were ready to march into battle against hunger and poverty.

Camp Rio Abajo, Puerto Rico — The Rainforest

If things can get worse, they will.

- Murphy's Law

It was dark when we arrived at the airport in San Juan, Puerto Rico, where we were met by several members of the camp staff. We climbed aboard buses that took us on a one hour ride to the rain forest near Rio Abajo. The buses got us as close as possible to our campsite, which was not nearly close enough. We got off the buses and struggled with our luggage across a wooden footbridge, and over rough ground. The women, for the most part, had on high heels, and sheath dresses. Those were the days when plane passengers dressed well. The dresses didn't give; the high heels did. They sank into the sucking mud with every step. We swore with every other step. We were overwhelmed by the humidity, and sweat oozed from every pore. It was close to midnight and I wondered how much hotter it would be during the day. We walked and walked. All we could see was blackness and more of the same. This must have been our first test of endurance. Finally we stumbled into an open area and saw our lodgings for the next 30 days.

One of the staffers yelled, "Tents for women straight ahead! Tents for men to the right! The latrines are behind the tents and down a slope."

Latrines? Tents? Oh hell, I thought, what have I gotten myself into? Maybe my mother was right when she warned me that I couldn't live like this. I certainly couldn't. I didn't want to live in a tent, or walk in the dark to a latrine.

Who knew what things were crawling around on the ground and inside the latrine? Where were the air-conditioned buildings? It was going to be a long 30 days. Nobody told us during the week in Baltimore that we would be living in tents and going to an outdoor latrine, or that we should have worn clothes more suited for walking in a rain forest. Our education was just beginning.

A few hours later, at 6 a.m. to be exact, we were jolted awake by a bugle. In my tent 20 sleepy women woke up wondering where they were and what that noise was. Before we could turn over to go back to sleep, we heard yelling about getting up, dressing and being outside in five minutes. Big Al, a camp instructor and a huge chunk of man, stood in the middle of the camp with a bugle making enough noise to be heard throughout the rain forest. We tumbled out of bed, remembered to shake our shoes and clothes in case scorpions had taken up residence, and trotted to the latrine to pee. There was no time to do anything else.

Al and the other instructors were yelling about jogging a mile, going through the obstacle course, and then coming back for breakfast. I was definitely not ready for this. We ran, or walked fast, and then hit the formidable obstacle course that quickly became everybody's nightmare. We were supposed to swing through trees on ropes, leap over sand traps, do chin ups, race up slippery slopes, race down slipperier slopes, and all within a very rigid time limit. We overlapped by a few days with a group of volunteer men heading for Columbia. Some had fractured arms and legs on the dreaded obstacle course. Our instructors wisely decided to eliminate the more physically demanding tasks for us. Once we got through the course, it was time to shower and dress for breakfast.

The rain forest was aptly named. It poured rain every few minutes it seemed. Anybody who knows anything about black women's hair, knows that the combination of water and heat will make it rise higher than any soufflé, and kink up for good measure. The heat was doing a number on my hair. One of my colleagues, Judy, who slept in the bed next to mine, asked in her usual friendly manner if she could feel my hair. I said sure, and hoped it would not cut her fingers. It was probably the first time that she had been so close to a black woman's hair.

She felt my hair and squealed, "Oh, it feels soft like wool."

Each day was different, and there were no dull moments. We were split into teams with a staff member as our team leader. Some teams dug a pool for the camp. That was a task I managed to avoid thanks to our team leader who never put our group to work in the pool. So my team did other things, including walking by the pool and smirking at those sweating blood down in the hole, digging for all they were worth. The kicker was that they would not get to enjoy the fruits of their labor, but the next group would.

Some of us learned that it was best to sleep in the clothes you planned to wear the next morning because by sleeping in them, they would be warm and dry, not to mention already on your body. If we left them at the foot of the cot, they would be cold, damp, and a scorpion might have bedded down in them. So we slept in our clothes, fell out of bed, and hit the tent flap at the first blast of the bugle.

After a few days in camp we were introduced to a man who would teach us "drown proofing." He was Freddy Lanoue, the swimming coach at Georgia Tech.

When he and I met it was a meeting of oil and water, or fire and ice. Lanoue was definitely a character and a brusque one at that. I did not like his southern drawl or his tyrannical manner. The fact that he was from Georgia Tech, an institution blacks were fighting for the right to attend, gave me another reason to dislike him. Lanoue had developed something called "drown proofing" that was supposed to keep one from drowning, even those of us who could not swim. This method was designed to help swimmers conserve energy if they had to remain in water for a long time, and it enabled non-swimmers to stay afloat with no effort. You had to stretch out on top of the water, with your face in the water, and lift your head every few seconds and take a deep breath. The air in your body would not allow you to stay under the water.

The struggle began. I had always enjoyed playing in a swimming pool, but Freddy almost cured me of that. At one session he ordered me to *jump* into the pool. I perched on the edge of the pool and slowly scooted forward. Telling me to jump into the pool was like telling me to throw myself off a mountain. Common sense told me that when I jumped into the water my butt was going to go straight to the bottom. I tried to ease into the water so that I wouldn't go to the bottom as fast as I would if I jumped in.

Freddy's face became redder and redder, and he shouted at me, "JUMP!"

I continued slowly scooting forward.

Finally he yelled, "Jump or you are going to hit your aaasss!"

Which is what I did, on the edge of the pool, but at least I softened my entry into the water. The staff seemed amused by my interaction with Freddy.

He hollered at me and I hollered back. In the end, he wasn't nearly as bad as I originally thought, and his method worked.

We were given an hour to rest after lunch. As we women lay in our beds with the tent flaps up for air, one of our guys, Ken Draigh, daily paraded from his tent to the showers with just a towel draped around him which threatened to come off at any moment. We hooted and whistled, but Ken seemed completely oblivious. We prayed the towel would fall off just to teach him a lesson. He insisted that he had the towel securely tied.

He said it seemed to be the only practical way to get to the shower and asked, "Why head for a shower fully dressed?"

My personal nightmare was the rope bridge that consisted of ropes strung between two trees, about 20 feet off the ground. They called it a Burma bridge. We had to walk across ropes and use the side ropes to stabilize the ropes under our feet. The secret was to push the ropes you were hanging onto OUT to the side which tightened the foot ropes that enabled one to scamper across; however, the tendency was to draw the side ropes into the body to feel some security which caused the footropes to become slack and one was highly likely to fall. Crossing that rope bridge was a terrifying experience. Once I yelled down to the instructor that the bridge was shaking.

He yelled back, "The bridge is not shaking, you are, and you're going to fall if you don't stop!"

Damn! He ordered me to stretch the ropes all the way out to the sides to make the bridge taut.

I peered down at the safety net that looked far away because it was. I knew that if I fell I would probably break something, and that would be the end of my Peace Corps career. I summoned up courage from somewhere, which was the whole idea, pushed the ropes away from me, and scooted across. Little did I know then that within a few months I would be living in a village with a rope bridge in the center of town.

We learned rock-climbing and rappelling. The first time I rappelled, my foot slipped. I heard the collective gasp of my fellow trainees as I swayed in the air. I held onto the rope with both hands as my body banged back and forth into the rocks. I shouted that I needed somebody to come and get me.

The instructor calmly said, "Nobody can get to you. You're dangling in the middle of the air."

I was painfully aware that I was dangling in the middle of the air. My only choice was to rappel correctly down the mountain, which I then did to the applause of everybody.

Rock-climbing entailed learning how to use pitons, cleats, correctly tying on a rope sling, and supporting colleagues as they ascended or descended. We learned to rely on each other as we often held the lives of each other in our hands. With one colleague at the top of the rocky mountain securing my rope, I had to find hand holds and toe holds on the rocky face in order to get to the top. On one climb, I fought for and found those sparse finger holds, and was moving up the mountain nicely when Mike, belaying above, yelled for me to stop. I assumed that he had to readjust the rope.

After a minute or two he yelled for me to continue climbing. He didn't tell me until we were back on the ground that he told me to wait because I was about to place my hand on a snake that had crawled out of the rocks, no doubt to see what the disturbance was on his mountain. Mike said he knew if he told me a snake was in the vicinity, that I, in all probability, would have immediately plummeted to the ground, bringing him down in the process. He was quite right. The most difficult thing to learn to do was to put both legs straight out against the mountain and push off, lightly touching the rock face every few yards with your feet. It was wonderful when it happened. When I tried to stay close to the mountain, which was my inclination, instead of pushing off, I banged into rocks all the way down that left me bruised from chest to knees.

Our training continued. At one point, each of us had to spend a night alone in the forest. We took Army rations and our courage. Each camp leader took a group of five or six of us several miles from our camp, and dropped us off one by one. One colleague chose to stay in a cave. I chose to stay in an open field. I wanted to be able to see all around me. Others in my group were concerned that cattle would come into the pasture the next morning. I knew little about cows, but I was certain that they would simply walk around me and not stampede in. I was more concerned about snakes and tarantulas. I hoped that they were safely ensconced in a cave and not out crawling around on the ground at night. Before we began this adventure, our camp doctor told us the greatest danger we would face overnight would be a tarantula bite.

He said, "Remember, while a tarantula bite is poisonous, you won't die. You'll wish, but it won't happen."

We began our trek armed with that advice. That night I tied my hammock between two trees and after falling out several times, I decided to crawl into my sleeping bag on the ground. Some lizards crawled in with me; at least I thought they were lizards. I never saw them, only felt them. I was afraid that I would mash them and I kept shooing them out, but they managed to get back in before I could zip up the sleeping bag. Finally, we all went to sleep. Apparently they were early risers because none were in the sleeping bag when I awakened the next morning.

The following week we were divided into groups of five woman or five men to spend four days and nights hiking and sleeping in the open armed only with a map, compass, a sleeping bag, two machetes and army rations. We were to leave messages at certain checkpoints. My group followed our map right into dense growth that even the machetes could not chop through. We were lost, but we were not concerned because we had been told that when we missed a checkpoint, our camp leaders would look for us. We later learned that nobody realized we were lost because they couldn't find the checkpoints either. By the third day we knew we were hopelessly lost, but we kept going. The hike began taking a toll on us.

One woman twisted her ankle; another said she had no feeling in one foot. Another one was unable to eat the army rations and was becoming light-headed. Meanwhile, the camp dog joined us. I thought he could lead us back to the camp. He didn't. We followed him out of the forest and into a swamp. At night he delighted in tormenting Elsie who was terrified of dogs.

When we bedded down for the night he nestled next to me until I went to sleep, and then he would go over to Elsie who immediately woke up screaming. I'd call him back, and go to sleep with him under my arm, only to wake up to Elsie screaming minutes later. Nobody got any sleep the night he was with us.

The next day our motley little group hobbled into a village. We immediately spied a car. We asked the car's owner to take us to our camp. He agreed, but said the dog could not go. I wasn't going without the dog. I said I would stay with him until a staff member from camp came for us. The others argued that we were told not to become separated, and especially now when we didn't know where we were. I refused to leave the dog because I didn't know if he could find his way back to camp. Somehow the others cajoled the man into allowing the dog in his car, and the five of us piled in with the big dog snugly in my lap.

Back at camp nobody seemed alarmed that we were the last group to return, that we arrived in a car, or that we had battle wounds. We cleaned up; some got medical care, and went to report on our adventure, anxious to let the staff know that we were safe. Imagine our surprise when we learned that nobody was looking for us. The staff didn't seem the least bit concerned. They said the maps were outdated, and nobody had checked out the area previously, but they were certain that we were astute enough to find our way back to camp. We were being tested on our fortitude, stamina and grit. We passed the test. By this time we were so highly motivated that none of us would have refused to try anything that was thrown at us. Everybody made an attempt which was the most important thing. Our group had bonded in Baltimore, but friendships were cemented during our camp trials in Puerto Rico. Thanks to our esprit de corps, we survived Camp Rio Abajo, even the women in their sixties. De-selection had begun and we lost several members of our group. The selection out process would continue throughout our university training. Our trophies from the camp were hardened hands, tight bodies, and a certainty that we could do the impossible, because we had spent one month doing just that. We had discovered great reservoirs of strength deep within ourselves that we didn't know we had. We were ready to face the world and teach Peruvians all about nutrition. But could anybody cook?

The University Of Puerto Rico — Rio Piedras

Smile…tomorrow will be worse.

- Murphy's Law

One really must be careful what one prays for. We lived for the day when we would finish our camp training and begin nine weeks of academic training in Rio Piedras at the University of Puerto Rico. When that day finally arrived, we were driven into the city where we lived with different Puerto Rican families. Pat Byrd and I lived on the second floor of a home. We shared a bedroom and a bath. We had a tiny kitchen and snacks were always available. We ate our main meals at the University of Puerto Rico where we had classes for 12 hours a day, including Saturdays. The Peace Corps had a large staff lined up to teach us. They taught us Latin American history, home economics, Spanish, Communist techniques, among other subjects. We sat through class after class, sometimes patiently, and sometimes not so patiently. For those of us who did not know any Spanish, we had Spanish classes eight hours a day. It was total immersion. Because of being so forcefully fed Spanish, I began to dislike it.

We were given a $14 weekly allowance called our "walk around" money. It didn't buy much, but then we had no need for much since our food and lodgings were supplied. Some of us used the money for cigarettes and exotic, tropical drinks at the Hilton Hotel's Trader Vic's. The days were long. They began with breakfast at the university from 7 to 8 a.m. for the few who ate breakfast. Some of us preferred to sleep later. Classes began at 8 a.m. and ended at 10 p.m.

On Saturdays our classes ended at 8 p.m. Finally, we rebelled and demanded a reduction in our workload. As a result, they reduced the beginning language classes to six hours a day. By now I not only disliked Spanish intensely, I hated it. We were told that Peruvians spoke the purest Spanish outside of Spain, and our instructors wanted us to speak pure Spanish. We picked up a lot of slang in Puerto Rico, some of which I had to explain later in Peru.

We learned that water in Peru and in most developing countries was unsafe to drink. All water used for drinking or for brushing of teeth had to be boiled for at least 20 minutes. We also learned that waste disposal was inadequate, and because food contamination was a constant that resulted in intestinal parasitic diseases, most of us would have almost constant diarrhea. Other maladies we would be exposed to included: high altitude sickness, rabies, leprosy, tuberculosis, malaria in the jungle areas, typhoid fever, infectious hepatitis, and bilharzia. Few of us would have electricity or indoor toilets. We were inoculated against as many diseases as possible. We were warned that some of us would die in airplane accidents. Nothing they told us made anybody want to return home. The gauntlet had been thrown down and we had taken it up.

A lot of class time was devoted to the subject of cultural differences. The guys were told they were going into a culture in which the men lived and died by being macho – domineering, aggressive, womanizing, and worse. Men drank heartily and often. For both sexes whenever the word, "Salud!" was said, you raised your glass and drank. To do otherwise was an insult to your hosts.

One night our youngest trainee decided that he needed to learn to drink in order to be more macho. He drank most of a bottle of rum and had to be rushed to the hospital to be treated for near-fatal alcohol poisoning.

We were told to be extremely careful when using the word "madre" or "mama" because in some Latin countries gringos had been killed for using the wrong word which inferred an unwelcome familiarity with the person's mother.

We had health and nutrition classes. We were told that whatever little we knew about health and nutrition was more than those we'd be working with knew. Our nutrition classes included learning to prepare what came to be one of my favorite dishes, Seviche, a dish of raw shrimp, onions, lime juice and hot peppers. It required no actual cooking because the peppers and lime juice cooked the shrimp without the need for heat.

The Peace Corps had nine weeks to give us a working knowledge of basic nutrition, planning and organizing a school breakfast or lunch program, teaching others to observe good hygiene, and preparing the food to be palatable. I didn't know how cornmeal mush could be made palatable. Puerto Rico had an extremely well developed school lunch program, and a breakfast program for pre-school children. We were divided into small groups to spend one week in various small towns to observe the Puerto Rican school breakfast and lunch program. Joanne and I went to Jayuya, a city some distance from Rio Piedras, where we worked in a school lunchroom, and lived with a Puerto Rican family.

One evening I happened to mention to our hostess that Joanne and I wanted to have our ears pierced, and asked if we could have it done there. She told us to drop by the hospital where she worked the next day after we finished our assignments. When we arrived at the hospital, we were immediately ushered into an operating room where it seemed the entire staff of doctors and nurses awaited us. They were gowned and gloved and ready for surgery. That's when we learned that our hostess was the administrator of the hospital. I was the first one to undergo the knife. I made certain they understood that I wanted my ears pierced and nothing else done. (I didn't know then, but later I learned about a man who went to a clinic in Mississippi to get help for a fish bone caught in his throat, and they circumcised him!) Hospitals can make mistakes. One doctor brought out an instrument that looked like a miniature saber. I was draped and prepped, the ear cleaned, and the operation began. They pierced the first ear and it hurt like hell. When they finished, I thanked them and prepared to get off the table.

"We have to do the other ear," somebody said.

"I've changed my mind," I replied. "I don't want the other ear done."

They insisted, and reluctantly, I let them pierce the other ear, and that hurt just as much as the first one had. Joanne was braver than I was and barely winced. The pain was worth it though. Back in the city we bought gold earrings and strutted around proudly to compliments from our fellow trainees.

When we finished our training we returned to our home cities to pack for Peru. I went home to Indianapolis to say goodbye to the family.

Every night I pushed the dresser drawers against the door to prevent Mr. Walt from entering my room. He said nothing to me, and I said nothing to him. I was an adult woman now, and I knew there was nothing he could do to me that I was going to let happen. Mother was not happy about me leaving the country, and that saddened me, but she perked up when a reporter, accompanied by a photographer, from *The Indianapolis Recorder* interviewed me at the airport and took my picture for their next issue. I returned to New York City to prepare for our final departure.

Shortly before leaving New York I received a call from Sargent Shriver that there had been a coup d'etat in Peru and while the new government said they welcomed the volunteers, the Peace Corps decided to delay our arrival until the situation was calmer. On August 8, 1962, we were sent to the Institute for International Living in Brattleboro, Vermont, until our government decided it was safe for us to leave for Peru. The Institute is located in a spectacularly beautiful area. The men lived in the Carriage House and the women lived in the main house. Our language and cultural classes continued, but we welcomed the extra free time we were allowed. We explored the beauty of Vermont in late summer and often walked to town. I enjoyed walking until one day a group of white teenaged boys yelled "nigger" at me from across the street. I was walking with three white companions. We all tried to ignore the word, and nobody commented. I was chagrined and angry at being called out of my name. I supposed that only a small number of blacks, if any, lived in Vermont, and I wondered why there was such hate in the teenagers. After that incident, I limited my walks to the countryside where I talked to the cows and their calves.

On September 7 we flew from Vermont to Miami, Florida, where we were to take an evening flight to Peru. The bus that met us at the airport in Miami had a huge banner on its side that read, "PEACE CORPS PERU II." We were elated. We wanted people to know that we were proud Peace Corps Volunteers, but the U.S. government officials accompanying us insisted that the banner be removed. They didn't want anyone other than Peruvian officials to know of our arrival. They were concerned about how we would be received by the Peruvians.

That evening we boarded our Panagra plane, an offshoot of Pan American, for Peru. We were the first group of volunteers going to Peru. We were welcomed by the flight attendants and the captain. Inside our souvenir menu was a special welcome from the airline that read: "PANAGRA is highly honored for having the opportunity to transport the U.S. Peace Corps Volunteers to Lima, Peru. September 7, 1962." The menu cover featured a stylistic and colorful drawing of an alpaca and El Sol (sun and money in Spanish). Our menu that evening consisted of filet mignon, garden peas, duchess potatoes, hearts of lettuce salad, and French pastry. It was our last taste of home.

We were supposed to land at some point to refuel; however, I overheard an official say we were not going to land because the pilot "thought" he could make it to Lima without refueling. My stomach turned over. I was already nervous at taking such a long flight, about 12 hours, and I thought they were foolhardy in hoping that the plane could make it to Lima without refueling. U.S. officials wanted to get us to Peru without anyone knowing about us until we were on the ground.

It didn't help that I sat next to Curt who kept me wide-awake by alarming me about the flames coming from the plane's engines, and alerting me to every bump and engine noise that occurred. I believe that was the night I decided I never wanted to fly again. Everybody was too excited to sleep. We ate, sang the Peruvian National Anthem, and talked about our host country. We were more than ready. The question was: Was Peru ready for us? We were about to find out.

Welcome to Peru

While each of us may not be poor, poverty affects all of us.
- Robert Kennedy

When our plane landed at the Lima airport around 6 a.m., from our windows we saw soldiers toting machine guns lined up on both sides of a path that led into the terminal. We had been excited beyond belief, but now we wondered why the soldiers were there with weapons out. We were not allowed to disembark. We sat on the plane for approximately 20 minutes. Our officials had left the plane and we had no way of knowing what was going on. Were we going to be shot on the tarmac? The plane which moments before had been filled with the sounds of laughter and joyful anticipation, was now quiet. Finally, we were allowed to leave the plane. When we disembarked, we walked single file between the Peruvian soldiers and into the terminal. Years later I watched our embassy hostages in Iran walking between raving Iranians who had held them prisoner for 444 days, and onto the Algerian plane that would fly them to safety. I thought they looked the way we must have looked that day in Lima. The hostages seemed unsure if they were headed to safety or to worse treatment. We did not know why we were being welcomed in such an unconventional manner. None of us had ever been greeted by soldiers and guns. Gone was the gaiety and excitement that we had felt at this marvelous opportunity to serve others.

We knew there had been a coup in Peru, and we trusted our government not to put us in harm's way, but now 43 Americans looked at those soldiers and their big guns, and wondered what we had gotten ourselves into. We were considerably subdued as we walked into the terminal. Inside the terminal Peruvian officials greeted us warmly, and explained that the soldiers were there to protect us against any potential problems at the airport. I wondered if soldiers were always going to surround us. The airport speeches were our introduction to Latin speeches. Each official who stepped to the microphone talked and talked and talked. The language was flowery and complimentary, but we were rocking on our feet to keep from falling over asleep. We had not slept on the plane, barely slept the night before our departure, and now our sleeplessness was catching up with us. It was nearing the end of winter in the Southern Hemisphere and Lima was quite chilly. A warm hotel bed was all that was on my mind. Finally, buses took us and our luggage into town, and to the Hotel Alcazar that came to be known as "the Peace Corps Hotel."

Lima was overcast. It was the time of year when the skies are perpetually gray due to the Humboldt Current that comes from Antarctica and up the coast of South America. At the hotel we were assigned our rooms, had breakfast and prepared to go to bed. The hotel rooms were cold. There was no central heating and the sheets were icy. I remembered a tip in training to iron the sheet before climbing into bed and then jump in. I had brought a travel iron with me, and every night in Lima I used it.

When we got up in the afternoon, after a few hours of sleep, we were ready to see Lima. Our arrival was headline news in the afternoon newspapers, and everywhere we went the Peruvian people hailed and welcomed us. We were a hit before we'd done one bit of work. We represented President Kennedy, a man they loved because he promised democracy and a partnership to our South American neighbors, and we were the first wave of those promises. One cultural custom bothered me. The shops were closed from noon until three or four in the afternoon for siesta time. People went home to eat huge lunches and take naps. It was called a siesta. I thought it odd. The stores stayed open late at night since they were closed half the day for naps. I came to embrace siesta time. When I returned to the U.S. Aunt Bess said I was the only person she knew who got up in the morning planning when she was going to take a nap. Peru was my introduction to a more relaxed world. Lima was an extremely noisy city. I noticed a constant pounding, and learned that because it was against the law for drivers to honk their horns, the frustrated drivers simply hung their arms outside the car window and banged on the side of the car door with their hands. The result was a constant thunderous commotion in the streets.

Cuzco, Peru

Never knock on Death's door, ring the doorbell and run (he hates that!)
- Anon

There is a saying that everybody wants to go to heaven, but nobody wants to die. After a few days in Lima, it was time to leave for our work sites. Some went by bus, but my group of 16 would be flying to Cuzco. We were told in training that Peruvians referred to one airline as "the death airline." They never said which airline that was. That morning found sixteen, green (in more ways than one) volunteers boarding a four-engine Faucett plane for Cuzco. The appearance of the plane didn't inspire confidence in any of us. It looked as if it had been put together with aluminum foil and thumbtacks. I knew this had to be the "death airline." Amidst the race to get strapped into my seat, frantically wondering how the plane could get off the ground, and fervently praying that it wouldn't, I discovered two long tubes attached underneath each window. The tubes in each row were for the people sitting in the seats ahead. The stewardesses explained that the tubes were for us to inhale oxygen. The plane was not pressurized.

A few minutes out of Lima we grabbed those tubes and sucked on them for dear life. Occasionally the oxygen supply was cut off when the people seated behind moved around and accidentally doubled or disconnected the air hose, and we were left gasping for air. I was fighting to keep down breakfast, drooling, and swallowing air. What a horrible sight and worse feeling.

When we landed in Cuzco, after a two and a half hour flight, and after they cleared the dirt runway of llamas, I floated off the plane from the infusion of oxygen and air. It was a good thing because Cuzco, at 11,400 feet above sea level, had little air to offer. We landed on top of a mountain and crawled off the aircraft. We had been warned that because of the altitude we might have some difficulty breathing for the first few days in Cuzco, and also that one alcoholic drink would make us feel as if we had had three drinks. We were also told that periodically we were to descend to sea level in order to keep our chests from expanding. Some of the women wanted their chests to expand. The Quechua have large chests, and it's been postulated that a large chest allows for increased oxygen intake. The lungs must work harder, and this expansion of lung capacity causes an increase in chest size. I was struck by the abnormally large chests of the diminutive Quechua Indians that enabled them to carry loads several times their weight. They were the beasts of burden.

Our group of volunteers was the first Peace Corps group in Cuzco. We arrived in September, the middle of winter in the Southern Hemisphere. All new arrivals to Cuzco are strongly advised to go to bed immediately to avoid altitude sickness, headache and dizziness, and to allow the body to become acclimated to the thin air in Cuzco. After a few days I was acclimated, or so I thought, and then the nosebleeds began.

One morning a bus took our small group to a village outside of town. We were there to view a school and its feeding program. We were greeted and began looking around when I suddenly felt my nose dripping.

I got out a tissue and saw I had a nosebleed. I was alarmed because I had never had a nosebleed. The bleeding worsened almost immediately. I went outside and Irene, another volunteer, who had seen the blood, followed me. By this time my nose was gushing blood. When our bus driver saw the problem, he said he would take us to a clinic. We boarded the bus just as the rest of our group came out of the building. We had had no time to tell anyone where we were going or what was happening. Some of the group saw us board the bus, and they suspected that something had happened. We sped to a "clinic." Blood was gushing from my nose and I had become very frightened. At the clinic I was immediately taken into an examination room. Irene spoke Spanish and translated. The medical person gave me an injection. I didn't want it because I didn't know how or if the needle had been sterilized, or what was in the medication. I did know that the nosebleed had to be stopped. After a few minutes it stopped and we reboarded the bus which had picked up the other volunteers and now waited for us.

Upon arriving back in Cuzco I got in bed per instructions. My roommate, Dorothy, was going to bring up my dinner. I was sitting up in bed reading when my nose began bleeding again. I tried to stop it and it began gushing. I ran down the hall in my gown and robe, flew through the lobby to the dining room door where I shouted for my roommate. She and other volunteers came running. I plopped down into an oversized chair outside the dining room. Some of the volunteers made me hold my head back. I would do that until blood slid down my throat, causing me to jerk my head up, which made my nose bleed more. Some of the volunteers got towels to hold to my nose. The floor was soon littered with bloody towels.

Our guys were shouting for ice, water and more towels. They would not let me move for hours. Finally, I was helped up the stairs to my room where I gingerly crawled into bed and went off to sleep with a towel at my nose, just in case. The next day Irene and I were taken to a local doctor. He said I needed to have the blood vessels in my nose cauterized which I did after one last nosebleed.

The city of Cuzco was much more than a step back in time. It was a giant leap into another world. It was very different from Lima, the capital of Peru. Lima was modern and bustling, whereas Cuzco was anything but bustling. There were few cars and fewer people on the streets in this ancient city of the Incas, and the fourth largest city in Peru. It is the capital of the Cuzco Province (state) and a haven for tourists en route to the ruins of Machu Picchu, the lost city of the Gods. This was the home of the Inca Empire and the richest city in Latin America some five centuries ago, until 1533 when Francisco Pizarro and his conquistadors arrived, slaughtered thousands and decimated the empire.

In 1962 Cuzco had a population of roughly 100,000. In the Quechua language Cuzco means heart, and indeed it was the heart of the ancient empire. The city is nestled in a valley surrounded by majestic mountains. The crest of the country is emblazoned on a mountainside and is visible from any point in the city.

Cuzco is the home of the descendants of the Incas, the Quechua, a tragic race displaced in their own homeland. Men, women and children carry ponderous burdens on their backs, and actually trot with them. Their life expectancy is 32 years. Many of the men wear sandals made from old tires. The women and children are almost always barefooted.

There are numerous Roman Catholic churches in Cuzco, each one features exquisite paintings and gold artwork. On religious holy days the statues of Jesus, the Virgin Mary, and some saints are brought out and carried through the streets in a procession which is when one can truly appreciate the gold and precious jewels that adorn the statues. Gold is everywhere in Latin churches. I was profoundly disturbed at the riches inside the churches while outside the Quechua people were barely able to feed themselves. I seldom went to church in Peru because the profusion of riches inside seemed obscene when one looked at the poverty everywhere.

A favorite place for volunteers to visit was Sacsayhuaman, just outside of Cuzco, formerly a sacred city of the Incas. These ancient remains are a tribute to the ingenuity of those who constructed it. It is said that it took several decades for 20,000 men to build the massive walls. Any one of the enormous stones could weigh more than 125 tons. The mystery remains as to how they are held together without mortar, and how they were moved from one place to another with men being the only beasts of burden at that time. These rocks are all that remain of a fortress that even the mighty Spaniards, who razed the rest of the country, were not able to destroy totally. Enough of the ruins remain to make one appreciate the incredible strength and labor that went into the building of this fortress.

Three of us moved into a large apartment which was frigid. It had a living room, dining room, three bedrooms, tiny kitchen and bath. There was no such thing as central heating in Cuzco. The first night at bedtime I kept my clothes on, and added pajamas, a robe, and an additional pair of socks.

The next day the three of us went to the market looking for warm blankets. I bought two items that the seller said were floor rugs, but looked like blankets to me, and they went on my bed. They were so heavy I could barely turn over in bed, but I was warm at last.

Driving on the mountainous roads was scary. During our training we were told that most of us would die in airplane accidents, but after arriving in Cuzco, I quickly came to the conclusion that most of us would die in road accidents. It was unnerving to drive along a road and see numerous small, wooden crosses indicating the site of a fatal accident. The crosses should have been - but weren't – a warning to drivers to slow down. The rutted unpaved roads in the mountains were barely one lane, and every few feet there was a blind curve. Lush valleys lay below while the great Andes Mountains soared above, but I was too afraid of an auto accident to appreciate the beauty.

I was amazed to see Quechua men openly urinating on the streets. The Quechua women, who wore voluminous, dark colored skirts decorated with elaborate embroidery, simply squatted, and you couldn't see what they were doing, but you could make a good guess. The women, unlike the men, were usually barefoot. They wore tall, white bowler-type hats, and their black, straight hair was always in two braids. Practically every woman carried a baby on her back swaddled in a brightly colored wrap. The women spun llama wool as they walked or as they sat on the ground selling coca leaves, ashes and limes. The men wore short ponchos, knee-length pants, vivid woolen caps with earflaps, and sandals made from old tires.

It is said the Quechua bathe three times in their lifetime: they are bathed when they are born; they bathe when they marry, and they are bathed when they die. That makes for a pungent body odor that permeates everything. When my trunk arrived back in the United States, I opened it and my nostrils were immediately filled with that special human smell that pervades Cuzco.

My two roommates were both New Yorkers. One was of Italian descent, quiet and rather plain. The other was Jewish, stylish and definitely a disco diva.

The other volunteers labeled us the "New York queens." Our apartment was large and would have been comfortable had I not been cold all the time. The complex was built in a semi-circle and each apartment was entered from the street. We had three bedrooms, dining room, and a tiny kitchen. The apartment did not come with a range. We used a Primus stove or two if we were baking.

We decided that living in the cold was one thing, but showering in the cold was quite another. We pooled our money and bought an electric shower. The problem was that the gadget had to be unplugged BEFORE we shut off the water. That meant you had to unplug the water heater with wet hands and body, and hope that you were not electrocuted by 220 volts of electricity. If we let the water run with the gadget plugged in until we dried off, that increased the electric bill considerably. When volunteers who worked outside of Cuzco came to the city, they usually stayed at our apartment. We always patiently explained how the shower gadget worked, but none of them was crazy enough to unplug the gadget with wet hands. We even posted a huge sign in the bathroom.

Nothing could get any of our visitors to unplug an electrical gadget with wet hands and standing in water. After two gadgets burned out, my roommates and I went back to taking cold showers. The plus was that we had fewer visitors.

Black-girl-in-town-blues

An eye for an eye only ends up making the whole world blind.
- M.K. Gandhi

The Peace Corps provided comic relief for the people of Cuzco. Me. They sent a black, American female to the capital of the ancient Inca Empire. The Quechua Indians were accustomed to seeing white tourists passing through Cuzco on their way to visit Machu-Picchu, but I was a novelty. I was the crowd-getter and the reason mobs of children followed us pointing and laughing. Some of them were about my color, but they knew that I was very different from them. Some adult Indians reached out to touch me because, I was told, some thought touching a black person would bring them luck. I secretly wondered if it was to see if the black rubbed off. At first, I tried to laugh it off, but inside I was deeply hurt. Some Indians screamed in horror and ran when they saw me.

When I first heard cries of "Negrita!" I thought it was their word for "nigger." I was told it meant, "little black." I didn't care if it meant "little goddess," I hated hearing the word. When I joined the Peace Corps it never occurred to me that a black American would stand out in a group of whites. I was long accustomed to being the only black or one of a very few blacks in a group, but I had never known such derision. The bonding experience with my fellow volunteers in Baltimore and at the camp in Puerto Rico had been so intense, that somehow I thought I would be seen simply as an American.

51

Instead there I was in Peru trying to help people who saw me as an object of ridicule. It was a jarring experience to have people look at me and burst into hysterical laughter. My insides twisted in agony. Some days I'd walk into a tiny store that sold matches, sodas and gum – called tiendas – and no one else was around. Minutes later when I turned to leave, I was always shocked to see a crowd of 10 to 15 people crowding the doorway snickering, screaming, and scrambling to get as far away from me as possible as I walked through them. I would smile and speak Spanish to them. This led to more uproarious laughter. At other times, I would simply smile and make a hasty departure.

The Peruvian view of race was never touched upon during our training, and the question of color had never come up in our cultural discussions. Odd that nobody thought of discussing race in a foreign country, especially at a time when race problems were foremost in U.S. news. It is said that in Peru people are not defined by their race, but their race is defined by their wealth. As has been the case throughout the history of the world, the indigenous people were shoved aside while the Europeans or descendants of Europeans plundered the land and its riches. In Peru it was the elites descended from Europeans who traditionally led the nation. They were not copper-toned, but mainly white. The fair-skinned people were the leaders as well as the wealthy landowners. The light-skinned mestizos came next, and finally the Quechua Indians whose birthright came from their ancestors, the Incas. As is true in many countries, the indigenous people are the least likely to have, or to acquire, wealth and power.

Our program involved overseeing the distribution of American-donated food that provided breakfasts for practically all of the poor children attending primary schools. When my two, white roommates and I visited schools in Cuzco, the officials greeted them effusively. They were polite to me during the introductions, but after that, they ignored me. Usually a teacher or principal would ask me several times where I was from. I patiently explained over and over that we were all from the United States.

A few minutes later a teacher would ask, "So you're from Africa?"

Or, "You are from Puerto Rico?"

If was as if they expected me to slip up and admit that I was not an American.

Finally, each volunteer was assigned several schools. At my schools the officials were rather brusque with me. When I arrived without my white colleagues, they looked behind me as if searching for the "bosses." They would inquire about the other volunteers, and when I explained that I would be responsible for their particular school, they looked quite stricken. As I talked to them about the breakfast program, they seemed to barely listen. I quickly got the impression that they resented having been assigned a volunteer who was not white. I thought that when the food program actually began, and they saw how much the children needed the food, they would get over their resentment that I was not white.

I noticed that when I visited other PCVs in villages outside of Cuzco, I was always greeted warmly by the people there. I never got the stares and histrionics. Perhaps, I thought, country people are inherently more polite than big city folks are.

I asked our Country Director, Frank Mankiewicz, for a transfer to a village. Frank was against it. He refused to believe that country people were more civil than the so-called city folk. When I was alone in my room, I cried a lot. I was far, far from home trying to express to a hostile (as I began to think of them) people the care and concern of all Americans, yet I was the butt of humor. I soon developed an irritating skin rash, and was unable to sleep. I finally had to see our Peace Corps doctor and unburden myself. He feared that I would have a nervous breakdown and advised Mankiewicz to transfer me to Lima.

I refused to go to Lima to work in the barriadas, slums areas perched on top of garbage heaps. We had a glimpse of those slums during our week in Lima. I wanted to stay in Cuzco where there was space, mountains as far as the eye could see, and the air was clear and crisp. I was also curious about the Quechua Indians and I was determined to work with them. I knew that I could not spend two years suffering stomach contractions, a rash all over my body, daily hot tears of self-pity, and anger at the people I was there to help. I prayed that a way would be found to enable me to remain in the Cuzco area.

The Peruvian doctor who had treated my nosebleeds sent my two white roommates invitations to a dance his social club was giving, but he didn't invite me. Jessica, a social butterfly, was excited about the event, but Irene saw it differently.

Jessica, danced around in the living room with her long, dark hair swinging and exclaimed, "What will I wear?"

"Surely you aren't going when Charlene was not invited," Irene snapped at her.

I jumped in, "It's OK. I know Jessica misses going out. Both of you should go."

Jessica looked stricken. I knew she really wanted to go to the dance.

Irene pressed on, "Are you still planning to go, knowing that one of your colleagues was deliberately excluded? What kind of person are you?"

As I watched from the sidelines, Jessica said to Irene, "I'm sorry you feel that way."

"I think you're being very selfish, thinking only of yourself. " Irene continued.

"You don't care that one of us was deliberately excluded from the invitation."

"Irene, let it go," I pleaded.

"I don't think I want to continue living in the same house with you," Jessica told Irene.

Irene, who didn't particularly care for Jessica in the first place, lashed out with, "And I don't want to live in the same CITY you're in! I'm going to request a transfer! I don't want to be anywhere near you!"

Dumbfounded, I looked at both of them and wondered what had just happened. In a matter of minutes, we three had gone from an invitation to them, no invitation to me, to one woman not wanting to live in the same house with the other one, and the other one refusing to remain in the same city as the other one. And I thought I had been the injured party.

Two weeks later on the night of the dance, the doctor arrived to pick up Jessica and Irene. I made a point of answering the door. The doctor was a short, swaggering man, slightly overweight, rather ordinary looking, with a light tan complexion. Irene was sequestered in her bedroom, and Jessica was not ready. I had looked forward to opening the door and seeing the doctor. I greeted him cordially, much to his discomfort, and invited him in to wait for

Jessica. When we were seated I took great pleasure in telling him that Irene would not be going since the three of us were not invited, and she felt that it was an insult of such magnitude that she could not possibly attend his dance. He squirmed in his seat, and his caramel colored face turned various shades of red. I was on stage and the curtain had gone up. I was in my element. I smiled at him charmingly. How I delighted in his misery. But deep inside, I knew that his misery was also mine.

The Kidnap Plot

The secret of reaping the greatest fruitfulness and the
greatest enjoyment from life is to live dangerously!
- Friedrich Nietzsche

John, our usually comical Peace Corps Leader, arrived at our apartment late one afternoon looking uncharacteristically somber.

"Frank is in town and wants to meet with you," he said flatly.

We were always happy to see Frank Mankiewicz, Director of the Peace Corps in Peru, who was based in Lima.

I asked John, "What's Frank doing here? Usually we know in advance when he's coming."

"I don't know," John answered, all business. "He just arrived and told me to bring you and Jessica to Ramon's office."

Ramon Paz was our Peruvian coordinator who worked with all of the volunteers in Cuzco. I immediately wondered if something had happened to our other roommate, Irene, who had been sent to Lima for medical treatment. I glanced at Jessica who looked as puzzled as I felt. We didn't quite believe that John didn't know why Frank was in Cuzco. In silence, he drove us to Ramon's office. Jessica and I greeted Frank with hugs as usual and he asked us to sit down. He and Ramon looked very solemn. We knew something was seriously wrong.

"I want you two to listen to me very carefully," Frank said.

He had our full attention.

"I came here because we've been told by Cuzco police that there is a credible plot to kidnap the three Peace Corps women in Cuzco city. Since Irene is in Lima on sick leave, that leaves the two of you."

"Fabulous!" I said.

"Wow, this is great!" added Jessica.

A volunteer in Bolivia had been kidnapped a few months previously and soon after released unharmed. The excitement during his capture and after his release was tremendous. He made the news in every weekly news magazine and newspaper in the U.S. He became famous. Jessica and I, both 25 years old and up for adventure, thought it would be fun to be kidnapped. We assumed that since the other volunteer had not been injured, our kidnappers would simply hold us for a few days and then release us.

We were going to be kidnapped! We almost danced a jig. Frank did not take our enthusiasm well.

After he recovered from our bizarre response, he said, "We are taking this threat very seriously. The police chief has sent out word to the streets that anybody kidnapping you will be dealt with severely."

"We don't want to appear to be scared because of the threat, so we're not going to remove you from your apartment," he continued.

Jessica and I sat there positively beaming.

Frank looked disgusted, but he continued, "We've asked the police to drive by your apartment periodically just to keep an eye on things."

He added, "We've also talked to some of your neighbors to ask them to be vigilant and to notify Ramon and the police if they see anybody suspicious around your apartment. John will be coming by several times during the day to check on you."

It was obvious that on the one hand Frank was relieved to see that he didn't have two hysterical volunteers on his hands, but on the other hand he appeared justifiably concerned that we thought this was a lark and we might not follow his instructions. We smiled at him brightly, while he glared as us in exasperation.

"Stay inside your apartment for the next few days," he admonished.

"Do not go to any of your schools until we give you the okay. Remember, we're doing all we can to stop this plot from succeeding."

Back at home Jessica and I enthused about how exciting it would be to be kidnapped, and wondered how we could get ready. We stayed inside and peeped out the windows frequently to see if we could see any kidnappers in the vicinity. We were ready to all but leave our door wide open to make it easier for them to get in. What were we thinking?

By the third day the kidnappers had not appeared and we were tired of staying home. Jessica suggested that we go to a movie that night. In the theatre we were watching a Doris Day-Rock Hudson film when suddenly there was a tremendous noise from outside. We heard booming and clashing and feet moving. Was it the kidnappers? Every head in the theatre turned toward the back of the theatre. I looked down at the seat in front of me; no way to get under it.

Jessica and I looked at each other with one thought: They are coming to get us! I hoped we would be lost among the movie goers. I cursed the day I thought it would be fun to be kidnapped. I will never know why we thought kidnappers would broadcast their arrival to a theater filled with hundreds of people, enter, and march throughout the theater looking for us, and then simply walk out with us. The noise increased in volume until everybody realized that it was a marching band passing by, which accounted for the cymbals, drums, pots and pans, and general clamor. At the end of the movie Jessica and I scurried home as fast as we could. We were ready to stay in as long as necessary. We never were kidnapped, and we never told Frank that we'd disobeyed and gone out. By that time we had decided that perhaps being kidnapped would not have been as much fun as we previously thought. On the other hand, it might have been.

Quiquijana

Not where I was born, but where it goes well with me is my home.
- Nigerian proverb

Some Quechua Indians said Quiquijana meant "fat, fat Jana," and others said it meant "bloody, bloody plain." Quiquijana, meant home to me. It was a place where I was loved by the people, and where I loved them in return.

A few months after my numerous requests for a transfer from Cuzco, a PC friend in Arequipa, another black woman, resigned. She was outgoing, hardworking and popular with the volunteers and children. I thought she was handling the race situation better than I was, but she had told me she was tired of being called "negrita" and laughed at by people. She had quit and returned to the U.S. I was sorry she had made that decision because she was exactly the kind of volunteer that the Peace Corps needed. I knew that I could never be comfortable living and working in the city of Cuzco, and once again I asked for a transfer to a village, and this time I told Frank that I was considering resigning. He reluctantly relented and sent me, along with Jean, a newly arrived volunteer, to visit a tiny village about two hours by train from Cuzco.

The moment I entered the village of Quiquijana, I felt welcomed. School officials greeted us, and we were taken on a walking tour of the community. They said the village consisted of 2,500 people, but it seemed smaller.

The Quechua men and women we passed gave us shy smiles and lowered their heads subserviently. Those of mixed heritage greeted us with warm smiles and waves. Some Quechua women sat beside the road selling chicha, a drink made from fermented corn, while others sold coca leaves and lime. The principal of the school and the teachers appeared to be of mixed heritage – Quechua and Spanish. There were no rude stares, and no hysterical laughter directed at me. I felt like a normal human being, no different from anybody else.

The townsfolk had built a little two-room house for its volunteers on the nuclear school grounds. This nuclear school was responsible for all schools in the outlying areas. The house had an outdoor kitchen, dirt floors and no electricity. The outhouse, which we would share with the school children and teachers, was almost one block from our house. A water pump was at the front of the school grounds, but we were prepared to carry water buckets. My heart told me this was where I was meant to be. They wanted us there, and we wanted to be there.

House in Quiquijana - 1963

A week later we returned from Cuzco with our belongings and discovered that our Quiquijana house had been painted a cotton-candy shade of pink after school officials learned they would have female volunteers. It was beautiful. Two dogs that belonged to the caretaker of the grounds immediately adopted us and only went home for meals and then returned to us.

The second day, walking through town looking for the post office, I saw to my horror that the post office was on the other side of town, connected by a swinging rope bridge high above loud, rushing waters that dashed on the remnants of the old bridge below.

Burma Bridge in Quiquijana - 1962

I was paralyzed with fright when I realized what I now had to contend with for the remaining 14 months of my Peace Corps service. I stood staring at the sight that back at training camp I was convinced was a figment of somebody's imagination, the dreaded Burma bridge. Jean immediately noticed my fear.

"I'll collect the mail every day. You won't have to cross the bridge," she said.

"But I have to cross it to get to the train station," I sputtered. "I have to force myself to do it." So I did.

The handmade bridge was constructed with wooden slats on top of ropes, with rope hand holds. A handmade bridge did not inspire any confidence in me. Some of the wooden slats were missing, so there were breaks in the bridge. Rushing water dashed on the rocks in the river below. I quickly discovered that when more than one person was crossing, the entire bridge bounced up and down, so I sometimes waited for others to leave the bridge before starting across. Gradually, without even realizing it, I graduated to walking across using no hands, often while reading my mail while others also walked on the rope bridge. Other people on the bridge no longer bothered me. I sailed across that bridge as if I had grown up walking across it. I was truly at home.

We began our breakfast program by teaching the Quechua mother volunteers how to prepare a delicious, hot breakfast and maintain hygienic conditions while cooking in the mud. We had to cook outside because there was no kitchen in the school. We used huge, industrial size pots to prepare the corn meal mush and the hot chocolate.

Jean and I worked with a local baker who prepared the rolls for the breakfast. Each child received two rolls, a bowl of mush, and a large cup of hot chocolate.

For most of the obviously appreciative children, it was their only good meal of the day. They were able to study better and to be better students with full stomachs. Another plus was the fact that school attendance increased since the children had to be enrolled in school in order to participate in the breakfast program. Our work provided instant gratification for Jean and me. We saw the children's cheeks filling out and the dreaded effects of kwashiorkor, child malnutrition, disappearing. Their little bodies filled out, and they were more active and attentive in their classes. It was a joy to be a part of a solution.

One of the mothers who helped prepare the breakfast every morning was Senora Wayna. She was very devoted to the breakfast program and never missed a morning helping prepare the food. She told us that her name meant "young" in Quechua. She seemed anything but young even though she had small children. Life is hard for the Quechua women. Senora Wayna had several front teeth missing, but that didn't take away from her lovely smile. Her entire face lit up when she smiled as she did often. She also sold coca leaves, ash and lime near the bridge along with other women. The senora often invited us to dinner at her home. The first time we went, I noticed several small guinea pigs running about on the floor. When we went to the table to eat, there in the center of the table lay a guinea pig on a platter, with his feet in the air, and teeth shining. I was repelled at the sight, yet I could barely take my eyes off it. Our hostess gave each of us some meat which I barely touched.

Throughout dinner I kept glancing surreptiously at the guinea pig, wondering how it had been killed. The head was there. Did they cut its throat? Jean eagerly ate the meat. The next time we were invited to dinner, again a guinea pig graced the table. I was nearly sick. I knew that the Quechuas did not eat meat every night, and that Senora Wayna was killing her guinea pigs in our honor. When we got home I told Jean that I was going to tell an out and out lie the next time I saw a guinea pig served up. Sure enough, a few weeks later we were again invited to our friend's for dinner. As the Senora reached for my plate, I demurred, saying that due to a stomach ailment our Peace Corps doctor had forbidden me to eat meat. That allowed Jean to eat my portion and then some. She thoroughly enjoyed the meat. I could barely eat with that little critter grinning at me from its central position. In the U. S. we think of guinea pigs as cuddly, furry, little pets for children, but to Peruvians, both at home and abroad, it is the food of choice.

Jean and I ate a lot of tiny, dried potatoes with aji, hot pepper sauce, canned Peruvian trout, and an occasional chicken brought from Cuzco during our monthly visits. We baked using a special oven that went on top of two Primus stoves. Banana bread was one of our favorites. We made doughnuts, and we improvised a toaster. It's amazing what one can do when none of the ususal accoutrements are available. We placed a small wire square in the center of a pan, put a slice of bread on top, and turned it when one side browned.

You Loved The Job.
You Were Miserable.

It felt like home.
  You were homesick.
    The country was breathtaking.
  The land was unyielding.
    The scenery was bigger than life.
  So were the insects.

- A Peace Corps Ad

The descent was steep. It was dismount, lead the horse, mount, dismount, and more of the same. I thought I couldn't do it again, but I did. I was exhausted and could barely get my leg over the horse's back to re-mount. The horse stood patiently each time as I wrapped both arms around her neck, lifted both feet off the ground, crawled up her side and fell into the saddle. This was the end of a two-day horseback trip high in the Peruvian Andes Mountains, an area called "the puna," the vast wasteland. We were visiting some of our truly remote schools, emphasis on remote; remote as in distant, out-of-the-way, isolated, far-flung.

Jean and I were excited when we learned we would be traveling by horseback because that was the only way to reach the area. I loved horses.

I had only been on a horse one time in my life, as a child, but as far as I was concerned, I could ride a horse. A male PCV, Jim, was sent from a neighboring village to accompany us. The Peace Corps did not want two female volunteers going to places no female volunteers had gone before, without an American male escort.

The rest of our party consisted of our local health coordinator, Senor Gonzales, and three Indian guides who journeyed on foot.

The sure-footed guides carried our sleeping bags and changes of clothing. They were also the only ones who knew the way. We left our village on a Tuesday at 7 am. The stated purpose of our trip was to visit the schools under the umbrella of our nuclear school, to observe their breakfast programs in operation, to meet the parents, and to let them know that even though their villages were at the back of beyond, they were not forgotten. We reached the first village after two hours of riding straight up a steep mountain, followed by one hour of descent. We arrived to find there was no school that day because the teacher had gone into Cuzco for the weekend and had not yet returned.

We continued on to the next school. Two more hours of riding brought us to Sachac, where the teacher was on a three-month leave of absence, and there was no replacement. We wondered why Sr. Gonzales had not sent messages ahead to be sure schools would be in session and teachers present, but we were too polite to ask.

Our lips were curved in permanent smiles. Our Peace Corps trainers had taught us well. We knew never to do or say anything that might even suggest an insult to anyone.

We headed to the next village. Our guides had hurried ahead to announce our arrival, and the entire village was out to greet us. We toured the school, and talked to the parents and the students. We stayed for lunch that consisted of hot soup and tiny, dried potatoes served with that delicious hot pepper sauce. After lunch it began to rain and get colder. Our coordinator insisted that we leave before the trails became too muddy.

He wanted to travel on to Urincuzco with Jim and one guide where they would overnight, while the other two guides and Jean and I headed for Llampac where we would spend the night. Jim was nonplussed by this decision since he saw himself as our protector and didn't want to be separated from us. Jean and I didn't feel that we needed protecting, and we wanted to get warm and dry. As Jim and Sr. Gonzales talked, we galloped off leaving Jim staring at our horses' rear ends. By now we were well over 13,000 feet high in the Andes. The rain was freezing. Suddenly, we began hitting steep, muddy embankments, and we had to get off and lead our horses repeatedly. When the rain stopped, the snow and sleet began. We arrived at Llampac soaking wet and freezing. Indian fathers were there to greet us. It was all I could do to smile and mumble salutations. I thought unkind thoughts about people living so far up in the mountains when there was plenty of space below. After a supper of hot soup, we were ready to go to bed. We were led to a cold enclosure, and "bed" was a cement slab over which our hosts stretched several animal skins, ponchos and our sleeping bags. We were too cold to even consider changing clothes. We slept in our wet clothes, on top of an icy, cement block, and inside our cold sleeping bags. We got little sleep because we coughed and sneezed all night.

When the sun came out the next morning, we got up and changed into dry clothes. Jim and our coordinator arrived and we prepared to leave, but not before the children had shown us charming folklore dances from that region. When we were ready to leave I was given a different horse than the one I arrived on because my original horse was pregnant and about to give birth.

I got on my new horse and sat in the saddle holding the reins with one hand while waving at those around us with the other hand. Suddenly the horse neighed and reared up and up. It was like a rodeo. I bounced up and down, in and out of the saddle for what seemed an interminable amount of time. I managed to hold onto the reins until someone got the horse under control. Once on the trail I discovered that my horse would not let another horse in front of him or allow me to guide him. Finally, I had to let Jim ride him because the horse didn't know or care where he was going; he just wanted to be in the front. We rode for hours hugged by the warm sun, and then we rounded a bend to an unbelievable sight.

Facing us was a straight path leading to the school gates, and lining each side of the path were village fathers, some playing instruments, all smiling, yelling and waving to us. As we rode through the middle of them, each father reached up to give each of us a welcoming abrazo, embrace. As I leaned from my saddle for hug after hug, I thought this must be how conquering heroes felt returning from battle to the adulation of their people. That extraordinary welcome was both overwhelming and humbling. I forgot my runny nose, sore throat, and throbbing head and just enjoyed this affectionate welcome. I wondered how and why these diminutive Quechua Indians would greet foreigners so effusively. But I knew it was because their children were being fed by the people of the United States led by President John F. Kennedy. They were thanking us. They had our President's word that life was going to be better for their children, and they believed in him.

They welcomed us in the only way they could by hugs and music and food. We were the direct links to helping their children have a better future. We rode into the schoolyard where the students stood at attention in their colorful fiesta costumes.

Their mothers squatted on the ground in their bright attire. We dismounted and after greeting the mothers we talked to the fathers. Among the Quechua, school is the business of men because as head of their households, they oversee anything that concerns the family. They also donate their labor to building schools and kitchens in various communities. We ate a delicious lunch prepared by the smiling mothers. We reluctantly left around 3 pm because Sr. Gonzales wanted us to descend and reach the main road before dark.

As we headed for home I began to feel the full brunt of the trip, the rain and the cold, my head cold, and the constant getting on and off the horse. I began to take chances. I stopped dismounting, remained in the saddle, and hoped the horse could make it up and down the steep trails. At one point Jim was adamant that I get off and lead my horse because we were approaching an area where there had been landslides. I dismounted and led my horse. I turned to look behind me to see if the horse was managing all right and I fell. My upper body was hanging over a cliff and I was looking straight down for thousands of feet. I was not injured, but I didn't move. I was tired and wanted to rest for a minute. Jim and our coordinator leaped to my side and snatched me off the ground.

"You see," I said, "I would have been safer on the horse."

Thereafter, they let me stay on my horse when I wanted to, and I wanted to stay on often, and did.

We reached the main road at 6 pm just as the sun sank. In that part of the world dusk does not exist. There is nothing between day ending and night beginning. One minute it is day and the next instant it is night. As we rode toward home, I felt exhilarated from our incredible journey and the people we'd met, who, I was convinced, exemplified the best of Peru.

The Death of a President,
November 22, 1963

Do not be afraid of those who kill the body,
but (they) cannot kill the soul...
- Matthew 10:28

Friday, November 22, 1963, Jean and I had gone into Cuzco to do our monthly shopping, to enjoy a hot shower, and to see other volunteers. We were at the supermarket in the checkout line.

I heard Jean say, "It's just another rumor."

"These people are always starting rumors," another volunteer added.

"What are they saying now?" I asked idly.

Someone replied, "They're saying President Kennedy has been killed."

"Oh, for pity's sake!" several of us said in unison, and dismissed the idea immediately.

Jean added, "Just another one of those crazy rumors."

Jean and I had just had lunch with some other volunteers who were in town to shop and all of us would be heading back to our villages the next day. The rumor was promptly forgotten and another volunteer and I headed for the dry cleaners. When I returned to the hotel the desk clerks stared at me as they usually did and it bothered me as it usually did. Somehow the stares seemed a wee different that day.

When I opened the door to our room Jean was crying as if her heart were breaking. I had never seen her cry before. Obviously something was wrong, but I didn't ask what. I must have sensed what it was, but I didn't want to know.

I hung up my dry cleaning and said to her, "It's time to go to the dentist."

She turned up a tear-stained, sorrowful face to me and said in a whisper, "Charlene, it's true."

My reaction was bewildering. I became angry, so angry that I wanted to slap her.

I shouted at her, "I don't know what you are talking about, and I don't want to know!"

Jean dropped her head into her hands and continued crying.

"We have to go to the dentist," I said impatiently.

As long as I didn't hear the words she was aching to tell me, I felt that all would be well and our world would not be rocked. How on earth did I know what I must have known? Jean cried all the way to the dentist's office, while I did my best to ignore her. In the empty waiting room we sat down to wait our turns. A radio was on, but we couldn't make out the words due to static and background noise.

Suddenly the static ended and we clearly heard the announcer say in Spanish, "President Kennedy has been assassinated in Dallas."

There it was. The words were out. I had heard them. I could no longer deny the tragedy. Like zombies we walked out of the dentist's office with no destination in mind. We wandered aimlessly, both of us sobbing. Back at our hotel we sat silently, each of us lost in her own thoughts and prayers.

"Who could have killed President Kennedy?" Jean said between sobs.

Silently I prayed, "Dear God, please let it not be a black person."

The next morning John picked us up to drive us to our village. We were all sad. Traffic on the narrow, dangerous roads seemed more chaotic than usual that day. A bus nearly ran us off the road. Through the bus window we saw the driver's mouth curved in a wide, manic grin.

At our house one of our dogs, JFK, came to greet us.

Jean yelled, "Get away! I don't want to see you!"

I hugged him, and I said to her, "It is not his fault that we named him JFK."

Jean and I spent the rest of Saturday in silence. No conversation was needed or wanted. I worried about my family back in the U.S. I wondered what would happen to black people after the death of the man we saw as our savior. I wondered what it meant for the Peace Corps. Would the new president want to end the program? My mind was in turmoil.

On Sunday Jean and I cooked the chicken we had bought in Cuzco on Friday. We cooked on our Primus stove in our tiny, dirt-floored kitchen. We didn't have refrigeration, but we thought the cold air of the Andes would keep our frozen chicken fresh.

We always bought a frozen chicken on a Friday to take back to our village on Saturday, to be cooked and eaten on Sunday. We ate lunch and gave the two dogs the leftovers. A few minutes later one dog began vomiting.

"Hmmm," I said to Jean, "I wonder what he ate."

Moments later she ran outside to throw up in the weeds. She had no time to run to our outhouse a block away.

When she came back inside, she said, "I know what he ate – that chicken."

Minutes later I began vomiting. Both of us soon became feverish and delirious. Suddenly I was thirsty. My mouth felt as if I hadn't had any water for days. I drank a glass of water. That caused more vomiting. I had to have more water even though I knew the instant it hit my stomach, I had to be on my way outside to throw up. Jean didn't seem to be as thirsty as I was.

In my delirium I heard myself repeating over and over, "We're going to die and nobody will ever know."

The night was long and miserable as we moaned loudly and tossed and turned in our beds.

On Monday morning the villagers began coming to our home to extend their sympathy at the death of President Kennedy. At first Jean and I took turns getting out of bed, opening the door, and falling back into bed. We could barely raise our heads. When I answered the door, I simply opened it, turned and stumbled back into the bedroom. I could have let in Jack the

Ripper. I just wanted to get back in the bed. I vaguely remembered people standing over us.

Julia, one of the teachers at our school, and a good friend of ours, arrived at some point.

I heard her say to someone, "They are too sick to have visitors. I'm going to leave my daughter here to answer the door."

I remember she wiped our faces and placed more covers on us. We alternated between chills and fever. Later that day I heard Julia and the school principal talking in our bedroom.

She said, "We have to get a doctor for them. We must telegraph Cuzco to contact the Peace Corps office."

By the next day we felt a lot better. That evening as I was returning from the outhouse, the dogs suddenly stopped and cocked their ears. In the distance we heard a car engine. I was astonished to see an aqua colored Peace Corps jeep appear out of the dust with our Peace Corps doctor and his wife.

Dr. Starr hopped out and said, "We just returned to Cuzco from visiting some other sick volunteers and there was an urgent message from your school principal that you two were dying."

"It certainly felt like it yesterday." I said.

His wife chimed in, "We didn't unpack. We got right back in the jeep and drove here."

After examining us Dr. Starr said, "It seems that you two had food poisoning. You're lucky. It could have been a lot worse."

We told him about buying the chicken on Friday, and cooking and eating it on Sunday. He warned us not to do that again.

Without refrigeration, he said, we had to eat the chicken the same day we bought it. That meant no more chicken for us because we always had to overnight in Cuzco due to the train schedule.

Dr. Starr and his wife brought news about the assassination, and he was able to assure us that our country would survive. Yes, it would survive, but I knew that it would never be the same. President Kennedy had appealed to many Americans, but he was noteworthy for his ability to reach out to blacks in particular. Black Americans were long accustomed to the "hurry up and wait" motto of the older, reserved civil rights leaders, and they were tired. In the early 1960s young blacks began sit-ins at food counters that refused to serve blacks, or that wanted them to enter via the back door; encouraged black voter registration, and refused to ride in the back of buses going to the South. It was the era of Freedom Riders, and President Kennedy and his brother, Attorney-General Robert Kennedy often had to send out federal troops to protect blacks and white supporters when the city and state governments refused to protect them.

As a presidential candidate, Kennedy won 68% of the black vote. When he became president, Kennedy took actions that no other U.S. president had taken. He appointed more blacks to administrative posts; he appointed black judges; he said he would end segregation, but it took his death to accomplish that. While the entire world seemed to mourn the loss of President Kennedy, black Americans were especially touched by his loss.

What Manner of Man Indeed

Injustice anywhere is a threat to justice everywhere.
-Dr. Martin Luther King, Jr.

For two days in the country of Peru, in the state of Cuzco, the lives of an Indian boy with a broken leg, his father, train conductors, doctors, nurses, a policeman, and two American women intersected. Jean and I unwittingly held the lives of two Quechua Indians, descendants of the noble Incas, in our hands. Jean and I lived in a two-room house on the school grounds in Quiquijana, a village in the Andes Mountains. Often we joined the children to play during the warm, midday recess. It was on one of those afternoons that I noticed Luis sitting off on the sidelines. I went over to ask him to join us. He said he had hurt his leg. I knelt down beside him to see how badly his leg was hurt.

"His leg is broken," one of the teachers shouted as she approached. Other teachers crowded around us.

I saw the pain in the poor boy's eyes as he stoically tried to keep from crying.

"There is nothing to do," one of the teachers declared, saying that there were no doctors in the village.

I nodded to Jean to help me, and together we carried Luis into the school. As she and I discussed what to do, one of the teachers went out and returned with a dark liquid that smelled of kerosene, cloves, and the outhouse.

She applied it to Luis' leg and covered it with bits of paper. That settled it. We knew we had to take him to Cuzco where there was a hospital. A train came through our village three times a week, and serendipitously this was one of those days. The train was due within the next two hours. A messenger was dispatched to Luis' village to get permission from his parents for us to take him to Cuzco. His father soon arrived with half of their village, and he agreed for us to take his son to Cuzco, but he wanted to go too. We agreed to pay the fares for both.

Jean and I packed hurriedly, and our group walked through town, across the rope bridge, and to the train station. I purchased first class tickets for the four of us. Moments later Luis' mother arrived with the rest of their village. They squatted around the boy laying on the floor and set up a loud wail. When the train arrived, Luis was carried on and stretched out in two seats. On both sides of the aisle there were double seats with a table between them. Jean and I sat opposite Luis, and his father sat across the aisle from us.

The train took off, and soon the conductor began collecting tickets. The father held out his ticket, but the conductor ignored the ticket and ordered him to the second class car. I asked the conductor what was the problem.

He replied, "He belongs in the second class car."

I asked, "Doesn't he have a first class ticket?"

He replied curtly: "It doesn't matter. Indians can't ride in the first class car!"

The conductor grabbed the father by his poncho to haul him out of his seat.

I leaped to my feet and thundered, "He's with us and he stays here!"

With my first three words the transformation was remarkable.

The conductor became all smiles. "Oh, Senorita, that's all you had to say."

I was angry that I had had to say anything. I thought of the irony of a black American abroad defending the rights of a Quechua Indian in his own country while in the U.S. we blacks were not so far removed from this same kind of segregation.

At the first stop Luis' father left the train, to use the facilities we assumed. After a few minutes the train began moving slowly. Jean went to the door looking for the father.

Suddenly she yelled to me, "Charlene, they won't let him on!"

I raced to the door. The father was running beside the moving train while trying to reach the door with one hand. His other hand was in the grip of the station attendant who was yelling that the father could not ride in the first class car. The train picked up speed. Jean and I stretched our arms as far as we could to reach the father's outstretched hand and we pulled. He was now stretched between the attendant and us. I knew it was dangerous for us to continue pulling because at any moment the father could slip underneath the train wheels. In one last burst of energy we yanked him aboard. He smiled his thanks and sank into his seat. Luis lay across from us wrapped in a blanket observing everything. We smiled at him, but inside I felt homicidal at the injustices his father was experiencing.

The telegraph system worked well, and our Peruvian coordinator, Ramon, and our Peace Corps Leader, John, met us at the station in Cuzco and took us to the hospital.

We left Luis in the care of the nursing staff who assured us that x-rays would be taken and treatment begun immediately. His father shook our hands and took off to stay with relatives - we hoped. We were running out of money and too weary to consider doing battle with a hotel clerk on behalf of the father.

When we arrived at the hospital the next morning Luis' father looked worried as his son writhed in agony. I pulled the sheet back expecting to find his leg in a cast. The leg still had the remains of that Quiquijana concoction on it. A kid in the bed next to Luis told us nothing had been done for Luis after we left the hospital the previous night. We queried the nursing staff and got excuses. Underneath was the unspoken but implied response: he's just an Indian. The staff had no idea that we would follow up on our mission of mercy. I asked for a doctor. None was in the hospital.

"Get some doctors in here!" I demanded.

I wanted to shake the hell out of the smug, complacent nurses. Outraged, I lambasted the nurses about their lack of consideration for this child. Luis had suffered all night due to their unconcern.

I shouted at them, "I want EVERYBODY doing EVERYTHING for Luis and NOW!"

I telephoned our coordinator, Ramon, and raved some more. He spoke to a nurse, issued orders, and said he would be there personally to see what was being done. Luis' father remained in the background, following meekly in the wake of the waves made by two dauntless volunteers, no respecters of the dominant and discriminating majority.

He looked on silently as this bold American woman said things he was probably afraid to think. Doctors quickly arrived. They began ministering to Luis and taking x-rays. We stayed at his side. Finally a doctor called us in to see x-rays of his leg and showed us where the bone was broken. He said they would put a cast on Luis' leg. He would spend a few more days in the hospital, and he would have to return to the hospital in six weeks to have the cast removed. An uneventful recovery was expected. The doctor said if we had not brought him to the hospital, he would have had a severe limp for the rest of his life.

When we returned to the hospital in the afternoon, Luis' father met us smiling. Luis was resting comfortably. Our confidant in the next bed told us the staff was taking good care of Luis. At one point his father slipped away quietly. Jean and I left moments later. We walked through the hospital doors feeling good. It was then that our eyes took in a scene from hell. We saw a policeman at the bottom of the hospital steps remove his gun from its holster, and aim it while yelling at a running figure to stop. We immediately recognized the running man as Luis' father.

Jean and I screamed in unison, "NO!"

I shut my eyes and prayed our screams would be faster than the bullet. When the policeman heard our screams he turned toward us and lowered his gun. We raced down the steps to him. The father stopped running, walked back, and stood close behind us. Two American women stood between him and a policeman's bullets. Nothing stood between us and the policeman's bullets.

I asked the policeman, "Que pasa? What's going on?"

Still gripping his gun, he replied, "I told him to clean my car."

I asked, "Does he work for you?"

"No," he replied.

"Do you even know this man?" I asked the policeman.

He replied haughtily, "No. I gave him an order to clean my car."

Furious now, I said, "He is not going to clean your car now or ever!"

Jean and I flanked the father; each of us took an arm, turned on our heels and walked away. The policeman still had his gun out. He was angry. Our backs were exposed. I wondered if he would shoot one of us or all three. He knew that Jean and I were Peace Corps volunteers, as did every citizen in the state of Cuzco. Would that matter? Those thoughts raced through my mind as we commanded our leaden feet to move. We never looked back. We walked a few yards to a corner, turned it fast, and sagged against a building, weak from fright. The father squeezed our hands in thanks, and indicated he wanted to keep moving to get further away from danger. We watched him scurry out of sight, running as fast as an undernourished Quechua man could run. I had one thought: had we been two seconds later coming through the hospital doors, Luis' father surely would have been killed solely because he refused a humiliating order. The next day Jean and I left Cuzco to return to our village, happy that we had saved Luis from being crippled for the rest of his life, but extremely troubled at the thought of what the rest of his life would be like.

During this time fathers from nearby villages came to Quiquijana to donate a day to help build a dining room and kitchen for the children so they would no longer have to eat their breakfast outside in the cold.

One day several weeks after the trip to Cuzco, as Jean and I returned from one of our other schools, we noticed a group of Quechua men sitting on the ground, resting their backs against our house. As we got closer we recognized Luis' father. He leaped up, grinning, and stretched out his arms to give us the traditional Spanish abrazo (hug). He then quickly dropped his arms. I knew immediately that he thought we might be offended because we were American women. We opened our arms to him and the three of us hugged tightly. Each father leaped to his feet and gave us an abrazo. These fathers had heard about the two Peace Corps women who had rattled the *status quo* in Cuzco and dared shout at those the Quechua viewed as authoritarian figures. We were legends in their community. Each little, wizened man held out his tiny, dirty pouch of parched corn inviting us to share their lunch. We accepted with gusto. Jean and I went inside and brought out glasses of cola for everybody. We all sat together on the ground, happily munching corn, and raising our glasses to toast the friendship of Quechuas and Americans.

Remembering: Requiem for a Departure

To be happy in one's home is better than to be a chief.
- Nigeria

All too soon it was time to leave Quiquijana. Jean had already left for a new assignment. On the day of my departure I awakened to a gray mist covering the mountaintops despite the brilliance of the day. As I lay in bed I could hear a lone flute being played in the mountains. It was a doleful tune. I opened the curtain over my bed, but could not see anybody in the mountains. The mournful Huayno music floated on air. Huaynos are a vibrant part of the Quechua cultural identity. The music has a melancholic sound even when the tune is lively.

What a joy it was to have served here. I learned a lot, much more than I could have ever taught. Quechua friends invited me to their homes for dinner; I sat on the reviewing stand on Independence Day with the town fathers; soccer games were dedicated to me; I danced at weddings; drank chicha (fresh, home-brewed beer made from fermented corn) with Quechua friends, and ate (or tried to) guinea pigs slaughtered just for me.

I remembered a teacher at our school telling us about a meeting of the town fathers. A group of rebellious Indians from the hills threatened to invade Quiquijana and cut the bridge that was the only way in and out of Quiquijana. The town fathers met and decided that there was nothing they could do about it.

Someone stood up and said, "Don't forget we have two Peace Corps volunteers here, and we have to protect them."

The men immediately went home, got out their ancient firearms and took up positions at the bridge, the small power station, and even sent a teenaged girl to spend each night with us until the danger was over. She was to explain to the invaders that we were Peace Corps volunteers, and our protectors felt that with those magic words we would be left alone. We trusted them and slept well.

When there were demonstrations and people yelled, "Baja, Yanquis! Down with the Yankees!" our friends assured us that didn't mean us. We were "voluntarias del Cuerpo de la Paz," not to be confused with other Americans. We were different; we were special to the people of the soil because we lived among them, had no more than they did, and we were helping in our own little ways.

A Quechua friend once asked me, "Senorita, why are you here living like this? We know you don't live like this in the United States."

I smiled and said I was there to let her and her people know how much the people of the United States cared about them, and to try to help alleviate their poverty, and to help their children to get an education so as to better their lives. I said that sharing their poverty spoke to the depth of my country's commitment to them.

One day our school principal asked me why my roommate and I did not like President Kennedy.

I was shocked and exclaimed, "We love President Kennedy."

He asked, "Then why would you name your dog after your President?"

I said, "It's an honor to the president to have a dog named for him. When Americans are fond of someone, they name a pet after that person."

I could tell that I was only confirming his notion of how crazy Americans really were.

He added, "I am amazed that the dogs speak English."

I tried to explain that it is the intonation they understand, but he and everyone else continued to marvel that the dogs "spoke English."

What memories I had. One of the dogs, JFK, followed me everywhere. When I went into town, he came along and barked and howled until he was let in wherever I was. He even walked across the swinging bridge following me. I was terrified that he would fall into the rushing water.

There was the day I took the train to Urcos to visit two other volunteers for the weekend.

As the train pulled away a man sitting across the aisle from me who faced the doorway said, "Senorita, here's your dog."

I couldn't believe it. I looked around and there was JFK sheepishly coming down the aisle.

The man asked, "Do you want me to throw him off?"

The train had picked up speed and I was afraid he would be killed if tossed from the train. I shook my head. JFK came to my seat and laid down at my feet. Moments later the train conductor came through.

He immediately saw JFK and thundered, "Whose dog is this?!"

I didn't say anything. I didn't know what to say.

The man across the aisle said, "The dog belongs to the senorita del Cuerpo de la Paz."

He had said the magic words: the Peace Corps lady. The conductor became all smiles and welcomed JFK. He wanted to put JFK up in the seat across from me. I was beyond embarrassed. I cringed in my seat. In Urcos JFK stayed in the backyard with the chickens and ducks and didn't bother them. On Monday morning we took the train back to Quiquijana.

Most of our Peruvian friends were too polite to comment on our Spanish. During our language training we were told that Peruvians speak the purest Spanish outside of Spain. In Puerto Rico the constant greeting on the street was, "Ola! Que tal?" Hi, how's it going? As I strolled through the streets of Quiquijana, I called out that greeting to everyone I saw.

Finally one day our coordinator groused to me, "Where did you learn that 'Ola! Que tal?'"

I said I learned it in Puerto Rico.

He grumbled, "No wonder."

Oops! That expression apparently was not considered "pure" Spanish. From then on I never used that phrase in Peru.

On another occasion as I was returning home from a trip to the post office I stumbled upon a party at the home of some Quechua friends. I was invited in and given a glass of chicha, a liquor made from corn. The glass was crusted with dirt, but worse, a huge fly suddenly dropped into my drink. Whenever someone said "Salud!" all glasses were raised and you had to drink.

I would glance at my glass, swirl the contents around a bit and when the fly was on the other side, take a quick sip. The "saluds!" came faster and faster. At one point I forgot to look in my glass, took a swig, and I felt the fly sailing down my throat. I suffered no ill effects.

I remembered the day we were almost out of toilet tissue and Jean had the Inca trots. Toilet tissue was not sold in our village, and I went on an errand of mercy. No train was due until the next day. I had to hitch a ride on a truck to Urcos where two other PCVs lived and either borrow from them or hope that their local store had toilet tissue. I walked into the middle of our village and waited with others for a truck to come through to hitch a ride. A huge truck finally came through and some people climbed down and others climbed up. I was prepared to stand in the back of the truck, but someone gave me a seat on a box and I sat down. Another volunteer, Jim, was also on the truck, heading back home to Urcos. We bounced along the bumpy mountainous roads and around curve after dangerous curve and finally arrived in Urcos. I got some toilet tissue and lined up to wait for the next truck going through Quiquijana.

In August 1963, Jean and I planned to go into Cuzco to attend a meeting, enjoy our monthly shower (bucket baths every night was our custom), and celebrate my birthday. We had told one of the teachers at our school how I was going to celebrate my big day. Later, I decided I wanted to remain alone in Quiquijana to meditate on my 26th year and to think about life after the Peace Corps. Jean went to Cuzco alone. The morning of August 13th dawned. I got out of bed to oversee the breakfast preparations.

Afterwards, on my way into town, I ran into Senor Gonzales, our coordinator, who was also the Director of Health. When he asked where I was going and how long I expected to be gone, I told him that I was on my way to the post office and would return shortly. On my return trip I stopped frequently to chat with various people in town as was my usual habit. I must have been gone for about an hour when I looked up and saw Senor Gonzales coming toward me, walking fast.

"Are you coming back?" he asked.

"Yes," I assured him.

We walked together down the road and turned into the flower-bordered school grounds, and there standing in front of the office were all of the teachers. Each one gave me an abrazo and said, "Feliz Cumplianos! Happy Birthday!" What a surprise. They took me inside the school where they had prepared custard and cookies. Then they sang, "Las Mananitas," the Little Mornings. This is the traditional Spanish birthday song that I loved. *"These are the little mornings that sang the King David, today we sing them to a loved one who happy will be. Wake up this early morning and the sun you will see.... We come in celebration of this special day just for you."*

And then to my absolute astonishment they sang, "Happy Birthday" in English. I began crying at the second word and I couldn't stop. I was deeply moved. How long these teachers must have practiced to sing a song to me in English. I was thousands of miles from home and these wonderful people gave me what I had never had before – a surprise birthday party, a gift from their hearts.

Pisco sours, that indescribably delicious national drink of Peru, made of Peruvian brandy, egg whites, sugar and lime juice, were served. My tears vanished. For the rest of the morning classes were held without the teachers. We drank more Pisco sours. Several teachers took chairs out onto the playground, someone got a guitar and we danced. The Pisco sours flowed. By noon we were all more than ready for the traditional siesta. That was a memorable birthday.

The time passed swiftly. Yes, there were moments of frustration and times that I asked myself what the hell I was doing there. But I had only to look around to see the answer. On the day of my departure, the town seemed draped in mourning.

I was leaving on the morning train to Cuzco where I would take Faucett Airlines to Lima and an American carrier back to the U.S. I swept the dirt floors, and dusted my clothes one last time.

I hugged JFK and Shaggy and thanked them for being wonderful companions. Their owner tied up JFK to keep him from following me to the station and possibly boarding the train as he had done before. My last tearful glimpse of him was of a sorrowful, sweet, furry face whose beautiful, wise eyes acknowledged that he knew my departure today was different. His mother, Shaggy, wagged goodbye with her tail. It seemed as if the entire village accompanied me to the train station, and what a sorrowing party it was. There were teachers, students, parents, school officials and everybody else. I wiped away tears constantly. My heart ached at leaving my village where I had been so loved and so welcomed by everybody. I didn't want to say goodbye to them. As we walked there was little talking. There was no need for words.

Everything had already been said; the rest remained in our hearts. The haunting flute music wafted over and around us. I strolled across the rope bridge – no hands! – while waving at the market women selling coca leaves. They raised their voices in an ululation saying goodbye. The train arrived and was delayed while each person embraced me. Finally I boarded the train. In my head was the mournful sound of a flute being played somewhere in the mountains. It was a melodic farewell, a requiem for my departure. As the train chugged away I stood in the doorway waving as tears obscured the last view of my village of Quiquijana and its extraordinarily loving people. I was on my way home, but in a sense I was leaving home, a home that would always be a part of me.

Coming Back Home

I look back at those days in amazement that we, the Kennedy Kids as some called us, thought that we could change the world with hope and love. It was the days of flower power, "Black is beautiful!" and the opening of doors, and optimism flourished throughout our nation and the world. We were all so innocent. We thought our country was omnipotent. War was a word for past battles. Vietnam had not become a household word. More and more African countries were becoming independent. We knew not of coups and tribal animosities. Social change was occurring everywhere one looked. And then something happened. It began with the assassination of President Kennedy.

Our politics turned ugly, and many Americans became disillusioned. Some politicians began working solely for big business interests, ignoring the American taxpayers who put them in office. There ceased to be any concern for those who had little or nothing. And as we were faced with assassination after assassination, we lost that innocence, that idealism, that faith, that fire with which we once lit the world. We began a descent into a murkiness that seems to increase rather than to decrease. Since the 1,000 days of John F. Kennedy's vision and spirit in the White House, nobody else has inspired Americans as he did.

Back in Indianapolis I was met at the airport by Mother, Aunt Bess, Uncle Rabbit and Uncle Charlie. It was good to see them after nearly two years away. As we left the airport I noticed that we headed to town and not to our house.

I idly wondered why. We drove to Aunt Bess' and Uncle Frank's and there we talked about Peace Corps and I handed out presents. I gave Aunt Bess and Mother beautiful alpaca rugs. Uncle Rabbit and Uncle Charlie got gorgeous face coverings worn by the Quechua men to keep their faces warm in the cold climate. I knew that my uncles often went hunting in the winter and these alpaca masks would keep their faces warm. The evening wore on and I was getting tired and sleepy.

Finally I asked Mother, "When are we going home?"

Aunt Bess and Uncle Frank left the room, and my other two uncles suddenly decided it was time for them to leave too. I began feeling uneasy. Finally Mother and I were alone in the living room.

She said, "Walt said you can't come back."

I looked at her incredulously.

She continued, "He doesn't want you in the house."

I was speechless. I never asked why. I knew why. I had not let his resentment or his treatment of me stop me from moving on with my life, being an accomplished Peace Corps volunteer, and seeing the world. Plus, I harbored a secret that he must have lived in fear of being revealed. Mother said she was getting a divorce and her attorney had advised her not to "abandon" the home, but to continue living there. I heard little else because my mind was reeling. Mr. Walt, the bastard who had sexually assaulted me, caused me and my mother a lot of grief, that bastard now had the nerve to say that I could not return to my mother's house. I was livid. I told Mother I planned to return immediately to New York, and using the money the Peace Corps had sent her to save for me, I would get an apartment.

Mother hung her head and said, "You don't have any money."

I asked, "But didn't the Peace Corps send $75 every month? You said you were putting it in the bank. I should have at least $1,800."

"I used it," she whispered.

"On what?" I tried not to shout.

"I needed the money for different things," she said.

I knew instantly that my money had gone for liquor. I burst into tears. Mother apologized and said she would pay me back. I knew that would not ever be possible. I felt sorry for her, but I had been counting on that money. I had no nest egg. I would again have to live with Aunt Alma in Harlem until I found a job and saved up enough money to move into an apartment. Aunt Alma was living alone in a one bedroom apartment and she welcomed me. Aunt Bess gave me money to help out until I could find a job.

Back in New York I was completely humbled by the reaction of people when they learned that I was a returned volunteer. Each person looked at me with admiration and awe, expressed respect for the Peace Corps, and said they were "honored" to meet a returned Peace Corps volunteer. They seemed genuinely proud of my small contribution to world peace. As I hunted for a job people always asked, "Why did you join the Peace Corps?" My reply was that I wanted people in other countries to know that Americans cared about them, and wanted to help them and the next generations to have a better future.

Thomas Merton said it better: "It is easy to tell the poor to accept their poverty as God's will when you yourself have warm clothes and plenty of food and medical care... But if you want them to believe you – try to share some of their poverty and see if you can accept it as God's will yourself."

By now reverse culture shock had sat in. I, and many of my fellow volunteers, found that the U.S. was not the utopia we had imagined it to be when we were overseas. One's own country seems so perfect when one is in another country experiencing hardships. How I looked forward to having an indoor toilet; getting a daily bath; talking on the telephone, being able to walk up and down supermarket aisles and buying ready-made products, and drinking water from the faucet instead of boiling it for 20 minutes. To all of us the U.S. was perfect. And then we returned. Within weeks I was ready to leave again. The pace of life was too fast. Everybody hurried. Nobody listened to my experiences. I had gone to Peru, I was back, and that was enough for everybody to hear. They wanted to talk about what people were doing on a soap opera, or what happened last week in their lives. This was not what I expected, and it amazed me. Americans on the whole are generally not interested in what happens beyond their borders, or even beyond their home towns. I wrote to Frank Mankiewicz and said I wanted to return to Peru. He wrote back saying that he had heard from many former volunteers asking to do the same. He talked about reverse culture shock for which nobody was prepared. Few of us had culture shock upon our arrival in Peru because we had been so thoroughly prepared for it.

Nobody told us about the let down we would experience upon returning to the U.S.

Frank suggested that I take a few months to see if that was what I really wanted, and if so, we would talk. Needless to say, after a few months I was over culture shock and enjoying the pleasures of being at home.

One cannot be a Peace Corps volunteer and not be changed. For most of us our Peace Corps service was the best experience of our lives. I wish every American could have the opportunity to serve abroad, and to live and work with people of other cultures. The Peace Corps allowed me the opportunity to experience that, and it was indeed an unforgettable and awesome assignment. As volunteers we tried to improve the lives of the poor and the disadvantaged – to teach, to encourage, to demonstrate, and to work beside them helping them do what they might have thought was impossible to do with little or limited resources. The Peace Corps philosophy is to help people to help themselves.

Peace Corps volunteers lack the official title of "diplomats" but they are truly ambassadors who represent the best of the United States. For most people in the host countries volunteers are their first contact with Americans. They have preconceived notions of what Americans are like from what they have seen in the movies, or have heard. In Peace Corps volunteers they see a very different kind of American. They see young and old, black and white and all shades in between, working hard with them, walking to outhouses like them, carrying water in buckets like them, eating the foods they eat, suffering illnesses they suffer, and sometimes dying of illnesses or accidents, as they do. Americans also love their Peace Corps volunteers. It was a unique concept in the history of the country – Americans going to live and to work with the poor of many nations.

Some saw us as brave Americans marching into the unknown, and indeed we did march into the unknown. We were not brave or foolhardy, we simply cared. Perhaps that should be the epitaph of the Peace Corps: We cared.

The world has changed. It too has lost its innocence. But good people will always be needed to lend a hand to those less fortunate and less vocal. And more importantly, good people will always be found. It is those people who are sorely needed to step up, to help inspire new generations, and to bring dignity and honor back to politics. We must serve humbly those less fortunate. We must speak for those with no voice. We must use our voices and our education to right wrongs. We must shake the consciences of others in order to help them to do that which is right, and above all, we must revive the spirit to do what Sarge Shriver told us at our reunion in 1986: "… to serve, serve, serve. And to always serve honorably."

Peace Corps — United Nations - Foreign Service Links
1964- 1972

"...need I add that I who speak here am bone of the bone and
flesh of the flesh of them that live within the Veil?"

W.E.B. Dubois

After my Peace Corps service I knew that I wanted to remain in the international arena, and to continue to serve others. I had no idea of what I would do when I returned to New York City, especially since I did not have a college degree. A lot of universities were offering scholarships to former volunteers, but I felt that since I had such a poor record at Indiana University, I would never be awarded a scholarship. I applied for a job at the United Nations, and I became a UN clerk. I moved from Aunt Alma's in Harlem to the YWCA on East 45th Street, just a few blocks from the United Nations. I was hired as a clerk and I took secretarial classes at night and moved up to the secretarial level at the UN. Working at UN headquarters was exciting. I loved going to the employee cafeteria eating foods from various countries, listening to the interpreters speaking the five official languages in the General Assembly, and seeing staff members in their various native dress. Several of my former Peace Corps buddies came to New York, and I always gave them a grand tour of the UN. In my office, Records Retirement, I worked with people from Australia,

Jamaica, Argentina, Yugoslavia, Panama, Colombia and a few Americans. Americans were in the majority since the UN was located in New York City. I saw many kings and queens who visited the UN, including the late King Hassan of Morocco.

It was exciting being at the UN at a time when many African countries were gaining their independence. For the first time in my life I saw men and women who looked like me as ambassadors from independent black countries. I was terribly proud of them. I found the West Africans especially warm and inviting, especially the Ghanaians. They often invited me to baby naming ceremonies, to dinners and to family celebrations. I loved most of their ethnic dishes, especially the hot, spicy dishes. The African diplomats from Francophone countries were elegant in their exquisitely cut suits. I was sorry that I could not speak their language.

While at the UN I began studying French. I would respond to a question certain that I had used a French word, but it was almost always a Spanish word. One day the instructor asked the class if anybody had noticed my accent.

A man from Uruguay said, "She speaks French with a Spanish accent."

Everybody had a good laugh and the instructor pointed out that the Spanish accent was better than having an American accent.

I became a volunteer at the African-American Institute, and one of my assignments was to help newly arriving African diplomats find apartments as close to the UN as possible. Whenever we arrived at the management office of a rental apartment, the manager looked at me as if I were something under his or her foot. I had telephoned to set up the appointment, but because I spoke correct English, they apparently assumed that I was white. I would immediately explain that the gentleman with me was a diplomat with the United Nations, and I would name his country.

Ah, the smile returned to the person's face. I, a common black American, was not welcomed to live there, but an African diplomat was.

The most exciting event that happened at the UN during my years there was a visit from Pope Paul VI on October 4, 1965. We received word that His Holiness was coming to the UN, and he wanted to meet with the staff, not just with the diplomats. Several thousand staff members wanted to meet the Pope and that was not possible, so they decided on a lottery system. Each office would be allowed a certain number of tickets and we had to draw. I prayed very hard that I would draw a ticket. The drawing was held at the same time all over the building, and in my office I drew a ticket. I was thrilled. I was definitely going to see the Pope. A few minutes later my phone rang and it was Frieda, my boss' other secretary in Archives. Frieda was Jewish.

She said, "Charlene, I just drew a ticket to see the Pope, but I want to give it to you. I would love to see him, but I know how special it would be to you."

I was overwhelmed with gratitude by her offer to give up her ticket because she knew I was Catholic and how meaningful it would be to me to see the pope. I was happy that I was able to thank her and to tell her that I had drawn a ticket. When he arrived, Frieda and I went together to hear the pope, and she was just as excited as I was. About 3,000 non-diplomatic staff members heard Pope Paul VI. I only remembered one thing he said.

"I have brought gifts for all of you."

A gift from the pope? What could it be? I couldn't wait, but I had to. I thought we would receive our gifts within a few days of his departure.

No gifts came. I waited another week and then I called the office of the Secretary-General. His secretary said the gifts would be distributed shortly. I waited two weeks and then I called again. This time I threatened to write to the pope and tell him that the UN refused to give us our presents, and I meant it. The secretary had to tell me the truth.

She said, "The truth is that the pope did not bring enough of the medals for all the staff and we had to figure out a way to tell him. That took us some time. Then the Vatican had to restrike the medals, which takes more time. But the medals are coming, and as soon as we have all of them, they will be given to the staff."

With that knowledge in hand, I waited patiently for our medals. And then came the day they were handed out in all offices. The pope sent each of us a round, bronze medal, about two inches in diameter. On one side is the coat-of-arms of Pope Paul VI and the words PAULUS VI PONT MAX, UN 4 OCT. 1965. On the other side is the Burning Bush and the words AMORIS ALUMNA PAX. This blessed treasure was tucked inside a little, brown suede envelope with the pope's coat of arms emblazoned on the front. It remains a much loved and treasured present.

I worked at UN headquarters for more than three and one-half years, and then I requested an overseas assignment. I had had a taste of foreign cultures and I liked it. Such assignments were limited since the UN was not involved in any skirmishes at that time, for which I was grateful. I was offered Dacca, East Pakistan (now Bangladesh). I leaped at the opportunity. The UN offered no training, and when I inquired of the personnel office as to what sorts of items to pack, I was told in no uncertain terms that, "This is the United Nations, not the Peace Corps." They should have added that it was barely one step up from being a Peace Corps volunteer. I was assigned as an international secretary to a Frenchman who, along with other UN officials in Dacca, was planning a new city.

The city of Dacca teemed with men, some whose bodies were barely clothed, some crippled, some with limbs missing, and some with faces deformed by leprosy. Children were often missing and it was said that gangs kidnapped them, crippled them, and then made them beg for money for the gang. The rare woman seen on the streets never had more than a skimpy piece of cloth barely covering her bony body. These were the poorest of the poor women. Hunger forced some of them to beg on the streets. The poverty was crushing. Over the next few days I was welcomed and feted by the UN international community that consisted of French, Indonesian, English, Australian, Turkish, Lebanese, and Jordanian. I was the only American. The French quickly became my favorite group because of their sheer exuberance.

Ali was my official driver in Dacca. Soon after arriving I needed to open a bank account for the UN to deposit my salary. Ali drove me to the bank, and he could not find a parking space in front of the bank. I kept telling him to let me out and then he could look for a parking space.

He kept saying, "No! I go!"

Me: "Yes, you let me out and then you go."

Ali: "No, I go!"

This yes, no, I go, you go business was making me dizzy. Plus I was getting nowhere. So I opened the car door and Ali had to stop. I got out and walked to the bank. Every man on the street stopped and stared at me.

It was as if they couldn't believe their eyes. I quickly realized that I was the only woman on the street as far as the eye could see. I looked at the men staring at me, and then I was hopping over what looked like splotches of blood all over the street. I later learned that it was betel nut juice. Every man in Dacca seemed to chew the stuff which turns the teeth red, and then they hawk red gobs of the juice everywhere on the streets. Passersby had to be watchful because those doing the spitting were not watching where the red juice landed. All of the men had red teeth from eating betel nut. Betel leaves are filled with a mixture of lime paste, cloves, camphor, coconut, cumin, tobacco and pieces of betel nut. The leaf is then folded into a small packet and people suck on it. It's quite disgusting. I tried it once because it was served in restaurants at the end of the meal. The lime paste causes the ingredients to break down fairly quickly and the aftertaste is like bitter spearmint. Betel nut is said to be mildly intoxicating and addictive.

Inside the bank I was even more of a spectacle. I did not know at the time that Pakistani women did not go out without a male with them, or that they wore burkas covering everything except their eyes, or that they rode in cars with curtains at the windows. It was show time every morning when I arrived at my office and walked up to the third floor. When I got out of the car there was a waiting gallery of men. Few Muslim women worked, and there were none in my building. Men hung on every step, in fact two and three to every step, watching as I walked up the stairs. Nobody ever touched me, and I never looked directly at any of them. I just held my head high, gritted my teeth, cursed them soundly in my mind, and kept stepping. I hoped those below enjoyed the view of my girdle.

The new apartment building I was moving into had three floors with two apartments to a floor. The owner and his relatives occupied the first floor apartments. I moved into one second floor apartment, and Marcel, a Frenchman with the UN, moved into the other apartment. A Turkish couple, also with the UN, moved onto the third floor. When I was shown my apartment I thought it was huge because I kept going in and out of doors. I did not realize that I was going in and out of the same rooms but through different doors. Each room had two or three doors in order, I later learned, for a Muslim woman to be able to get out quickly if a man entered the room. I actually had only three rooms. A huge room that I used as a dining room, living room and bedroom. The kitchen was outside the apartment in a room off the balcony, as were the servant quarters.

95

The main mode of transportation in Dacca was "baby taxis" (motorized, three-wheeled contraptions with 2 seats in the back). They went at breakneck speed throughout the city, while competing with cars and rickshaws.

Marcel was the only single man with the UN and I was the only single woman, so we were always invited together to dinners or parties. Everyone wanted an even number of people at the dinner table. The UN community thought Marcel and I were having a hot love affair because we lived in the same building and would share one of those dangerous forms of transportation when going to somebody's home for dinner or a party which was practically every night.

My new supervisor was from Russia and he was accompanied by an interpreter even though his English was as good as mine when he occasionally slipped and said something in English or corrected his interpreter.

The UN community got a kick out of a Russian being assigned an American secretary. I knew that he understood everything I said to him, but he always waited for his interpreter to speak. It was terribly time consuming. Most of our UN community assumed that the interpreter was there as a watchdog.

Eventually, after being thrown together constantly, Marcel and I became more than friends and the next thing I knew, we were engaged. As time went on, Marcel began making our marriage plans. Frankly, I had not thought much about it because he was a divorced Catholic. I put off having that discussion until I could no longer avoid it. I had to tell him that I would never feel married to him because the church would not recognize our marriage since he was divorced. It took me many years to become Catholic, and I was not going to give it up to marry a man who was nice, but was a divorced Catholic. On the other hand, maybe I was not that much in love with him. By the way, did I mention that he was impotent?

In the marketplace Western women were always accosted by beggars, especially lepers. I was often tapped on the shoulder and when I turned to see who had touched me, I found myself looking into a face lacking a nose or a mouth. They depended on shocking women to get them to give them money to get rid of them. More aggressive Bengali men would pinch a woman's bottom in the marketplace. Finally the UN advised women to avoid going to the market unless accompanied by a man.

When the British granted India its independence in 1947, they divided India into two countries, Pakistan for Muslims, and India for Hindus.

However, East Pakistan and West Pakistan were separated by 1,000 miles of India, as well as by language. During my final year in Dacca, the political situation heated up considerably. West Pakistan felt totally alienated from the east. At one point West Pakistan considered passing a law requiring people from East Pakistan to have passports, certain vaccinations, and special permission to enter West Pakistan. The East Pakistanis were outraged. That idea was quickly dropped. I noticed that the Bengalis were, for the most part, considerably darker in complexion than the West Pakistanis. Language was another difference. In the West they spoke Urdu, and in the East they spoke Bengali. Zahid, a Pakistani friend whom I knew from New York came home to Lahore and visited me in Dacca. He had never visited East Pakistan before. It was an exercise in frustration for him.

He said, "Charlene, this is a part of my country and yet I can't even communicate with people here. Nobody speaks Urdu, and I don't speak Bengali."

The fact that few West Pakistanis could talk to the East Pakistanis was one reason for discontent on both sides. The other reason concerned Sheikh Mujibur Rahman. The Sheikh headed the Awami League, a political party that opposed the military government of Ayub Khan. He led protests against the ethnic and institutional discrimination of Bengalis. In 1968 he was tried for treason. It was said that he had conspired with the Indian government. That was the beginning of days and weeks of rioting and shootings. The students would demand that any car on the streets have a black flag waving in solidarity with them. Our UN office had warned us to never attach black flags to our cars so that nobody could say the UN was taking sides.

We foreigners in Dacca knew that if Sheikh Rahman were found guilty, the streets would run with blood, including ours. He was found guilty and instead of being executed, he was imprisoned in East Pakistan. Those opposed to the government in power, students, in particular, wanted him released from prison. They continued rioting. The battle see-sawed. One day the students would riot, and we were told to stay in on the advice of the police and the UN office. The next day the students would warn people to stay at home because they were going to retaliate.

I remember one day Maklouf, who was number two in the UN office, called me at work and said, "Charlene, I want you and the Russians to leave the office now and go home."

He sounded very calm which was totally unlike Maklouf. He was always very excitable.

I immediately realized how serious the situation was, and then he added, "Charlene, first send the drivers out to get black flags to put on your cars."

That meant all hell was breaking loose. I ran into my boss' office and told him and his interpreter and we sent our drivers for the black flags. As I got into my car with my driver I realized that I had to ride shotgun. I would have to be his other set of eyes because he had to watch the road. I wanted nothing more than to cower as close to the floor as possible and remain there until I reached home. I watched rooftops and street corners, praying that I would see a brick before it hit one of our car windows. We should have been safe flying the black flag, but it was a United Nations vehicle, and I didn't know whether the students regarded the UN as friend or foe. The riots and demonstrations went on for over one year.

At the time of my departure from Dacca I counted that of my last 365 days there, I had had to stay inside over 200 days. The UN Turkish couple who lived over me would come down, Marcel would join us and the four of us would share our precious cans of caviar or paté, open a great wine or a bottle of champagne and have a picnic. There was no television and none of us had a radio.

Marcel completed his assignment and left Dacca one month before I was due to leave. I was in French class one evening when the door opened and my housekeeper stood there looking traumatized. I raced to the door. Abani had just walked me to my class. When we left, Marcel's former housekeeper, Sunil, had been ironing. Ahmet, my Turkish neighbor, ran out with me. Abani told us that when he returned to the apartment Sunil was gone along with the hot iron, liquor, and other things.

I walked into my bedroom and began saying, "Well, at least he didn't get my suitcase…"

And then I screamed because the suitcase was gone. That suitcase contained my plane ticket back to the U.S., emerald earrings that Marcel had given me one Christmas, and a pearl necklace for which I had selected loose, Baroque pearls in Hong Kong and had strung. I was almost sick. Ahmet and Abani went to get the police. They returned and the police refused to talk to me. I had to leave my apartment and stand on the balcony while Ahmet talked to them. He was very apologetic, but we were in a Muslim country and he was Muslim. They would have talked to Attila the Hun or any man, just not a woman. I was furious. Abani told them in detail what was in the suitcase. I had forgotten some things.

He knew because often he was in the bedroom cleaning when I had the suitcase open. It had contained various sweaters – never needed in Dacca – and other items. The police said they would go to Sunil's village and look for him. The next day Abani asked me to let him go with the police, otherwise, he said, they wouldn't go, but would say they had gone. Next, all of the Buddhists servants in Dacca came to see me as a group to apologize for Sunil's theft. I was extremely surprised. They expressed their regrets, and promised that they would find Sunil.

I let Abani go to Sunil's village with the police. When they returned, the police brought back Sunil's little brother and locked him up. They said that would encourage Sunil's parents to turn him in. I was appalled, but everybody said that was the only way I would ever get my belongings back. The little brother revealed to the police that Sunil had a friend who was a teacher. When the police went to the teacher's school, he was not there, but in his desk they found my plane ticket, pearl necklace and the emerald earrings. The police brought the items to Ahmet for me to identify. Ahmet and the police came to my apartment and when I got my hands on my things, it would have taken an act of God to get them out of my hands. I knew that I was leaving the country in two weeks, but I didn't want the police to know that because I knew my items would simply disappear. They were not happy about me keeping my belongings, and they insisted that I sign a statement that I would present these items at the trial. I signed the document that I would present the items at the trial and I added: "… if I am in the country." The police said they were not going to release

Sunil's brother until the parents produced Sunil. I felt sorry for him, but the pressure was on the parents.

The police were also searching for the teacher. I had the feeling that once I left the country, all charges would be dropped against Sunil and the teacher.

It was down to my last two weeks in Dacca. I was getting out of the rioting and political wrangling, and going to be free to walk down the street without my cook beside me. The airlines went on strike and the airport closed. The household packing companies went on strike. It became dizzying. The banks were closed. Everything was suddenly shuttered. I fumed and wondered why everything closed down just days before I was due to leave. I had only seven dollars in hand. Even if the airport opened, I could not leave the country with seven dollars to my name.

One afternoon I went upstairs to visit a Turkish friend, Nevine. As we chatted on the terrace some beggar women passing by saw us and began begging. I opened my purse and dropped my seven dollars to them.

Nevine said, "Didn't you say you only had seven dollars? How could you give your last seven dollars away?"

I looked at her and I said, "Nevine, there is nothing I can do with seven dollars. But it will buy them food for a week or more."

I remember she looked at me in amazement and said, "You are such a good person."

I said, "Not at all. They can do so much more with those few dollars than I can."

Later, when I returned to my apartment and saw the furniture, the refrigerator, the air-conditioner and other things I had not been able to sell, I felt very down. I figured I would just have to leave it in the apartment.

Before the day ended, a Pakistani friend arrived to buy everything and she paid me in cash. My prayers were answered.

After one week we learned there had been a coup in West Pakistan, but the news was kept secret because the government was afraid that Dacca would secede, which it would have. Since India would not give Pakistan permission to fly troops over 1,000 miles of its territory, the troops had to come to East Pakistan by ship which took one week. Only when they arrived was it announced that there had been a coup in West Pakistan. The airport opened along with all other businesses. Farewell activities began in earnest for my departure. I was homeward bound after two tumultuous years. Two years later, after the Indo-Pakistan war of 1971, when Indian troops helped East Pakistan, Bangladesh was created.

Author in front of the Taj Mahal in India - 1969

Enroute to the U.S. I stopped in New Delhi and Agra, India; Katmandu, Nepal, and Beirut, Lebanon. I could walk in New Delhi without being stared at. Visiting the Taj Mahal was a dream come true. I remember being cold in Katmandu, and feeling warm and wonderful while marveling at the beauty of Beirut. I received word on the plane that Rome had no hotel rooms and I continued on to Paris. I had planned to spend just a few days in Paris, but I spent one month there. I stayed with Marcel's mother and I fell in love with Paris and could not leave. But as magical as Paris was, I knew I had to be at home on Mother's Day, and I was. Back at the UN I queried personnel about a transfer to UNESCO (United Nations Educational, Scientific and Cultural Organization) in Paris. I was told to write to UNESCO. That organization replied that they could not offer me a position while I was in New York, but if I were in Paris they could.

Author in Dacca, East Pakistan - 1968

I handed in my resignation at the UN, and over Mother's objections, I moved to Paris. What a leap of faith. Aunt Bess encouraged me to move to France, for which Mother never forgave her. I sailed to France on the glorious ship, *Le France,* in October, 1969. I left New York with one trunk, five suitcases, and several large packages of framed pictures from Thailand. It was a five day ocean crossing and I was so busy with shipboard activities that I never went out on deck to see the ocean.

We arrived in Le Harve, a port city in France where I was to take a train to Paris. The porters in Le Harve were on strike. My trunk and paintings were going into storage until I could find an apartment in Paris, but the five suitcases were going with me. As I stood wondering how I was going to manage getting the suitcases to the train an old French porter came to my rescue. The other porters booed and jeered, but he ignored them and loaded my suitcases on his dolly and we walked to the train.

Before leaving New York I had written to the YWCA in Paris to reserve a room. I had heard nothing from them. I then sent a telegram to them shortly before leaving the U.S. I foolishly assumed that their silence meant consent. I arrived at the YWCA in Paris around 9 pm at night. It was on the third floor of a building that had no elevator. I could only carry up one suitcase at a time and I made five trips. It took quite awhile because I had to rest after each trip up the stairs. Finally, all five suitcases were outside the door of the YWCA and I went in. I was told that I had no reservation; they had never heard of me, and they had no rooms available. I was speechless. The receptionist told me there was a hotel on a street about a block away. It might as well have been on the moon.

I knew there was no way I could go back and forth picking up one suitcase at a time. I should have just camped out at the YWCA for the night, but I was so upset that I began taking my suitcases back downstairs. I didn't know what I was going to do. I lugged the suitcases out to the sidewalk. The street was narrow and not well lit. I stood looking up and down the street for a taxi. Not a single car passed by. I said a silent prayer. Moments later I heard a car door slam, and I looked down the street and saw a taxi sign light up. It was a miracle. I ran down the street, tears streaming, waving and babbling. The taxi driver got out of his car and approached me.

He said, "It's all right. It's all right. Whatever it is, it's all right."

He opened the taxi door for me to get in. I waved at my suitcases half-way down the block. I couldn't speak.

He said, "I'll get your suitcases. You just stay in the car."

After collecting my suitcases he got in the car and asked, "Now what's the matter?"

I told him that I thought I had a room at the YWCA, but I didn't, and now I needed to go to a hotel. He said that would be difficult because an auto show was going on in Paris and most hotels were full. I began wailing again.

He said, "No, no. Don't worry. I won't leave you until we find you a hotel."

He was truly heaven sent. We went to four different hotels. He went into each one to ask about a room. There was no room to be found.

Finally he said, "If we don't find a hotel room, you can stay at my house."

I began crying, "I want my own room!"

He said, "I want you to have your own room, but if we can't find one..."

Finally, we stopped at the fifth hotel and he went in.

When he returned he said, "You can stay here just for tonight. Tomorrow you have to find something else. And you must stay in your room. "

I hugged my angel in disguise and gave him a good tip. He saw me to my room with my luggage, and repeated that I should stay in my room. I didn't understand why he was so insistent that I remain in my room, but as I heard doors opening and closing all night, I realized it must have been a hotel where prostitutes brought their johns. I didn't get much sleep that night. The next day I called a friend of a friend from Mali who was a delegate to the UN, and she invited me to stay with her and her mother until I found housing. She was from Martinique. Within a week I had found a tiny studio apartment in the 16th arrondisment near the metro station, Chardon LaGache. My trunks were delivered and I got settled, I was ready for a job at UNESCO.

I went to UNESCO, filled out the necessary paperwork, and was told that since I was a senior secretary from headquarters, it should not be long before

I was called. It took them one year to contact me and when they did I had another more interesting job as a verbatim reporter at the Organization for Economic Cooperation and Development (OECD) which I did not want to leave. I loved Paris. I loved the wines, the cheeses, the fresh baked baguettes, and it was a good thing because that's what I lived on. I was poor in Paris, and that was no fun. Friends I had met who worked at the U.S. embassy thought it was a joke when I said I had no money. They took trips and bought imported American foods at their Commissary, and their housing was paid by the American embassy.

I had other friends from various countries who were also near penniless. We had wonderful parties. Each person would bring a loaf of French bread, or a piece of cheese, or paté, or a bottle of wine, and by sharing we were able to eat, drink and have loads of fun. During my nearly three years in Paris I was fortunate enough to visit Mont-St.-Michel for a weekend; one day was spent in Champagne country; one week in Rome, and a weekend in Holland visiting a Dutch friend. There was so much more that I wanted to see, but I couldn't afford to.

At the end of three years I was a bit tired of Paris, and a lot tired of being poor. I loved Rome, but I didn't want to learn another language or to look for another job. Through one of my former secondary school teachers, I learned of the availability of numerous university scholarships. I decided to return to Indiana University to complete my B.A. degree. I was accepted and I left Paris. I returned to the U.S. on the beautiful ship, *Le France.* That was one of its last voyages before it was retired. At lunch and dinner each table was kept stocked with bottles of red and white wines. What a treat!

In 1972 I enrolled at Indiana University (IU) in Bloomington. I was awarded several scholarships, including the Ernie Pyle Journalism Scholarship, and one from the American Newspaper Publishers Association. I completed four years in two and one-half years, including summer classes. Shortly before completing my studies at IU, a friend with the State Department called and suggested that I might be interested in the U.S. Information Agency. I had never heard of that agency, and neither had most Americans. It was the agency charged with making U.S. foreign policies more acceptable to foreign governments.

Creative writers, thinkers, and cultural types were what this agency wanted. I later learned that some of my colleagues referred to USIA as "the propaganda branch of the U.S. government." I contacted USIA, filled out the paperwork, passed all security clearances, went to Washington for exams and meetings, and I was duly sworn in as a Foreign Service Officer. That was definitely one of the happiest days of my life.

Acronyms

USIA – U.S. Information Agency (US)
USIS – U.S. Information Service (abroad)
Ambassador – Chief of Mission
DCM – Deputy Chief of Mission
PAO – Public Affairs Officer
CAO – Cultural Affairs Officer
IO – Information Officer
FSN – Foreign Service Nationals (local employees)
UN – United Nations

Diplomacy

1976 - 1995

We are born naked, wet and hungry, then things get worse.

- Anon.

Foreign Service Officers are under the jurisdiction of the U.S. Department of State. Some Americans know what the Department of State does, and others have no clue. It is the department that handles foreign affairs matters for the federal government, and it is a part of the Executive Branch of government. The Secretary of State is the fourth in line for succession in the death of the president. In other countries this department is called the Ministry of Foreign Affairs which is a more apt title. Heaven forbid that we call it the Ministry of Foreign Affairs.

A friend said some people would think that department was responsible for match-making with foreign spouses, and "ministry" would cause people to think it had to do with religion. If we called it the Department of International Relations, some would think it had something to do with sex.

We then come to the title of Foreign Service Officers. The first reaction of people is to assume that we are in the military. When we say we are members of the diplomatic corps, their eyes glaze over. Some of us wonder what's present or lacking in our culture that prevents people from developing a world view. American Foreign Service Officers are diplomats who represent the government and the people of the United States. A wag once described a diplomat as "one who can tell you to go to hell in such a way that you look forward to the trip." Diplomacy has, in many instances, replaced war as the means for winning hearts and minds; it is an instrument of foreign policy. An embassy is usually composed of public diplomacy, political, consular, administrative, and economic sections. The embassy reports to the State Department in Washington on conditions existing in that particular country, and recommends ways for the U.S. to assist in order to achieve the goals sought by the United States.

For example, if a country is run by a dictator, the U.S. embassy will closely monitor the treatment of political activists and journalists. The American officers will work to encourage democracy through the distribution of publications designed to foster such democracy. They will invite American political scientists and other speakers to address specific groups in that country. They will also provide fellowships to students and professors to study or do research in the United States. They will also meet as frequently as possible with the leadership of that country, and through the art of diplomacy and gentle persuasion, they will push for democracy. Diplomacy is a wonderful way of demanding and at the same time damning another country using the flowery language of poets and kings.

The United States Ambassador does not pick up the telephone and ask the Minister of Foreign Affairs of Mwaqadachi, "Why the hell did your government bus workers to our embassy to deface it with paint?"

Instead, he sends a formal diplomatic note stating: "The Ambassador of the United States presents his compliments to the Minister of Foreign Affairs and has the honor to refer to the recent incident in which unknown assailants adorned our embassy with paint. We would appreciate the removal of said paint and the prevention of such in the future. The Ambassador of the United States avails himself of this opportunity to assure the Minister of Foreign Affairs of his highest consideration."

In other, plainer words, we are mad as hell, we want you to know it, and we want you to take full responsibility for the paint thrown all over our embassy. Yes, indeed we have the honor, such as it is, to address His Excellency in exaggerated language to complain, to lament, to scold, to grumble about some wrong doing or other, but it is all done in the language of diplomacy.

Another mode of communication is the *diplomatic note* that informs the host government that the U.S. ambassador will be unavailable to attend the annual Hog Swilling Contest.

There is also the *aide-memoire* that reminds the host government of something the U.S. expects the host government to do. All of these methods of communicating with host governments have one point – to keep the channels of communication open.

Be the face of America to the World ...said the pamphlet from the U.S. Information Agency (USIA). I heard and answered the call to become a U.S. Foreign Service Officer. In the U.S. the official name for our agency was the United States Information Agency (USIA), while overseas we were known as the United States Information Service (USIS). Most Americans have never heard of USIA because by an Act of Congress that agency, now absorbed into the Department of State, was not allowed to disseminate information in the U.S. It was feared that an unscrupulous president could use USIA to further his personal political goals. For that reason, none of our publications, of which there were many, could be disseminated in the U.S.

Our job was to win the hearts and minds of audiences abroad; to advance the causes of freedom and democracy throughout the world, and to make some of our unpopular foreign policies more palatable to an overseas audience. Some called our job propaganda. Propaganda is information. In short, our job was to make our government look good and we excelled at that. Our cultural centers included a library, often the only one in town. We offered educational fellowships, exchange programs, and we promoted the best art and culture of the U.S.

Our Fulbright scholarships and fellowships paid for U.S. professors to teach abroad and for professors in the country we served in, to come to the U.S. for research; for American graduate students to research and teach abroad, and we brought American experts in economics, government and politics to address foreign audiences. We also sponsored visiting American cultural groups in order to expose foreign audiences to American culture seldom seen outside of the movies.

In many remote countries suffering from drought, poor education, corruption and economic distress, American diplomats are there trying to promote democracy, to win friends and influence people. There and everywhere one finds American officers putting their lives on the line to explain, cajole and to educate those expected to be the leaders of tomorrow, thereby advancing U.S. interests and democracy. We love the travel, the learning of new cultures, and in most cases the incredible warmth of the people. I have discovered that while some people in foreign countries might not like U.S. policies, they usually like Americans. They can and do distinguish between American individuals and our government. If they like you as a person, and trust you, doors open that would not ordinarily be accessible to American diplomats.

We don't live grandly, certainly not in the third country posts in which I served, but residences are large for those with representational responsibilities. That is because USIA officers had representational responsibilities and were expected to entertain often and well. Entertaining is not done for the sheer sake of entertaining, but rather for the opportunities inherent in meeting government officials outside the formality of an office, and being able to talk informally.

The exposure to American hospitality and living standards are welcomed by those host government officials. Servants are necessary to maintain the household.

Many Foreign Service Officers experience almost daily occurrences of: power outages, debilitating heat, poisonous snakes, cancelled flights, frustration that things don't work as efficiently as they do in the U.S., among other annoyances. All of our assignments are challenging. Many diplomats work in countries mired in poverty and lacking infrastructure. We often find ourselves in the midst of coups, or standing in pouring rain with an ambassador with our best shoes sinking into the mud, or explaining to black Africans our barely disguised racist policies toward South Africa in the '80s. I have bathed in dirty water from the day before because there was no more water; swooshed newly born, deadly mamba snakes down the bathtub drain with bleach, and explained to host country officials that countries do not have friends, only interests. This is the Foreign Service. It is people like me representing you, the people and the government of the United States, trying to promote democracy.

We live and work in countries often ruled by corrupt officials, with high mortality rates, rampant diseases, poor medical conditions, difficult working conditions, frequent power surges, and often no power at all. Even under those conditions we strive to promote the image of the United States, meet with government officials, be responsive to the ambassador and assist other embassy officials, lament the lack of competent staff, and celebrate small triumphs. We then go on to other countries when our tour of duty ends, and we do it all over again. We love it. None of us would trade our jobs for any other in the world.

It is unfortunate that for the past few years there has been, and continues to be, is a target on the back of anyone working at a U.S. embassy. We have lost many dedicated officers and Foreign Service Nationals. Not enough can be said about local employees who work with our embassies. American officers come and go. The dedicated local people, who often work at our embassies for years, are those who provide the continuity, who in many instances "teach" the incoming Foreign Service Officers. Often they too are at risk because they work for the U.S. embassy.

Another component of our mandate is to tell our government about the people and country we work in, in order to help them make better and more informed decisions on matters of importance for both countries. That is not always appreciated by our officials. Former Secretary of State, Henry Kissinger, who swore in my class of officers, spoke to us after the swearing-in.

He complained, "Too often Foreign Service officers become advocates for the country they work in."

His remark surprised me. Who better to tell our government of the thinking going on in our host country than those officers who are working there?

The popular image of the Foreign Service is of diplomats standing around sipping champagne, being chauffeured in limousines, and hobnobbing with heads of state. We do all of that and more.

Before USIA became part of the State Department, a friend with State said to me, "I would love to be a USIA officer because you do fun things, but you work all day and then in the evenings you host or attend dinners, receptions, or present visiting speakers at your centers. When I finish work, I want to go home."

I laughed and replied, "We are the fun agency, and we have to love what we do!"

I certainly loved it!

I Speak for this Black Woman

All my work is meant to say, "You may encounter
defeats, but you must not be defeated."

- Maya Angelou

Black Foreign Service Officers are a special, rare breed. We are few compared to the density of white, male officers. Black, female officers are seldom seen as individuals, but rather as we have been depicted all too often in the media as evil, nappy-headed, ball-busting bitches. You learn to laugh as you bridle your tongue and your stomach does flip-flops. We see events and situations through different prisms than whites. We also identify more with the poor people in the countries in which we work.

America is represented by dynamic, professional, and exceptional black officers, each of whom has truly earned his or her place in the diplomatic community. As Paul Laurence Dunbar said, "We wear the mask that grins and lies." We put on that mask along with an invisible coat of armor to go out and face the other, whiter world. It is not an easy thing to be black, but I doubt that any of us would trade it for anything else. We can laugh in times of trouble. We can even laugh at ourselves. It is our way of keeping sane. Can whites imagine what it's like to have a total stranger look at you in hatred, or call you a "nigger"?

In 1948 there were only five black men in the Foreign Service. A few more were allowed in during the 1950s, but most were restricted to serving in Africa and the Caribbean, or the "Negro circuit" as it was called.

Early in the 1960s the U.S. Information Agency (USIA) began actively recruiting blacks. As a result, some outstanding blacks went on to become ambassadors because of their USIA careers. In 2005 blacks constituted 6.5% of the Foreign Service. Despite some strides made by blacks, we remained limited in where we could serve, and faced injustices in our performance reports. The Foreign Service has always been regarded as a stepping stone for privileged, white Protestant males. Due to court cases brought and won against State and USIA by women and blacks, the doors have opened wider for the Foreign Service to better reflect the nation it represents. Some still resent seeing blacks and other minorities building exciting careers, and the "old boy network" still prevails in the halls of the State Department. Despite the obstacles, our nation has an unprecedented number of black female and male ambassadors proudly representing their country. USIA is now a part of the State Department, and while the mixed marriage of USIA and State Department officers is not perfect, one can only hope that the State Department will recognize and reward the superior ability of USIA officers for their talent in mixing freely with the people of various countries, as well as for their unique creative abilities.

As a Foreign Service Officer I represented all Americans, and did so proudly.

When President Ronald Reagan grandly introduced his policy of "constructive engagement" toward South Africa, it was especially humiliating for a black American officer to attempt to justify this policy.

That policy was the U.S.' way of ignoring sanctions imposed on white South Africa for its violent and destructive policies toward black South Africans, and a way to continue to support white South Africa. Reagan's Assistant Secretary of State for African Affairs, Chester Crocker, said that by offering carrots and retiring the stick, the South African government would be more encouraged to ease its policy of apartheid. That was a lie. Black and white Americans marched in protest against what they saw as a wink and a nod from U.S. officials to a rabid and unapologetic South

African government. In fact, our policies encouraged the South Africans to become bolder in their violent oppression of blacks. They tried to eliminate any liberation movements in South Africa or neighboring countries. Black activists were jailed, killed, or simply disappeared. The white South Africans viewed the U.S. as being their best friend and felt they could do no wrong because the U.S. was backing their incredibly vicious treatment of blacks. More and more American businesses discontinued doing business in South Africa. Our policy was regarded as immoral and disgraceful by most. When the United Nations' Security Council wanted to impose sanctions on South Africa, the U.S. was the only country to veto the resolution.

While castigating "the cycle of violence" in and around South Africa, the U.S. refused to cast the blame where it should have been, on South Africa itself which was trying to consolidate its power and dominance in the region. Our policy was despicable, and black officers had to defend it. Fortunately I was in Liberia during this time and people there knew and understood that any words of defense vis-à-vis "constructive engagement" were simply from a script I had to follow.

I was sworn to uphold the policies of any U.S. government in power, even if I detested those policies. Nobody in his right mind could have thought that any black officer could agree with such a policy. Even if our own government could not see the ridiculousness of its policies, fortunately, those who mattered could.

Welcome to the Foreign Circus

I am the darker (sister). I, too, am America.

- Langston Hughes

The first part of our Foreign Service training in Washington began with 12 new USIA officers and 20 new officers of the Department of State. At age 39 I was the oldest. I was also the only black in the group. Everyone was curious about me, and possibly because they were aware that we were being scrutinized on camera, most made an effort to be pleasant to me. I have always lacked self-confidence, but usually hid it successfully. I had learned early on to have a thick skin because of my upbringing, and my exposure to people behaving differently to me. That toughness worked well for me in the Foreign Service. Day after day I heard colleagues making arrangements to go to lunch, or to see each other over the weekend. I smiled and wished them a good weekend.

As a group we visited each U.S. government agency and were lectured on what each agency did overseas. We looked forward to the visit to the Central Intelligence Agency (CIA), and their speakers proved to be as interesting as we thought they would be. We read briefing books prepared for the White House when foreign dignitaries were coming to the U.S. We saw movies demonstrating what U.S. spy planes can do. We even had lunch in the employee cafeteria. A curtain separated us from undercover CIA agents dining at the same time. All of us wanted to peek behind the curtain, not that we would have known who we were seeing, but it was tempting. All too soon our visit was over.

The official who briefed us at the Department of Agriculture opened with a poorly chosen reference to a racist joke their recently fired, Secretary of Agriculture, Earl Butz (a Hoosier) told a group of journalists. Butz had joked that the only thing black men wanted was "loose shoes, a tight p----, and a warm place to s---." He was outraged when it was reported in the media. The rest of the country was outraged that he would say such. The official greeted us.

I was startled when he opened our meeting saying, "We know what you all want."

Most of the group guffawed. A few of us did not. At the end of our agency visits, we returned to USIA to discuss the visits. I stood and said I did not appreciate the reference to Earl Butz' sick joke. My fellow USIA trainees looked at me as if I were a lunatic. However, two male State officers stood and said they too did not appreciate it. I was proud of those two State officers, and I was profoundly disturbed that my USIA colleagues, with whom I would soon be working, apparently thought nothing of the sick joke or how I could be insulted by it.

Our training continued. We saw movies of American hostages. We were told about the "Stockholm syndrome" phenomenon where the hostage begins to identify with the kidnapper because that is the person the hostage depends on for food, for life. This syndrome was identified in 1973 when hostages were held for six days during a bank robbery and after being released, were sympathetic toward their captors and rather scornful of the police trying to free them. We already knew, but it sure didn't help to be reminded, that the U.S. never negotiates for its hostages. The officials tried to soften the news by saying that the U.S. expected the host country government to negotiate for our release.

We were taught about driving defensively. Officials wanted us to have hands-on training to learn defensive driving and evasive driving techniques, but money was not available for training. We were told to vary our routes to and from the office and our residences. That's all well and good if one is stationed in Paris or London, but in third world countries where most of us serve, there is usually only one way to get from here to there. So we watched the movies and hoped we never had to execute any of those moves.

When our basic training was completed, our State colleagues returned to the State Department to begin training for their Economics, Political, or

Consular cones. USIA officers were tested on our language aptitude because the agency wanted to put some of us into Thai, Russian, Arabic, Japanese or Chinese classes, the so-called "hard languages." I certainly wanted no part of any of those languages, and I came perilously close to getting a score that would have put me into a "hard language" class. We began learning how to work a video camera, thread a movie projector, introduce speakers, clever ways of entertaining, and the best part of all – how to bid on the country you wanted to work in. Everything depended on which countries were available at the same time you were. In one sense we were in luck because we would be heading to our assignments in the summer. Summer is when most FSOs leave their posts for vacation and move on to other posts. That is when schools are out. Single officers don't have to worry about schools, or so they think.

Only after arriving at a post do you realize how important it is to know if your supervisor has children, and how old they are, because that determines when they will want to go on vacation. They naturally want to vacation when school is out.

That usually leaves a junior officer to take vacation in January or February, not the ideal vacation months. Vacation planning is crucial because the U.S. Congress mandates that all Foreign Service officers must spend 10 working days in the U.S. every two years. That is called Home Leave and it is not charged against annual leave. Congress reasoned that since we are out in the field telling people about the U.S., it would be smart to require us to return every two years so that we know what is going on.

As USIA officers we were either junior officers in training (for the first year only), Cultural Affairs Officers (CAO), Information Officers (IO), or Public Affairs Officers (PAO), who head the agency at our posts. Presently they are all identified as Public Diplomacy Officers. When the list of available posts came out, most of my class wanted Europe. There were two European posts on the list, Russia and Greece. I wanted to go to a black country. The only black country on the list was Haiti. At that time the U.S. did not send single people to Russia on the theory that single people could easily be compromised sexually and blackmailed. The one guy who wanted to go to Russia was engaged to be married. He received the assignment, and he did get married before leaving for his new post. When the countries were announced I was awarded Haiti. I was deliriously happy. I was also the only person who wanted to go there. Nothing I heard or would hear about Haiti discouraged me.

I was assigned to a refresher course in French since I had lived in France and spoke French, or so I thought. At the Foreign Service Institute the instructors are native speakers in every language offered there. I took an oral exam before beginning French classes.

When the exam ended one of the testers said to me, "You are incredible. You speak French so fast and so fluently that we have to listen very carefully to hear your mistakes."

That was the whole idea. In Paris I spoke fast, dropped endings, threw in slang, and it was to hide the fact that I didn't know French grammar. I spoke like a real Parisian. The testers alerted the French instructors to make me speak clearly and slowly. That was my undoing. We changed instructors every month in order to prevent burnout of the instructors or students. The instructor would ask me a question, I'd snap out the answer and he or she would go to the next student.

Suddenly they would remember the caution about me and say, "Mademoiselle Duline, would you repeat that slowly, s'il vous plait?"

When I repeated it slowly it was wrong, of course. I reached the point where I didn't want to open my mouth. I found French grammar extremely difficult and I just wanted to babble fast so nobody could hear my mistakes. While the French instructors complimented me on my Parisian accent, they all forced me to slow down and to enunciate every word. The struggle was on. Language classes were rigorous. We had classes from 9 a.m. to 4 p.m. five days a week. We had a ten minute break every hour, and we had three hours of homework each night.

Outside of class we were expected to read, listen to tapes, radio and TV to test our understanding of French. In the midst of this intensive language training, I began the numerous inoculations I needed for Haiti. My arm felt like a pin cushion. One inoculation was particularly painful for days afterward. I could not bear anything touching that arm. I could barely move the arm and when I did there was excruciating pain. I could not sleep on that side of my body for about a week. It even hurt for the shower water to hit it. Then came tetanus shots, gamma globulin, polio, and on and on. Between the inoculations and studying for my final French exam, I was miserable.

I was extremely anxious about my final French exam. I knew what I didn't know, but I hoped the testers wouldn't know it. The American linguist apologized that she would not be able to listen to my exam because she had an outside appointment. I didn't care where she was going to be; I just wanted the exam to be over. On the day of my exam I walked into the small examining room looking like a thunder cloud and feeling the same. The two testers I had previously were seated at the table. I was chagrined. They knew me. Did they ever. The tester I had had as an instructor greeted me in French as did the other tester. I replied in French while thinking mean and evil thoughts. They were slouched in their chairs. My former instructor told the other tester that I was going to Haiti. He lazily asked what I would be doing there. I rattled off a response, but in my head I was shouting, *"Start the damned test and stop this silly chatter!"*

That silly chatter went on for several minutes.

Finally one tester said, "Well, the oral part of the exam is over. It's time for the reading part."

That's when I realized the exam had begun when I walked into the room, and I came undone. The minute I knew the exam was underway, I couldn't read or translate anything. They were very patient with me, but it was as if I had never seen a word of French.

The linguist, listening to me in another room, after assuring me that she would not be present, said later, "Your spoken French was flawless. You didn't make one single mistake when you were speaking, but the minute you realized the test had started and you had to read and translate, you went to pieces. What happened?"

Indeed, I, too, wanted to know. I was given six more weeks of French. Finally I passed the damned test and I was on my way to Haiti as a junior officer in training, but I was so intimidated that I did not want to speak any French. The Foreign Service Institute had ruined my French along with my confidence.

The Magic of Haiti
1977-78

We have dared to be free; let us dare to be so by ourselves and for ourselves.
- Jean-Jacques Dessalines, Haitian Hero

Discos throb with sensuality as black bodies hugged tightly together swivel and sway to a beat that is hot and sassy, not to mention sexy. This is the dance of the nation, the sexy meringue, a hip-rolling dance that leaves one breathless and weak in the knees. This is Haiti where the poverty is disheartening and overwhelming. The weather is hot and the rainy season unforgiving, but the landscape is lush and green with swaying trees, and red with poinsettias blooming everywhere. Haiti is mystical and enchanting. It's the world's first black republic, born in the blood of its patriots – Jean-Jacques Dessalines, Henri Christophe, and Toussaint L'Ouverture. It has been, and remains, the poorest country in the Western Hemisphere. Despite 19 years of occupation by the U.S. military, there is nothing to show for such occupation: few paved roads, and no infrastructure. There is incredible music and equally incredible poverty. On verdant hillsides, trees drip with breadfruit, mangoes, and bananas. Rum is the national drink. Rum punch is the drink of choice, and no bartender spares the rum. The Barbancourt Rum Distillery in Petionville, in the hills overlooking Port-au-Prince, welcomes visitors and offers samples of rums with exotic flavors such as hibiscus, apricot, mango, papaya, coconut, anise, nougat, and mint among other flavors.

The heat, the gaiety, the laughter, the dance, the passion for everything, the vibrancy of people, flowers, and art everywhere the eye looks – this is Haiti. The country throbs with passion and colors that form the creative artwork on buses, doorways, and everywhere else. The air vibrates with the sounds of distant drums from high in the hills above the city. The language of France is the rhythm in the ear, along with Creole, Haiti's special language. Haiti attracted me like a magnet. From the moment that I stepped off the plane onto Haitian soil, I was enchanted by the people, the language, the food, and it was the first time for me to be in a country where blacks were in the majority and blacks ruled.

Haiti is hot. I don't mean the kind of heat that causes one to perspire. I sweated buckets of sweat. I began sweating when I stepped off the plane, and I did not stop sweating until I left one year later. Every crack and crevice of my body oozed sweat. My dress stuck to my slip which stuck to my panties which were plastered to my butt. I tried to discreetly dab the sweat pouring down my face, but tissue sticks in pieces to wet skin, so out came the handkerchiefs. I often yearned for a towel. Being discreet be damned, I wanted to envelope my entire body in something that would dry it.

Haiti is indeed a magical island. There is beauty and art as far as the eye could see: art on buses, known as Tap-Taps, on billboards, and on buildings. I stayed at the San Souci, an old gingerbread-type hotel, surrounded by exquisite tropical flowers. The hallways were dim, and the rooms were ancient.

I never wanted to look under the bed for fear of finding dirt as old as the earth, or skeletons. I was entranced with the lush, tropical beauty and people filled with the joy of living, no matter how poor.

The evening I arrived, I was met and taken to my hotel by the Cultural Affairs Officer. I barely had time to change and rush to a reception given by my supervisor, Frank Gomez, the Public Affairs Officer (PAO). I ordered a gin and tonic and began meeting and greeting. We were outside on Frank's terrace and the night seemed to get hotter. The one gin and tonic didn't help to cool me, but made me feel even hotter. I was also beginning to feel giddy. That night I promised myself that I would never drink alcohol at receptions, but would instead ask for a glass of tonic and lime. I also remembered being told during our training that the majority of FS officers became alcoholics because of the low cost and the availability of liquor. I decided that I would not become one of those. Only at dinner parties did I allow myself to enjoy fine wines.

I assumed that on my first day I would go into the office, meet everybody and then be taken out to look for housing. Big mistake. I arrived at the office and the PAO said we were going to the Ministry of Foreign Affairs. I had on a lovely three piece pants suit, but not quite the thing for the Ministry of Foreign Affairs.

I asked, "Can I go wearing this?"

Frank looked me up and down and said, "Well, I guess you'll have to."

That was the last time I wore slacks at any post.

I worked in each section of the embassy for one week to get a feel for an embassy. They knew better than to let a new officer handle visas, but I did spend time in the consular section. In the political section I could barely organize the files because I kept stopping to read fascinating cables of some historic events. I spent time working with our cultural branch situated in a gorgeous, old gingerbread house where our library was located and where English classes were offered for a small fee. I also did everything the PAO did. He took me to daily Country Team meetings where the ambassador met with all the heads of U.S. agencies and where one really learned what's going on in the country. I attended all official events to which the PAO was invited. He took his job as my trainer seriously, and was determined that I would learn every facet of USIA and embassy operations. I was the third officer at a two-officer post. I indirectly supervised four senior resident professionals. I acted as liaison officer to the Agency for International Development (USAID), and helped develop programs to increase awareness among priority audiences of U.S. assistance to Haiti. I assisted the CAO in implementing the post's seminar programs on foreign policy, communications, American society and others, ensuring emphasis on the human rights objectives of our post. I gained a working knowledge of all the media products used in our office, and I was an active participant in policy and program planning.

I had to find my own housing. The first house I wanted the General Services Officer did not approve of for security reasons. Soon I found a gorgeous house that he did approve of. This house had a swimming pool, and was ornately decorated with fancy metal grill at the doors and windows.

One wall in the living room was carved teak. On the ground floor were servant's quarters, and a carport. On the second floor were two bedrooms, two baths, living room, and a huge balcony surrounded the upstairs. I used the balcony outside of the kitchen as my dining room. The owner of the house, who lived next door, had about 40 plants on my balcony which she took care of. There was also an artificial tree on the balcony where a family of green lizards lived. I had never felt so relaxed and happy in a foreign country before. Everyone did not share my joy. Such was the case with many of the embassy wives. They were bored. They could not get jobs. The local economy had no jobs for wives of diplomats. They had servants and nannies, so there was little for them to do at home. They met in morning coffee klatches that quickly turned into alcoholic, pity parties. Things reached such straits that the Department of State sent a psychiatrist from Washington to talk to them. Months later I found out about this from an embassy secretary. I bristled when I asked my boss why I had not been notified of the psychiatrist's visit.

He laughed and said, "You are the last person who needed to see the psychiatrist. You're the happiest person here!"

Meanwhile, Baby Doc, Jean-Claude Duvalier, ruled from the palace surrounded by his late father's henchmen, and tried to keep an eye on his ambitious sister. At the age of 19 this youth took over the reins of government shortly before the death of his father, Francois Duvalier. The son continued the country's legacy of torture and abuse of its citizens, especially journalists and human-rights advocates. Neither man did anything to help the people of the poorest country in our hemisphere to rise above their poverty.

While the rich continued to enjoy their riches, and the poor got poorer, our small embassy staff worked diligently to bring democratic changes to the nation. My year of training as a Foreign Service Officer was underway.

Our foreign policy goals in Haiti were to promote human rights, to plan and implement programs rather than reacting to events, and to help alleviate poverty and under-development, and to establish institutional linkages, sorely lacking due to Haiti's isolationism – not entirely self-imposed. I had been at the post for one month when we learned that Ambassador Andrew Young, our UN ambassador, was coming to Haiti. My boss was away on vacation, and the Cultural Affairs Officer said he was far too busy to help in planning for the Young Visit. Before arriving in Haiti I had read an article in the USIA newsletter about a high level visit to another country and the exhaustive preparations such a visit entailed. I knew media arrangements had to be made immediately and they had to go smoothly. We needed telex machines, press rooms and telephones that worked. When I tried to discuss the visit with the CAO, he brushed me off. I went to a friend, the General Services Officer (GSO), out of sheer frustration. We could not wait for the return of the PAO. The GSO explained this to the Chargé who called me in and gave me carte blanche to work on the visit. Ambassador Young was coming with 12 aides and 13 reporters. I set up two press rooms with telex machines and phones that miraculously worked throughout the three day visit. I stayed with the press and saw to it that they got to and from various places. A veteran correspondent with the Young party said press arrangements in Haiti were the best in the 10-nation trip.

My boss, Frank, accompanied Ambassador Young and the U.S. Chargé d'Affaires into the meeting with Jean-Claude Duvalier, and acted as interpreter. The remaining Country Team members, including me, were in a waiting room. I had asked Frank what I should say when I met President Duvalier.

He said, "Don't worry. You won't be meeting him."

When the official meeting ended, President Duvalier accompanied Ambassador Young out of his office and he was face to face with the rest of the official Americans from the embassy. We leaped to our feet and Frank realized that introductions were in order. As I moved down the line, my mind was working furiously about what to say. I remembered that at some point one of my French instructors had said a woman did not say, "Enchante, charmed" to a man, but rather a man said it to a woman. But it was all I could think of, and that is what I said to the president. I have no idea what he said because he barely opened his mouth. I had met my first head of state. Never mind that he was a boy dictator, a despot, a sybarite, a puppet of his father's henchmen, and evil personified. I had met my first head of state and I floated out of the palace that day.

I had a friend in the U.S. who was from Haiti. He was excited when I told him that I would be going to his country, and he promised to visit while I was there. A few months later he visited me briefly, and spent the rest of his time in the provinces. A few days after his planned departure, I received a frantic call from him saying that the police had taken him off the plane, held him for several days, and had just released him. He came to my office and relayed information that I had just read in our Secret files, but had no idea that a member of his family was involved.

In 1973 U.S. Ambassador Clinton Knox had been kidnapped by three Haitians. They demanded the release of 31 prisoners, a ransom of $70,000, and a plane for their safe passage out of Haiti. The Haitian government claimed to have only 12 of the 31 in custody, and agreed to release them. The kidnappers' demands were met, and our ambassador was released, thanks in part also to the good offices of the Canadian and French ambassadors. One of the kidnappers was the brother of my Haitian friend, and because of that kidnapping, my friend had been told when he left the country that he should not return. I asked why he came back knowing that he was not supposed to. He said he felt safe in returning because I was there as a diplomat. I groaned. Now he was afraid to go back to the airport even though he had been released from jail. He wanted me to accompany him to the airport. I had no intention of doing that; I was concerned that both of us would be jailed. I consulted with my boss, who contacted a political officer at the embassy, who met with my friend. They arranged his departure date, and the political officer went with him to the airport, saw him on the plane, and waited until the plane departed. I hoped he would not return under my watch.

I had a wonderful housekeeper named Janine. Janine was like a mother to me. When I was ill she would send the gardener up the road to pick some leaves for her to make a tea that always cured me.

I'd say, "Janine, the dogs and cats have peed on these leaves."

She'd reply sweetly, "No, Mademoiselle."

I wasn't convinced, but her tea always worked.

Janine's daughter had a baby and she took some time off to be with her. Her sister, Sophie, came to work in her place. When we were out of permanganate tablets to wash vegetables in, Janine knew to use a *drop or two* of Clorox bleach to wash the lettuce for salad. I came in one evening from work and there was a strong smell of bleach throughout the house. I assumed it had been used to clean the floors. I ate dinner that included a salad and later went to bed. Sophie went downstairs to her quarters and Dominique, the gardener, gatekeeper, and pool keeper, went to his quarters. I woke up a few hours later with excruciating pain in my abdomen. I rang for Sophie. I didn't know what she could do, but I wanted somebody to know how sick I was. She and Dominique flew up to my bedroom. Suddenly I remembered the strong odor of bleach. I asked Sophie how much bleach she used in my salad.

She said she used one-half a cup. Damn! No wonder I was dying or so it felt. Dominique looked shocked too. He knew Janine only used a drop or two at the most. For some reason it never occurred to me to call one of the Haitian doctors the embassy used. Perhaps it was because Sophie immediately ordered Dominique to go and pick certain leaves. I was too sick to protest. He returned quickly and Sophie fixed a cup of tea. I managed to sit up in bed to drink it, but I was still in agony. She and Dominique looked frightened and concerned. Almost instantly the pain subsided, and finally it was completely gone. I went back to sleep. I learned the next morning that Dominique had slept on the floor outside my door in case I became ill again. Poor Sophie could not apologize enough. I didn't eat any more salads until Janine returned.

In Times of Trouble, Don't Call the Embassy!

May God preserve us from, "If I had known!"
- Hausa, Nigeria

A movie critic reviewing a movie about an American in trouble in China said the U.S. Embassy was as helpful as a can of grease in a kitchen fire. That statement is not completely wrong. Most Americans are unaware that a U.S. Embassy is not in a foreign country to serve Americans, but to discuss foreign policies, to relay messages between governments, to influence people, and to report on political happenings in that country. Mr. and Mrs. America go gaily off to East Hell, and assume that the U.S. Embassy is there solely to bail them out of any difficulty. Be disabused of that notion. Embassy officers are there to maintain cordial relations with the foreign government, not to offend them. Of course, in an emergency – a death, a missing American, lost passport, etc. - embassy officers are at your side, doing the best that they can do for you.

Diplomacy has changed drastically over the years. Diplomats, especially American diplomats, are no longer protected by their special passports asking that all courtesies be extended to them. Instead, in some instances, carrying a Diplomatic Passport is an invitation for kidnapping or death. In fact, after several plane hijackings in which Americans were targeted, most

Foreign Service officers carried a personal passport in addition to their official passport.

In some instances, we were required to carry two passports. Before South Africa became free, other black countries would not allow passengers to enter their countries if they had a South African visa in their passports. That applied to diplomats also. When I was assigned to Swaziland, next door to South Africa, I was issued a special diplomatic passport good *only* for South Africa. I also had my other diplomatic passport for all other countries. My third passport did not identify me as a diplomat in the event of a plane hijacking. When I left for one country a friend, Dorothy Whitehead, gave me a half slip that had a hidden compartment in which one could hide money and passports. That was a welcomed gift because I always wore dresses when traveling to or from Africa in the '70s and '80s. In Tanzania women were not allowed to wear slacks or mini-skirts; men could not wear bell-bottom trousers or have long hair. In fact, during my years in Africa, I never wore slacks or even had any in my wardrobe.

I always felt safe in foreign countries before I became a Foreign Service Officer. In various countries I would hotfoot it to the U.S. Embassy to let them know I was in town. I was certain the embassy would take care of me if there were any problems. Much later I learned that in a crisis, such as when there has been a coup and renegade soldiers are shooting anything that moves, the U.S. Embassy is the LAST embassy to make a move to get its citizens out. We are not going to be seen as fleeing a country. Oh no! We like to hang tough, get out and about and see what is going on in the streets. Such activity on our part looks good in our performance report by which each officer is judged against other officers.

The promotion board might read: "She braved danger, going where nobody else with any intelligence dared to go, did excellent reporting on the executions, but did not survive to see her name in lights at the airport in Mwadagido."

For Americans in trouble in foreign countries, U.S. embassy personnel can do little other than notify your family that you are in the hoosegow, sick, dead, or have been sentenced to 50 years in prison. Sometimes embassy officials are allowed to visit and may take you candy and cigarettes, if permitted by the host government. They will provide you with a list of lawyers and interpreters, and try to dissuade the local authorities from using you for target practice.

Each Foreign Service officer has to be Duty Officer for a week until he/she reaches the level of head honcho of his/her respective agency. Duty begins on a Friday evening when the embassy closes, and lasts all weekend, and after hours for one week. I came to dread the weekends when I was Duty Officer. The Marine guard on duty at the embassy had to know where I was at all times. I had to know the location of the police station, the hospital, which consular officer to contact, etc. At that time USIA officers did not receive any consular training, and knew nothing about issuing visas or shipping bodies back to the U.S. We were happy in our ignorance. Currently all officers receive consular training.

One consular officer gave me some great advice, "The first rule of thumb is to get them (Americans in trouble) out of your territory."

It wasn't long before I had occasion to remember that advice, and to use it.

Mr. Handsome

A poor mulatto is Black, a wealthy Black is mulatto.
- Haitian Proverb

During the 1970s Haiti was a magnet for unstable Americans prone to getting into trouble. That was particularly true, it seemed, whenever I was the Duty Officer assigned to handling emergencies after the embassy closed. One Saturday morning in October I woke up early to prepare for a Halloween party I was hosting that night. I was the duty officer again, and I hoped the weekend would be quiet. That hope was quickly shattered when a Marine guard called early that morning to say that an American was in jail and wanted help from the embassy. I figured that I would make a quick trip to the jail to see if he was being taken care of, and get back to my party preparations.

At the jail I was ushered into an official's office. As I walked in, I saw the man's nameplate on his desk and inwardly I shivered. This was the man the Haitians called "The Beast." It was said he was extremely rough on prisoners. I introduced myself. He was polite to me, and sent for the prisoner. Mr. Handsome was escorted in. He was an African-American, extremely good-looking, over 6 ft. tall, and appeared to be in his mid-30s. He was also light-skinned, a fact that figured prominently in his story. Despite being wrinkled, his linen pants and jacket still managed to testify to their elegance and cost.

Mr. Handsome was dispirited. I introduced myself and told him I was from the American Embassy.

He handed me his credit cards and passport. I looked at them, and when I tried to return them to him, he ignored my attempts. I asked both men what happened. Mr. Handsome began his story in English, and at the same time The Beast began interrupting in French. I was trying to understand what had happened, as well as translate into French Mr. Handsome's responses.

Mr. Handsome said, "I was walking down the street and a beggar kept bothering me for money."

As he continued, The Beast shouted, "You said you didn't …!"

I soon found myself shouting back, "What he meant was…"

I tried to understand what Mr. Handsome was saying. The Beast was unrelenting in his questioning and interruptions. I kept telling The Beast that I was not Mr. Handsome's attorney, and occasionally I remembered it. I was not going to let The Beast judge and sentence him right there. Sometimes I would go back to being diplomatic, but would soon find myself shouting again.

Mr. Handsome was charged with beating a Haitian beggar with a whip. He might as well have tried to bring down the government. Haitians have always fought against slavery and anything that smacks of slavery. In the 1600s the French had over 500,000 slaves in Haiti. Some were black, and others were the offspring of black slaves and Frenchmen. They were called mulattoes, and they were favored over the pure black slaves. The French were incredibly cruel to the slaves, often branding, mutilating, sealing them inside barrels lined with spikes and rolling them down mountains. The first major slave rebellion was led by Toussaint L'Ouverture in 1791.

In 1801 Napoleon Bonaparte sent troops to retake Haiti, but he was defeated by Jean Jacques Dessalines, who became Haiti's first chief of state.

Mr. Handsome's story was that the street beggar had been bothering him and he asked a shopkeeper how to get rid of him. The shopkeeper gave him a "whip," that the shopkeepers used to chase away beggars. One might ask if Haitians used "whips" why couldn't Mr. Handsome? Mr. Handsome was *not* Haitian and he *was* light-skinned like the mulattos the black Haitian slaves had overthrown centuries ago. There would be no mercy shown him. The

Beast said Mr. Handsome would be appearing in court shortly where a judge would sentence him. I was alarmed and protested that he needed a lawyer. I handed Mr. Handsome a list of Haitian attorneys as compiled by the embassy, and asked him to select one for me to contact to represent him. He refused. I explained that American diplomats were not allowed to select attorneys for Americans, and that he needed an attorney. I urged him to select one from the list. He was lethargic and uncooperative. I wondered if he were hung-over or drugged. I knew that both of us had to be alert in court. Just before entering the courtroom I called the Consul General, a low-keyed, basically useless man as I was to discover. He promised to meet us.

As Mr. Handsome and I walked into the courtroom the judge looked up and said in French, "You again! I advised you to leave Haiti several days ago!"

I translated for Mr. Handsome and asked how the judge knew him. He mumbled that he had an incident in a hotel with a taxi driver. He had no idea that the man who suggested he leave Haiti was a sitting judge. Mr. Handsome was called before the bench and I approached with him.

The judge asked him in French, "Do you speak French?"

I replied, "No, he doesn't."

The judge then sent for an interpreter to interpret French and Creole into English and vice-versa.

While we waited, Mr. Handsome turned to me and asked, "Do you know where to send my body?"

I didn't respond.

He then complained, "I haven't had anything to eat or drink since early yesterday."

It was now noon.

I addressed the judge, "Your Honor, Mr. Handsome hasn't eaten since early yesterday. Would it be possible to get him something to eat or drink?"

The judge immediately took some money from his pocket to pay for food and drink for Mr. Handsome who refused the offer.

I radioed the Marine House and told them I might need two or three Marines to help get this man to the airport if he were released. They agreed to stand by. I also called two Haitian friends and asked them to go to my house to help my housekeeper decorate and get the house ready for the party.

The interpreter arrived, and Mr. Handsome was called before the bench. As I listened in horror, he said to the judge, "I am an expert in karate. I have asked Ms. Duline to send my body to my mother. But I know karate and I will use it."

At that point, I opened his passport and made a note of his mother's name and address. I was beginning to think I might have to contact her.

The Swiss manager of the hotel where Mr. Handsome stayed was in court to ask for payment for Mr. Handsome's room. He was petrified when Mr. Handsome talked about his karate expertise.

He pleaded, "Your Honor, maybe we should have a policeman here in the courtroom."

I silently agreed with him, but the judge didn't seem bothered and ignored the request.

Mr. Handsome, standing before the judge, began slowly unbuttoning his shirt.

I leaped to his side and asked, "What are you doing?!"

He replied, "I'm ready to die."

He removed his shirt.

I said, "Nobody's going to die! Please stop taking off your clothes."

I didn't know what was going to happen, but I knew it was not going to be pleasant. Over the din of my thundering heart, I heard the hotel owner wailing for a policeman. This time the judge sent for one who came in and stood next to the judge. I didn't think this was what Mr. Hotel Owner had in mind. By this time Mr. Handsome had removed his shirt and sandals, and was about to remove his pants.

I pleaded with him, "Please, please, put your clothes back on."

I wondered what he was going to do. I didn't know if he was going to try to hurt or kill somebody, and if so, who? That was the all-important question. Who? I didn't like the possibilities since I didn't know if he regarded me as a friend or one of "them." More importantly, I didn't want to see him shot down in court.

I had a duty to help him, but now we both needed help. I had no idea that the U.S. Consul General had arrived and was sitting in the back of the room. As far as I knew, I was on my own. I was beginning to think that someone had drugged Mr. Handsome. I talked fast, and finally got him to put his clothes back on. The judge smiled at me patiently. Mr. Handsome continued muttering about dying, and karate, and me shipping his body to his mother. I was really worried. I knew that his fate rested in my hands, and that was a horrible feeling. This man was well on his way to jail or worse, and only a junior officer-in-training, at her first post, and her first court appearance, stood between him and whatever, and whatever was getting closer and it didn't look good. I sent up a prayer to St. Jude, the patron saint of impossible causes.

The trial began. Everybody had a story to tell. The man who was whipped was there. He was not injured, but the fact that this American had had the audacity to lash him with a whip was cause for him to be indignant. Never mind that shopkeepers used them on beggars all the time. I asked to see the whip. I had imagined something similar to a cat of nine tails. The infamous "whip" looked exactly like a shoelace. It was about 18 inches long, and could do no harm to anyone. That, of course, was not the point. It was incredible to me that we were in a court of law because of a shoelace. Witnesses were called including the hotel owner who testified that he was owed for five nights, and he wanted Mr. Handsome out of his hotel. Money was not a problem. Mr. Handsome had thousands of dollars in Traveler's Checks that The Beast had handed to me.

The judge was patient and made sure Mr. Handsome understood everything said in court. When Mr. Handsome complained that he was tired of standing, the judge allowed him to sit. Again he was offered food and drink, and again he refused. He continued asking me if I knew where to send his body.

I wanted to yell at him, but I managed to say between clinched teeth, "Will you please stop asking that?"

I desperately hoped he would be allowed to leave the country. He was a sick man, and jail time in Haiti would do him no good. I thought that if he were not drugged, perhaps he was having a nervous breakdown. I felt sorry for him. From his identification I knew that he had a high level job in the U.S. He was in the wrong country at the wrong time of his life. He never appeared to be angry, just sad and resigned. After listening to all of the evidence, the kindly old judge fined him $300, ordered him to pay his hotel bill, and to leave Haiti within 24 hours. I was relieved, but not for long.

Mr. Handsome said, "Wait, I'm not sure my life is worth $300. I have to think about it."

He actually stood before the judge deep in thought. I suggested to him that he stop that nonsense, pay the fine and go home. He continued to think about it. The judge looked at me sympathetically and waited. Glancing around, I noticed the U.S. Consul General sitting in the back of the courtroom as if he were a spectator. I threw a pleading look at him, but he sat there looking back at me. After some thought, Mr. Handsome agreed to pay his fine and hotel bill.

I peeled off the Travelers Checks, which he signed. At last, I thought, I was finished and could go home. I radioed the Marines and said they would not be needed. Fool that I was.

The hotel owner then petitioned the judge to have someone from the embassy accompany Mr. Handsome to the hotel to get his belongings. He was afraid to have Mr. Handsome loose in his hotel without an embassy presence. The judge requested that I accompany Mr. Handsome to and from the hotel. I gritted my teeth.

As we left the courtroom, the Consul General came up to me and said, "I will wait in the hotel lobby while you go up with him to get his belongings, and I'll take him to the airport."

Once in his room, Mr. Handsome plopped into a chair. I urged him to begin packing while I called the airport to make a plane reservation for him. The hotel owner lingered, for which I was grateful. I did not want to be alone with Mr. Handsome. He would not pack. I wanted him on the next flight leaving for the U.S., so I packed his suitcase. When I finished, Mr. Handsome refused to leave. He said he wanted to rest. So did I. I pleaded, prodded, and by the time he finally agreed to leave, he had missed the flight. It was back to contacting airlines to see what was leaving Port-au-Prince. I no longer cared where it was going. I remembered the advice I had been given by the consular officer to get problem folks off my turf. I wanted to get Mr. Handsome on the first thing smoking. I found a flight going to Puerto Rico, and I convinced him that he could easily get a flight out to Washington or Baltimore from Puerto Rico.

Actually I did not have a clue, but I was not going to let him spend another minute in Haiti, let alone a day or two to wait for a plane going to the Washington area. I grabbed Mr. Handsome's suitcase and escorted him to the lobby where the Consul General waited.

He cautioned me, "I'll take him to the airport, but if he refuses to get on the plane, he's yours again."

The Consul General had not done one single, helpful thing all day. I, on the other hand, had spent the entire day with a man obviously off his rocker and quite willing to get both of us shot. I had acted as counselor, confessor, and second at a duel, and Mr. Consul General was generously going to take him to the airport, and if he balked at getting on the plane, the problem was back in my court. I wanted to fall on my knees in gratitude after kicking him in the balls, but being the consummate junior diplomat that I was, I smiled and thanked him. I was homeward bound to prepare for my party. I arrived at home just in time to change into my Halloween costume. I held my breath until after the scheduled departure of Mr. Handsome's flight.

Several days later I learned that Mr. Handsome did indeed create a ruckus on the plane. Our ambassador's wife happened to be on the same flight. Did I do Mr. Handsome a disservice by getting him out of Haiti? I think I served him well. Had he caused any more problems in Port-au-Prince, he definitely would have gone to prison. At least in Puerto Rico he was on U.S. territory.

Voodoo

The magic remains in Haiti, but the spell crosses the sea.
- Haitian proverb

Haiti is a magical and mysterious country, and most people think of voodoo when they think of Haiti. I was more than a bit interested in voodoo when I arrived in Haiti. When slaves were brought from Africa they mixed the Catholicism of Haiti with their own deities, and the result was voodoo or other beliefs their ancestors had practiced for centuries, such as Santeria in Brazil. Voodoo is regarded as a peasant religion, and I respected it as such. Whether they admit it or not, most Haitians take voodoo seriously. Despite having read and heard many negative things about voodoo, oddly, none of it bothered me. Haitians always say that voodoo is never used to harm anyone, only to benefit them. Ghedes are said to be naughty, mischievous spirits who delight in sexual humor. October is the month of celebrations honoring these spirits of debauchery and lewdness. One Friday night two Haitian friends who worked at the embassy arrived at my home with the mother of one of them.

She said, "I understand you want to see some voodoo. Let's go."

I had been told that she was a mambo, a priestess, for Baby Doc Duvalier, i.e. his fortune-teller. So it was with awe and trepidation that I hurriedly prepared to leave with them. I felt perfectly safe, and invited a newly arrived colleague to go with us. He, too, was excited at the idea of going to some real voodoo ceremonies.

At the first site there was such a crowd of people that I wondered how I would see anything. But the moment my guide walked in, paths parted for us and we were taken to the front row where seats were quickly made available. It was obvious that my hostess was prominent in voodoo circles. There was much kowtowing to her and to us as her guests. The large room was hot and steamy. Drums throbbed while several priests, called houngans, and women, called mambos, danced in trance-like states, and the air was filled with a rum haze. The participants dancing took a mouthful of rum and spewed it out in a fine mist. From time to time I used to practice on my balcony spewing out rum in a mist, but decided that I'd rather drink the rum than spit it out which was what I was doing. It never came out of my mouth in a spray. The drumming and the dancing are to invoke the spirits or loas as they are called, to take possession of their bodies. Animal sacrifices are offered to the loas in an attempt to appease them to gain their favor for better health, food, money or other needs. The animals are usually goats, sheep or chickens. Their throats are slit and the blood collected in a vessel and drunk by the mambos and houngans. The rum and the heat were intoxicating. The beat of the drums was infectious. At one point, I knew that if my hostess got up to dance, I would too. After all, I had studied Afro-Cuban, and Primitive-Haitian dancing in New York City. I watched the goats that were going to be sacrificed. I felt very sorry for them, but I could not allow my mind to dwell on them. This was not the time to get into a pissing match about animal rights.

At the next site I decided to stand at the edge of the crowd. I was too hot to be engulfed by more heat down front. I might as well have been drinking the rum rather than inhaling it because I felt intoxicated. There was more dancing by people seemingly possessed. Again I watched the goats standing so innocently. When their throats were slashed, I could only close my eyes. I was unable to move due to the press of bodies against me. The heat was overwhelming. Sweat oozed from every pore. My floor length cotton dress was as wet as if I had stood in a rain shower. My head throbbed with each drumbeat, and I felt that if I got one more whiff of rum I would be absolutely drunk. Finally my guide made her way back to me and asked if I wanted to go to a third ceremony. I had to decline. I was honored to have been invited to accompany a mambo to some real ceremonies. I wanted to learn more about voodoo, but then I wondered did I really want to know. Some odd things had happened to me during my one year in Haiti.

One Saturday afternoon I was alone in the house, cooling off in my bedroom when there was a knock at the door. I thought Janine, my housekeeper, had left, but I yelled for her to come in. Nothing happened. I looked at the door and could see the space beneath the door and no one stood there. I opened the door calling Janine's name. She was not in the house and all of the doors were closed and locked. I shrugged and returned to reading. There were three doors in my bedroom. One door led to a hallway, one was the bathroom door, and the other door opened onto the balcony. The knocks started coming on the outside door or the hall door.

It could happen during the day or at night. It was always when I was alone. I finally mentioned it to a Haitian friend.

He asked, "Do you pray every night before you go to bed?"

"Yes," I replied.

He said, "Just make sure you do."

Oddly enough I did not ask any more questions. Maybe I didn't want to know any more. Weeks went by and just when I had almost forgotten about the knocks, they returned. I would be awakened late at night by the knocks, listen to the silence, and go right back to sleep. Amazingly enough the knocks did not frighten me. Even odder is the fact that I never mentioned the knocks to anyone else.

I was preparing to leave Haiti after completing my one year of training. I was very sad at leaving Haiti, but I was excited about going to Africa. Haiti had been the perfect assignment. In the FS everyone says your first post is always your favorite post. Haiti was beautiful, the Haitian people incredibly accepting and wonderful, and our office staff was superb in helping me to learn and to grow into a good officer. I was no longer a junior office. I was now a full fledged Cultural Affairs Officer (CAO) assigned to Dar es Salaam, Tanzania.

On my last day in my house, I walked into the kitchen and suddenly I saw a huge, dark creature flying about the kitchen. It was a butterfly, but it was the largest butterfly I had ever seen. It must have been at least six to eight inches across. As it flew around the kitchen, Janine and I dodged it. I was fascinated and repelled at the same time. I told Janine to have Dominique, the gardener, kill it. She looked at me oddly and got busy doing something. I noticed that she did not call Dominique right then, but assumed that she would. A few days before this incident, I had had a conversation with some Haitians about gigantic Haitian butterflies.

I was told that certain colors of butterflies meant certain things. I thought this butterfly was black and that meant death. That was the last thing I wanted to see or hear about before I got on a plane going to the U.S. A few minutes later I walked back into the kitchen, and again I told Janine to call Dominique to kill the huge butterfly.

She said softly, "Mademoiselle, Haitians don't kill those butterflies because they represent our ancestors."

I thought: more superstitious foolishness.

Instead I said, "Janine, you are a Catholic. You're not supposed to believe that."

She looked at me with her big eyes in that tiny body and said, "Oui, Mademoiselle, quand meme..." Yes, but still...

We determined that the butterfly was not black, but dark brown. I asked her what that color meant. She claimed not to know, but I didn't believe her. I felt that she didn't want to frighten me. The butterfly disappeared only to turn up again hours later. Janine tried to make me feel better by saying that it was a message from one of my deceased relatives. For a moment I wondered which relative and what the message could be, but quickly dismissed those thoughts as nonsense. I never saw the butterfly again.

Evening came and there was an eeriness in the house. The air seemed alive and moving. A friend from the State Department was in Haiti on temporary duty, and she was staying with me. We were exhausted from my farewell activities.

We sat in the living room relaxing and chatting. The balcony surrounded the house on three sides. Gail was sitting with her back to the balcony, and I sat facing it.

Suddenly she asked, "What's all that noise?"

I instantly became aware that there was movement in the air.

Without hesitating I said, "It's the wind blowing the plants."

As I finished the sentence my eyes strayed to the plants on the balcony and not one leaf was moving. I prayed Gail would not turn around. I wondered what the noise was. Were the spirits speaking to me? If so, what were they saying?

A few minutes later an obviously nervous Gail said, "I can't stay in here any longer. I'm going to bed."

I said, "Me too, and I'm sleeping in your room tonight."

I got my things from my bedroom and joined Gail in the guestroom. I also locked the bedroom door. We turned out the light and talked for a few minutes. Just as I was drifting off to sleep I heard that dreaded knock on our bedroom door. I wanted to ask Gail if she heard it, but I hoped she was asleep. I said nothing.

I lay there and gloated, "This is the last damn time I'll have to hear those knocks!"

That was my fervent hope, but remember the Haitian proverb says, "The magic remains in Haiti, but the spell crosses the sea."

That it did!

Welcome to Tanzania

1978-80

If there is no struggle, there is no progress.
- Frederick Douglass

From Haiti I had returned to Washington for six weeks of learning the rudiments of Swahili, one of the two official languages of Tanzania. The other one was English. I had a private tutor who was a graduate student from Tanzania. He was completing his doctorate. Some days he was lethargic from being up all night studying, and other days – most days – I found the language impossible to learn. I was accustomed to Romance languages and I found it extremely difficult attempting to make sense of a language that used a string of consonants in the same word.

One friend gave me some advice when she learned that I would be going to Africa.

She said, "A long time ago somebody gave me some advice that I am passing along to you: 'Always remember that if an African can't eat it or screw it, he'll tear it up.' "

I laughed and promptly forgot those words of wisdom.

Also during those six weeks I was seeing a psychotherapist in an attempt to get over my fear of flying. I had chosen a career that enabled me to see the world, unfortunately I had to get on a plane to see it. I was terrified of flying.

Whenever I had to fly I began living the nightmare weeks in advance. I knew I could not go on like that.

I needed help, and I remembered reading about football players and Hollywood stars who used hypnosis to get rid of that morbid fear. That was the answer as far as I was concerned. I hoped the costs would not be astronomical, but somehow I would pay it. I began weekly hypnosis sessions with a psychotherapist. I never felt hypnotized, but I remember one day as I sat in his outer office I was very aware of all the noise coming from the street, K. Street. I wondered why on earth he would have his office on such a noisy street. Plus the telephones were ringing off the hook outside of his office. It seemed chaotic.

The doctor called me into his office and he began saying, "From now on you will only hear the sound of my voice."

Suddenly I was aware that I no longer heard the din from the street or the telephones ringing in the outer office. All I heard was the sound of his voice. I was amazed. I was not asleep. I was very aware of his every word. This was not my idea of hypnosis. He prescribed tranquilizers that left me barely able to move. I never told him how lethargic the medicine made me feel. I kept taking it and simply went through the weeks in a daze while trying to learn a new language. My sessions ended when the doctor wanted me to take a test flight to New York and I refused. I complained that I didn't feel hypnotized. I expected to be out cold. He said I would not be in a trance during the time I was on a plane, that he was teaching me relaxation techniques to deal with my anxiety. I had thought I would be in a self-induced trance anytime I flew. What a bitter disappointment that was.

The good news was that finally I was off the medication and the end of functioning like a zombie. The bad news was: how was I going to remain in the Foreign Service and not fly?

It was time to fly to Tanzania. I was anxious, but not as much as before my sessions with the doctor. I smiled and grinned at my desk officers in the African Area Office and everybody was excited for me, and inside I was thinking: *Damn! I have to fly 8 hrs. to London, sit for 6 hrs. at the airport, and fly another 12 hours to Dar-es-Salaam! I can't do it!* But I did it. I flew off to Tanzania with a cigarette in one hand, and my rosary in the other.

I learned during those long flights to and from Africa, that I could not remain tense for 12 or 18 hours. At some point I began to relax, at least until we hit an air pocket or two, and then I went rigid again. We made a stop in Djibouti at 1:00 am, and everyone had to leave the plane. We stepped off the plane into searing heat. I learned the temperature was 110 degrees. Had I been assigned to Djibouti, I think I would have gotten back on the same plane. We were directed into the terminal. They searched us as we got off the plane and again as we got on the plane. We had been isolated in one room for about one hour, I wondered what they were looking for. I was hot, sleepy and now unnerved. I was now in Mother Africa.

Tanzania is a poor country, and for those interested in its socialist experiment, it is a fascinating one. I had looked forward to going to Africa for years. I had met West African diplomats and their families at the United Nations in New York, and I thoroughly enjoyed being with them. I had always wanted to go to Africa, and now here I was.

I wondered what Tanzania would be like when I read the Post Report that advised officers assigned there to take cartons and cases of food and household items, and anything that we could not live without for two years. I went to a wholesale store where I bought cases of Kleenex, canned vegetables, canned meats (including canned bacon), peanuts, detergent, bath soap, hair shampoo, lotion, cocktail napkins, dinner napkins, and toilet tissue for two years. How does one know how much toilet tissue to buy for two years? I kept a record of the amount of toilet tissue I used in a month and multiplied it by 24. I then added more for the times I would have diarrhea, and more was added for guests using the facilities at dinner parties and receptions. In all I took almost a three-year supply, and when I left Tanzania there were four rolls of toilet tissue remaining. That was cutting it close.

Before leaving the U.S. I ordered a Peugeot car from France. Peugeots were said to be the best cars for the washboard roads in most of Tanzania. I was advised against getting automatic transmission and air-conditioning by the Peugeot Company in Paris. They said if either broke down I might not be able to get repairs done in Dar es Salaam. Imagine my surprise when I arrived in Dar and found there was a Peugeot garage in town and the mechanics had been trained by Peugeot headquarters in Paris. That was the last time I lived in

Africa without an air-conditioned car. It was expensive for the government to ship cars to Tanzania because they had to be crated. It seemed that sometimes our cars were accidentally dropped into the ocean during the transfer from the ship to the dock. Fortunately, there were a small number of countries for which cars had to be crated.

The first thing I noticed upon arriving in Dar es Salaam was the majesty and massiveness of the baobab trees. They are huge. They are said to be the oldest trees in Africa. The trunk of the tree is spongy. Baobab trees look as if they are upside down, like the roots are in the air with no leaves, while the leafy portion would seem to be in the ground. One legend says a good fairy cautioned the baobab tree against letting wicked spirits reside in its branches, but the baobab ignored the fairy. Finally, one day in a fury the fairy hurled the tree upside down and into the ground, and that's why the roots seem to be in the air. The baobabs are magnificent.

After having breakfast at the PAO's residence, he took me a mile or so up the road to my residence. We both were on Toure Drive. On one side of the road there were huge houses, and the ocean was on the other side. As we drove along I admired the azure blue of the ocean. We turned and drove down a long, long driveway, about the equivalent of one block. On one side were high weeds. On the other side was a compound of houses, an Italian compound I learned. Facing me was a huge, three-story house. It appeared vacant, gloomy and certainly not welcoming. My heart sank. I had never liked being alone in a house, large or small. Years earlier the embassy had purchased large houses for its diplomats with representational responsibilities because we were expected to entertain.

On the ground floor were a large living room, a large, formal dining room, huge kitchen, bath and shower, and spacious front and back hallways. On the second floor was a huge, master bedroom, and full bath. The suite overlooked the back yard. On the third floor were three bedrooms and two bathrooms.

I was told that my predecessors preferred a bedroom on the third floor because it overlooked the ocean. I too chose the third floor for my bedroom. I was introduced to my housekeeper, Valentino, a surly looking young man. I could tell it was going to be a long, long two years. By now I had been up for almost 48 hours and I promptly went to bed. When I awakened Valentino had left. I looked in the fridge to see what I could have for dinner. The wife of the PAO had proudly told me at breakfast that she had bought some basic food items for me. The fridge contained milk, eggs and potatoes. I don't drink milk, and I couldn't cook eggs without oil. Fortunately at the Paris airport I had bought a *saucisson,* a hard salami and some French bread. That was my dinner.

I arrived in the middle of a five day holiday – a no-no in the Foreign Service. The next day I was left alone. Valentino didn't even show up. I ate more of my saucisson. The third day the PAO and his wife arrived to take me shopping. I don't like outdoor markets where meat fresh off the hoof hangs everywhere; there is a lot of dust and dirt, and people are yelling at you to buy this and that. When I was finally able to go to the office, one of the local staffers, an Indian girl, offered to take me shopping on the weekend. At last, I was able to cook and to eat a decent meal.

Supposedly my house had not been closed up, yet every time I moved other things also moved. There was more wildlife inside than outside. It reached the point where I didn't move from a chair unless I had something in my hand to spray the damned things. The only spray item in the house was a can of Spray and Wash for clothes that I had packed in my suitcase as a last minute item.

It was wonderful for killing insects. I kept it beside me while seated, and in my hand when moving around the house.

At night the house seemed to talk. When I was downstairs reading, I heard noises upstairs. When I went upstairs to investigate, I heard noises downstairs.

It took awhile for me to realize the thundering sounds came from the ocean across the street. I had no idea that the ocean was so loud. I was so scared in that huge house. I wondered how I would live there for two years. I felt as if I were alone on an island. On one side of me was an Italian compound with high walls. On the other side was a Danish family who I rarely saw. I didn't sleep well. I locked the door to the hallway on the third floor and sometimes locked my bedroom door. I was painfully aware of how vulnerable my house was. The third floor had a wrap-around balcony. In all embassy residences the door to the sleeping quarters had to be strong enough to deter, or slow down, intruders, to give the residents time to call the police or the embassy for help. My house had so many doors and windows in the huge house that a thief could easily enter without me hearing.

In my early weeks in the house I began to see things out of the corner of my eye. I was driving myself crazy in that huge house. One of the guys in my office asked one day if I was interested in having a puppy. I leaped at the chance to have another living, breathing body in the house with me. He took me to the home of a Danish couple whose Labrador dog had had puppies six weeks previously. Their mistress picked up one of the puppies and handed it to me. I noticed that it was a female. I cuddled her while asking for a male puppy.

The woman bent down to look for a male and I tried to lower the puppy I was holding, but she refused to move, and stayed where she had buried herself, in the crook of my neck.

The owner said, "Oh, she likes you, look how she wants to stay in your arms."

It was love, and I took her home. I named her Happy because she seemed so happy. I bought a bed for her and put it beside my bed. I knew that with Happy in the house with me I would no longer be afraid. Or so I thought. I soon noticed that when I heard a noise and looked at Happy she'd be looking at me with a wild eyed expression that seemed to ask: "Did you hear that?" I would rush upstairs to check and whisper to her to guard the downstairs. She was too little to go up the stairs. When she became older she went down the stairs ahead of me in the mornings. I stood at the top of the stairway. At the bottom Happy looked left and right and into the living room and then back up at me as if to assure me that it was safe to come down.

The house had a lot of geckos, tiny, transparent members of the lizard family. They ran up and down the walls and across the ceilings, but did not bother me. I welcomed their company. They were impossible to catch due to their swiftness. They were cute and I enjoyed them. They made a clicking sound. I became so accustomed to that sound that when I didn't hear it I wondered where they were, and whether they knew something that I didn't know and were hiding.

It took baby geckos a while to get the hang of clinging to the ceiling, and often they fell, usually on top of my head. I simply reached up and removed it from my hair, and set it on the floor where it would scamper away.

Tanzania was going through some dangerous times. I had one night guard who arrived at 7:00 p.m. and promptly crawled into the glider on the front terrace and went to sleep. I asked him to at least stay awake until I went to bed. Thieves were breaking into homes and holding up restaurants. In the restaurants frequented by Asians the robbers forced the women to disrobe to add further insult. I had begun getting massages twice a week. My office mates tried to discourage me from going there because they reasoned the business could easily be held up. I dismissed their fears until one day I noticed a guy loitering outside the business. I did not want to be naked on the massage table when thieves held up the place, so I discontinued getting massages. A few weeks later the massage establishment was held up.

Tanzania was where I became aware of how single, female officers are treated by Foreign Service families at a post, versus how a family is treated. A single female is rarely invited to the homes of families. A single male is always in demand. Families are treated like gold. A wife who arrives at a post with her husband and children is almost always assigned to another wife who shepherds her around, introduces her to other wives, and tells her all the tips of shopping. In Haiti, I didn't need this and so I didn't miss it or even know that was the custom. In Dar it was only due to the kindness of the local secretaries in our office that I was taken shopping until I learned where to go on my own.

Joel Levy, Information Officer, arrived in Dar shortly after I did. He and his wife, Carol, were Kosher Jews, and the parents of two small children. I was always honored when they invited me to their home for Friday evening Seder. I enjoyed witnessing their observation of their faith. Carol was frank and outspoken, too much so for some people. She and Joel were tremendously funny and kept me laughing.

One of the Information Officer's chief assistants, Tom Mweuka, was from Malawi. He and others in my office worried about me and insisted that I needed someone more serious to guard my residence at night. Tom got a guard he knew personally who came to live in a small house on my grounds.

I now had two night guards. I was especially nervous when thieves began putting ether into air-conditioning vents, and breaking in while the families slept. Some families nearly died when too much ether was used. The situation worsened around us. All embassy families were frightened.

When wives told me how scared they were in the house with a husband and children, I wondered how the hell they thought I felt being alone in a huge, three story house. I, too, was terrified and didn't need to hear their tales of fear. We all knew of night guards who were being killed or badly injured in their attempts to stop thieves from entering homes. I was advised by Americans to give my guards a thermos of coffee and buttered bread at night shortly before I went to bed. That worked fine until the city was without flour for months.

Our tiny commissary had flour and other essentials trucked in from Kenya and I began baking French baguettes for official dinners. The guards seemed put out that there was no bread for them. They informed me that they did not want coffee if there was no bread.

I said, "Fine," and that eliminated a nightly task for me.

The American community noticed that when thieves broke into the homes of East Indians, they killed them. That was an indication of the continued hatred toward Indians, hatred that began years ago when England "owned" parts of Africa. The British brought Indians from India to be the middle men between the British and the Africans. They acted as overseers and ran businesses, and in many ways they too became the oppressors. This did not endear them to the Africans. Even now, years after independence for those countries, the hate remains on both sides. Many East Indians spoke of wanting to move to Canada. Others worked for the American government long enough to qualify for immigration to the U.S. and then they left.

When thieves broke into the homes of black Africans or foreigners, they tied them up, but did not hurt them. The first items they took were always food items. Only after cupboards and refrigerators were cleaned out did the thieves look for money, jewelry, and electronics. Tom insisted on getting a second night guard for me so that I would have two. The second guard was from an ethnic group that used bows and poisoned arrows, and was generally feared. I never found him asleep at night. The embassy paid for one and I paid for the other one.

I had been in Tanzanian for approximately three months when there came a knock on my bedroom door in the middle of the night. I sat up in bed and thought, the spirits have crossed the ocean as the Haitian proverb says. For the next two years the Haitian spirits knocked on my bedroom door every three or four months to let me know they were still around. Perhaps they protected me from danger since thieves never broke into my residence. As in Haiti, I was not frightened by the knocks, just mildly annoyed when they awakened me. Once I realized it was just my Haitian spirits, I turned over and went back to sleep.

East Africa is Different

If there is no struggle, there is no progress.
- Frederick Douglass

Dar es Salaam, Tanzania was my welcome to Africa. It took me awhile to adjust to the quiet reserve of Tanzanians. I looked forward to going to work every morning because every day was completely different from the day before. Many Tanzanians still had ideological hang-ups about the motives of embassy officials, and they also had a somewhat austere approach to dealings with foreigners in general. That placed some hurdles in the way of what in other parts of the world would be considered normal professional and representational contacts. My work environment could truthfully be called challenging.

Our hours were the same as the Tanzanian government hours, 7:30 am to 3:30 pm, with no lunch hour. The PAO brought his lunch in every day and ate at his desk. The Information Officer and I did not bother with lunch. I was always at my desk by 7 am which meant I left my residence at 6:30 am. If I left later than that, I ran into rush hour traffic, and often was stopped for long periods by the country's crown jewels, beautiful peacocks, that sometimes strolled in the streets to the dismay of rush hour drivers.

As the Cultural Affairs Officer I was one of three officers. I supervised the work of five Foreign Service National (FSNs) employees in the cultural section and the library, and I had the overall responsibility for an exchange budget of $290,000.

I worked closely with government ministries, the university and the institutions that were training grounds for the future leadership. I encouraged those institutions to establish linkages with American counterparts. I also planned and implemented a series of seminars, lecturers and exhibits to support U.S. objectives in the areas of foreign policy, economics, and management and administration.

In Tanzania, the government exercised far more control than most countries over the participation of its citizens in our exchange programs. There were some elements in the government who were deeply suspicious of our motives. Each exchange grant was the subject of delicate and sometimes prolonged negotiations with government officials. I always had to use an acute degree of political sensitivity, tact, and patience, which is, of course, the very definition of a diplomat. We operated in a climate that largely defined the U.S. and its foreign policy in negative terms. As a socialist country Tanzania was definitely at odds with the capitalist U.S., and vocal in its criticism of U.S. involvement in Vietnam, and Zaire.

The U.S. policy toward South Africa was attacked as being dominated by economic considerations while ignoring the questions of racial equality and human rights. Tanzanians avowed African socialism because of the emphasis on human dignity and cooperation. They viewed the U.S. system of democracy as being exploitative in social, political and economic affairs. Much of this changed in 1977 when President Jimmy Carter came into office with a different approach to black Africa. The U.S. and Tanzania began collaborating on gaining independence for Namibia and Zimbabwe (Rhodesia).

I quickly discovered that if Tanzanians liked you personally, it was far easier to work with them. For some reason they seemed to have liked the three USIS officers. In fact, members of President Nyerere's Revolutionary Party made steady visits to our offices requesting scholarships and study projects in the U.S. I had unprecedented access to officials at every level of government as well as at the University of Dar es Salaam. This was surprising because while political relations between the U.S. and Tanzania had improved, the previous period of prolonged hostility left a residue of suspicion about our motives. This was compounded by Tanzania's espousal of a militant form of socialism. Tanzanians were not admirers of the U.S. government, but they were admirers of what we had to offer: Fulbright fellowships, and opportunities for university professors to do research in the United States, and the chance to meet visiting American economics experts as well as political scientists.

We three USIS officers had good relations and easy access to President Julius K. Nyerere. President Nyerere was unusual for an African president because he set the example for his people by living simply. Whenever our office had visiting high level Americans, President Nyerere always received them at his home. We sat on his front porch in rocking chairs, and drank orange juice or lemonade, and enjoyed his hospitality. Visitors included then-DC Mayor Marion Barry, Mohammed Ali, Ambassador Andrew Young, among others.

Author greeting Tanzanian President Julius Nyerere at his residence - 1978

President Nyerere and I attended the same Catholic Church. He went to daily Mass. I learned this during my last year in Dar when I attended daily Mass during Lent.

There was also a small dog who attended daily Mass. I never saw him with anyone, and he was always in his pew when I arrived. Once there was a lot of loud noise outside of church, and the dog jumped to the floor, trotted down the aisle to the doorway where he peered out as if to reprimand the culprits, and then trotted back up the aisle to his pew having reestablished order. I was utterly amazed. President Nyerere came into church very humbly and nobody approached him. If anyone wanted to talk to him, they did so outside of church and in a certain corner. His bodyguards kept their distance.

Tanzania - airport arrival of Muhammed Ali - 1979

The ruling party of Tanzania was the Chama Cha Mapinduzi Party (CCM, The Revolutionary Party of Tanzania). Tanganyika gained its independence from the United Kingdom in December 1962. In 1965 it became a one-party system. Zanzibar overthrew its ruling Sultan in 1964, and united with Tanganyika a few months later. The new nation combined the names of Tanganyika and Zanzibar for Tanzania. Nyerere was president of the country, and the president of Zanzibar remained the head of Zanzibar, but also became the vice-president of Tanzania.

One of the country's major institutions was Kivukoni College, the ideological training center of the ruling party. Middle level and top level government officials were sent to this institute for consciousness-raising. The three USIS officers could visit Kivukoni College and take visiting American speakers to lecture there.

On the other hand, embassy officers such as the Ambassador and the Deputy Chief of Mission (DCM) had to request official permission to visit Kivukoni, and it was never granted during the two years that I was in the country or in previous years. The first time I planned to take a visiting American speaker to the college I mentioned it to our new DCM.

He said, "Oh, good. I'll go with you. I've wanted to go there. "

I said nothing, but as soon as I returned to my office I told the PAO. He immediately called the DCM and told him that he would have to request official permission from the Ministry of Foreign Affairs, but that it was highly unlikely that permission would be granted. It wasn't.

Meanwhile, I was busy familiarizing myself with the people and the country. I worked with various Tanzanian government officials to select outstanding students for our exchange program; identified future leaders of the country to visit the U.S. on 30-day international visitor programs to become acquainted with the U.S. and worked on identifying American speakers to help carry out mission objectives.

One of our visiting speakers was Sanford Ungar, journalist and former head of the School of Journalism at American University. He and his wife, a medical doctor, arrived in Dar a day after my hundreds of boxes of household effects had been delivered. I had not opened any of them. I took the Ungars to one of the better hotels where I had reserved rooms for them. They had asked me to remain to have a drink with them. I waited in the lobby which was a mistake because minutes later they returned with their suitcases. They seemed to be in a state of shock. They explained that they could not stay in that hotel. I didn't ask why.

I simply said, "This is the best hotel in the city."

They looked at each other and I could see they were ready to return to the airport.

I added, "You could stay at my residence, but I haven't opened any boxes and I don't know where the sheets are or anything else. "

They leaped at the offer, saying, "We'll help you find them."

So I took them back to my residence and we opened boxes until we found sheets and towels. I began preparing dinner only to discover that the gas bottle was empty. I was chagrined, but not for long. I got out an old Primus stove, fired it up and cooked steaks on it like the professional that I was. The Ungars were delightful people who took everything in stride. Only that hotel room seemed to have upset them.

I decided to make the film, "Roots" the centerpiece of Black History Month in 1979 since it was available to our post during February. The PAO told me that before my arrival when the prospect of bringing "Roots" to Tanzania was first discussed, it was the consensus of the Country Team that it would not be effective and that showings should be restricted to embassy staff. I was amazed that white Americans felt so much guilt about slavery that they didn't want anything seen or said about it outside of the U.S. The entire world knew that there had been slavery in the U.S. All of Tanzania was excited about the showing of "Roots," and it was a smashing success. The Minister of National Culture opened Black History Month and had his first exposure to the USIS Cultural Center. Some 5,000 people saw the film in three weeks. We worked long hours, gave up weekends and traveled upcountry to ensure that many Tanzanians could see it. The film enabled us to make numerous new Tanzanian friends. One year later when the movie was offered to us, we again showed it to an overflowing audience.

When the U.S. recognized Red China, the Chinese Ambassador in Dar es Salaam invited Kent, Joel and me for an incredible dinner on board a visiting Chinese ship. We ate thousand-year old eggs, jelly fish (I even had a second helping!) and other delicious dishes. The dinner was a thank you from the Chinese Embassy. I had let their embassy borrow the movie, "Roots." After we showed one roll of film, a Chinese driver rushed it back to his embassy, and returned for the next roll. We had the film for a short period of time and then it had to be sent on to the next post on a long list of posts waiting for the film. The Chinese knew it would be a long time, if ever, before they would have another opportunity to see the highly acclaimed film, and we did not have room in our small auditorium for their personnel to join our audience. As the three of us enjoyed our Chinese dinner, we could not help but be amused that USIS officers were feted by the Chinese Embassy before the U.S. Ambassador was. It wasn't only the hearts and minds of the Tanzanians that we won.

Race Relations

When you clench your fist, no one can put anything in your hand.
- Alex Haley

The U.S. is not unique in its race problems. Relations between the East Indians and black Africans of Tanzania often reminded me of relations in the U.S. between black Americans and white Americans. East Indians have been in Africa for generations and they own nearly every business in the country. The British brought in East Indians as barriers between the British and the Africans and their job was to oversee the black Africans. I immediately noticed that East Indians looked down on the black Africans, and there was little or no socializing between the two groups. Neither group cared much for the other group.

My chief assistants in the cultural affairs office were two Tanzanian Indians, Kalim and Nagri. The Information Officer, Joel's two chief assistants were black Africans, Tom from Malawi, and John, a Tanzanian. The Africans and the East Indians tolerated each other. Whenever the two African honchos on Joel's staff got angry with either of the two East Indians on my staff, they gave *me* the cold shoulder for a few days, as if whatever the problem was, was my fault. But they soon got over it. The black Africans in our office were thrilled to have a black female officer there, while the East Indians were anything but thrilled. Our staffs represented a microcosm of the racial and ethnic complexion of Dar es Salaam.

It was not a naturally cohesive unit, but I tried to exercise scrupulous fairness in dealing with them, and I worked hard to make use of the talents and potentials of each. Nagri, the librarian, was always polite and correct with me. He was an older man, content with his job and the cachet it gave him in the East Indian society, but it took him awhile to warm up to me. He and I worked closely together in updating the library collection to make it better reflect USIA policies and the post's objectives. We built up a good core collection and increased our periodical collection. I was to bring American culture to Tanzania, not just white, American culture. Our library had no African-American magazines, and very few books by African-American authors. I changed that situation as I did at every post when handling cultural affairs. It never seemed to have occurred to white officers that Africans identify with black Americans and want to see and read more about and by them.

For my first celebration of Black History Month my office was planning to show "Roots" and have other activities. Nagri and I worked closely to plan the month's activities since the library would be the central point. I knew what I wanted the cover of the program to look like. I could not draw, but I told Nagri that I envisioned a tree like the huge baobab, with its roots in the air, centered on the cover. I wanted the names of the generations in the film born in the U.S. printed on the branches, and below the ground level, on the tree roots, I wanted the names of the ancestors who came from Africa on the slave ships. Nagri found an artist who drew exactly what I wanted and our relationship was cemented.

Kalim was a different story. He seemed especially resentful, and was barely civil to me. Kalim was tall, handsome, and cunning. I always had the feeling that he had some scheme up his sleeve. He accompanied me as I made courtesy calls on various government, university, and museum officials, among others. I noticed that he went through doors ahead of me, walked in front of me, and generally treated me as if I were somebody tagging along with him. All right, I thought, I'm a woman in a predominantly Muslim country, so I'll grit my teeth while he gets accustomed to the idea of reporting to a black female.

Kalim's office was downstairs, and several times I walked in to hear him speaking rudely to black Tanzanians seeking scholarships. I cautioned him about that more than once. Finally I warned him that he would be fired if he continued speaking to blacks in such an insulting manner. Kalim had worked for our embassy for nearly 20 years and was soon going to be eligible to emigrate to the U.S. along with his family. The threat of being fired should have rattled him. He spoke incessantly about two previous Cultural Affairs Officers, both white females, who were obviously malleable in his hands. He wrote to them, and several times he told me that one or both of them would be sending for him. I hoped it would be soon. My resentment toward Kalim was increasing. One day when we were out he pushed the wrong button.

I found myself saying in a controlled, low, dangerously angry tone, "You will NOT go through doors ahead of me and let the door close in my face. If you cannot walk beside me, you WILL walk behind me. You WILL treat every African who comes into our office with dignity and respect. Do you understand me?"

The air was cleared and Kalim realized that he was going to have to be a gentleman in order to work with this black woman. It took a while, but Kalim and Nagri became joys to work with. The cultural section was finally welded into a well integrated and harmoniously functioning unit.

My boss wrote in my performance report,

"She has won the unqualified respect of her two senior Foreign Service National (FSN) employees — both males with long service at the post, and only an embryonic level of raised consciousness about the managerial talents of female officers."

Kalim's wife, Fatima, was the catalyst who really helped us to cement our friendship. She and I hit it off from the beginning. I think Kalim was afraid that his wife would get ideas from me that would not be to his liking because suddenly, Fatima said, he insisted that she and his teenaged daughter begin wearing burkas, the black garments some Moslem women wore in Tanzania. When I first met her, she did not wear a burka. On every Tanzanian holiday Fatima would send me a huge tray of delicious Indian dishes. How I looked forward to those days. I told Fatima that my tongue leaped for joy at the delicious taste of spices and herbs totally unknown to me. Each dish was a new taste sensation.

One of the Information Officer's chief assistant's, Tom, taught me to drive a stick shift. I had been advised to purchase a car with manual gears and I had ordered a French Peugeot which took several months to arrive. I had to learn to shift gears, and also to drive on the left side of the road.

Every day after work Tom and I got into the office's big van, and every day would find me looking down at the clutch and the accelerator, or at the gears, while the van ended up on the wrong side of the road. I know the drivers coming toward me were happy when I finally learned to shift AND stay on the left side of the road.

I stripped the gears, hit the brake when I wanted the clutch, killed the motor, and was a general hazard on the road. Tom never lost his patience, and when my car arrived it drove like a dream because I knew how to drive using a stick shift.

The Indians in Dar must have had resources at the dock that told them whenever a new car came into the city. The day after my new Peugeot arrived I had visits from three Indians offering to pay me double or triple what I paid for my car, THEN and THERE, and they were willing to wait for two years to receive the car when I left the country. They could not import new cars into the country, and they were willing to pay any price to purchase cars that had belonged to foreigners. Because they could only pay in Tanzanian rupees, they paid in advance so that the seller could use those rupees during his stay in Tanzania because it would have been impossible to change that much money into dollars when leaving the country. I was flabbergasted. I refused their offers. Throughout the two years I had many offers from Indians, but I decided early on that I would sell my car to a black Tanzanian who had little or no chance of purchasing a relatively new car, simply because they could not match the prices offered by Indians. Just before leaving Dar, I sold my car to a black Tanzanian for the price I paid for it which allowed me to purchase another Peugeot with a left hand drive for my next post.

Tanzania, at the time I was there, was the only U.S. embassy in the world that owned a beach house. I was told that when former Secretary of State

Henry Kissinger visited Dar es Salaam, he wanted to swim in the Indian Ocean, and was appalled to learn that the embassy had no beach house for his privacy. Shortly thereafter, the embassy purchased a beach house. The ambassador would occasionally invite embassy personnel to a beach party. An invitation from the ambassador is akin to a royal command. I had to attend even though I would break out in huge, itching lumps from waist to ankles when I was in the sun for an extended time. My skin became discolored and horrible looking. Our embassy doctor said that was due to the combination of the sun and the anti-malarial tablets that I had to take. We all took the tablets, but they seemingly affected everybody in different ways. I always wore a long, cotton dress with long sleeves, and a straw hat to the beach and tried to keep out of the sun.

I had to become accustomed to being the only female at dinners or at receptions. In Tanzania the men never brought their wives to official dinners or receptions. If I hosted a dinner or reception I was almost always the only woman there. The only other female officer at the embassy was a consular officer who had few representational responsibilities, and our circles were very different. I quickly became accustomed to sailing into all male affairs and being the only woman, and I began to enjoy it.

When Do We Eat?

"I've had a perfectly wonderful evening. But this wasn't it."
                                                    - Groucho Marx

It was the fanciest dinner party I had ever attended, and I left hungrier than I had ever been. The evening began with a phone call from the Deputy Chief of Mission (DCM). He asked - a euphemism for "command," - if I would be his hostess at a dinner party he was giving that evening. He explained that his wife was out of the country, and the woman who had agreed to be his hostess just telephoned that she was ill. I needed to be at his residence in two hours. I assumed it would be the usual dinner party, and wondered why he needed a hostess. As I dressed for the dinner I fumed. I didn't particularly care for this DCM. I found him rather cold and pretentious. I wondered why he hadn't called the wife of a senior officer who had some experience being a hostess. I arrived early at his residence as Foreign Service officers are required to do. The first thing I noticed was the dinner table. It appeared to be about one block long. Then I realized that several tables had been put together to make one extremely long table. The DCM informed me that the dinner was to bid farewell to departing U.S. Ambassador James Spain. The guests included Prime Minister Benjamin Mkapa, who later became president of Tanzania; the Foreign Minister who was the only other woman at the dinner, and other high ranking Tanzanian officials.

When we went into the dining room, the DCM motioned where I was to sit. I could barely see him at the other end of the table. To my right was the guest of honor, Ambassador Spain, and to my left, Prime Minister Mkapa. A waiter stood behind each chair. I was stunned.

If they could see me now, that little gang of mine...

The soup course arrived. I tried to see if the DCM had lifted his spoon because the ambassador and the Prime Minister were not going to lift theirs until I lifted mine. Finally, I picked up my spoon. Oh, it was going to be a long, long night if I had to keep guessing what the DCM was doing at the other end of the room. I managed to take two spoons of soup and one swallow of wine, and then my plate and glass were snatched away.

The fish course was served and with it a superb white wine. I wondered if the DCM was inhaling his food at the other end because at my end we only got to have a bite or two of food and one sip of the wine. I blinked and my plate and wineglass were whisked away. I was a bit surprised. I don't care much for fish, but I would have liked to savor my wine.

I'm eating fancy chow and drinking fancy wine.

The meat course arrived along with an exquisite red wine. This time I decided that I would somehow hang on to my glass of wine and not relinquish it until it was empty. It was going to be a challenge to cut the meat, eat, talk to the Foreign Minister and my ambassador, and hang onto that glass. I was tired of the servants yanking away the wines that got better and better. Not only that, but I had barely tasted the food. I was invited for dinner, and dinner I wanted.

I thought I would surely be able to enjoy my glass of wine during the main course. Alas, it was not to be. Again the waiters snatched away the plates along with the wine glasses. Somebody in the kitchen was enjoying a lot of wine. I was beginning to feel a bit disgruntled. Dessert arrived along with champagne, and toasts were made to the outgoing ambassador. Ah, I thought, I can now relax because nothing will follow this course, and I can enjoy my champagne.

They'd never believe it, if my friends could see me now.

I had taken exactly two sips of champagne when the DCM asked us to adjourn to the garden. The waiter behind me assisted in moving my chair so that I could stand up. I turned around to pick up my champagne glass, but it had been whisked away. I was furious.

"Where is my champagne?" I demanded.

"Gone," he said.

Hell, I could see that! Feeling homicidal and undiplomatic, I stomped out into the garden wanting the evening to end then and there. I had done my hostess bit and I was ready to go home. No, I didn't want any coffee, cognac, or crème de nothing. I wanted some food and champagne, in that order. I sat in the garden hungry and sullen. After a few minutes the Foreign Minister got up to leave. I trotted behind her, saying goodnight to all. The DCM stared at me, but I was beyond caring. I had not had any dinner and I was hungry. What more could he do to me?

As we walked out to the driveway, the Foreign Minister asked with a smile, "Aren't you the hostess? How can you leave early?"

I replied without a smile, "The DCM is probably asking himself the same question."

She chuckled and stepped into her chauffeured car. I drove home in a huff.

I had never been so hungry in my life. I went in and made a peanut butter and jelly sandwich, disgusting food that I eat only if there is absolutely nothing else to eat. For the rest of the evening I kept saying to myself: I'll just be damned.

The DCM never said a word to me about leaving early, or even a word of thanks. I think we both said to ourselves: never again. Later I laughed when it occurred to me that that's how the rich stay slim. They take one or two bites of those sinfully rich dishes and then the food is whisked away. No wonder they can go through eight or more courses. I'll bet they go home hungry too. Finally, I had something in common with the rich and famous.

If my friends had seen me then, they would have died laughing!

Nightmare

Death gives no answer.

- Jabo, Liberia

In Tanzania nightmares did not always happen when one was asleep. For some of us nightmares were frequent due to the anti-malarial medication we were obliged to take to prevent a malaria attack. Nightmares were the stuff that made me shiver the next day when I remembered bits and pieces of what I dreamed the night before. I wish with all of my being that what happened had been a deadly dream and that I might have awakened to the heat of the African sun and left what had happened behind in my dreams. One nightmare occurred while I was awake, at least I think I was awake. How I wish I had not been.

A friend invited me to a party at her apartment on the campus of the University of Dar es Salaam. The university is eight miles from the center of the city. I disliked driving anywhere in Dar es Salaam, but especially to the university. During the day the streets were crowded, and traffic was fast since that road was the closest thing to a highway insofar as it led out of town. At night the roads were pitch black in the absence of street lighting. That Saturday evening I took one of my two night guards because I knew I would be returning late, and cars, especially diplomatic cars, were often stopped by thugs. In fact, the day I arrived in Tanzania a secretary at our embassy was medically evacuated. She had been driving down a road at night and came to a roadblock.

As soon as she realized the men who stopped her were not wearing police uniforms, she tried to drive on, but the thugs had placed various gear on the road that immediately flattened her tires. She was yanked out of her car and raped by the three men. I knew the same thing could happen to me, but I felt better having a guard in the car with me.

That evening I picked up an American expatriate, Jim, and his two children. Jim was a professor at the university, and had lived in Dar for many years. He did not have a car, and I was glad to have the company of him and his children. The party was a fun evening of laughter and dancing, and we left around midnight. My guard sat in the front passenger seat. Jim and the kids settled in the back seat. As we drove down a dark road leading to the main street, I saw a man dressed in white weaving in the road ahead of me. There were a number of little drinking bars on the side of the road, and he apparently had just left one. He was on the side of the road facing me. He saw my lights and moved over to the other side of the road. A moment later I noticed car lights turning onto the road at the other end. I sped up to pass the man so that when he drifted back across the road, which he would have to do in order to get out of the way of the oncoming car, he would not be in my path. As I continued down the road, I passed the other vehicle, a pickup truck, and idly noticed that it was moving fairly fast.

Seconds later my mind screamed, "He's not slowing down!"

At that instant we all heard the sound of the truck hitting the man. The driver never sounded his horn. The sound was overwhelming. A fast moving truck had struck the soft body of a person.

It sounded as if a huge tomato had been squashed under foot and burst. I could not see this in the black African night, but I will never forget the sounds. I slammed on the brakes and we all looked back. The night was black and the car windows were fogged. We could only see the rear lights of the truck receding in the distance. The driver never touched his brakes to slow down or to stop.

Jim cried out, "He's gone! He's gone!"

I knew he meant the man who had been walking in the road was dead. The kids began crying. I didn't know what to do. I wondered if we could find him on the dark road. I thought perhaps we should follow the truck driver. A myriad of thoughts swirled through my mind. Where could we find a working phone to call the police, and would they say they had no gas, as was the usual response, and tell me to pick them up? I was too shaken to even attempt to drive back out to the university area. I would never be able to find that spot again. Thoughts crashed around in my head. I struggled for answers. The crying of the children got louder. Jim finally convinced me that the man had died instantly, and that there was little that we could do. I didn't see how the man could have survived that powerful blow by the truck. We could no longer see the lights of the truck. And then I made a decision that will haunt me the rest of my life: I decided to drive on. I was convinced the man was dead. There was no talking in the car; just the sound of the kids sniffling. At their home, Jim tried to console me by saying that there was nothing any of us could have done, and that the man was dead the instant the truck hit him. I wanted desperately to believe Jim.

When I reached home I immediately telephoned the police and tried to describe the area of the accident. They promised to send someone to the site immediately. I felt a bit better, but there was no sleep for me that night or the next. I kept hearing the sound of the truck slamming into a human body. Maybe he didn't die. Maybe he was knocked into the bushes, and nobody knew he was there. He was somebody's son, husband, father, brother. I felt like a criminal. I wanted to go back to the university road, but the times were too dangerous, plus I was too shaken to get behind the wheel again. I berated myself. I abandoned a human being. In my heart I did not think he could have survived the impact, but perhaps he had survived. He seemed drunk, but he was alert enough that when he saw my headlights he moved to the other side of the road. His back was to the approaching truck and he could not see it. The truck driver did not sound his horn or slow down. I wondered if he deliberately hit the man in white. I had no answers.

On Monday I drove to work at 6:30 a.m. as usual . My mind went back to Saturday night and the incident. At the office I told the PAO about the incident, and asked him to call the police to ask about the condition of the man. He called and was told they had no record of my call reporting the incident. I was devastated. The police had not gone out to look for the man.

When they reported back to the PAO, they said there was no sign of such an accident. A tiny thought, a flicker of hopeful light, wormed its way into my mind: perhaps the man had crawled to safety and help. Perhaps he did. I pray that he did.

Ambassador Andrew Young...
Up Close and (Almost) Naked

If you're going to play the game properly, you'd better know every rule.
                                                        - Barbara Jordan

There he was, polished orator, right-hand man of Dr. Martin Luther King, and beloved Ambassador Andrew Young, Jr., wearing only a bath towel. The highly respected Ambassador Young was leaving his post as ambassador to the United Nations over a flap about him meeting with a representative of the Palestine Liberation Organization. The U.S. government claimed that it was not an authorized meeting. Shortly before he resigned, he made a farewell swing through Africa where he was loved. This was his second trip to Tanzania during my tour there. It was a bittersweet farewell.

Ambassador Young was one of the younger ordained ministers in the civil rights movement with Dr. Martin Luther King, Jr. He was with Dr. King when he was assassinated. He represented Georgia for three terms in the United States Congress until President Jimmy Carter appointed him Ambassador to the United Nations. His appointment was controversial because of his empathy with Third World countries. When it was revealed that he had met with a representative of the Palestine Liberian Organization, President Carter asked for, and received, Ambassador Young's resignation. Many people thought Ambassador Young was a scapegoat who met with the

PLO representative at the request of the U.S. government, but no government official would ever admit to that.

Ambassador Young and his wife, Jean, stayed at the residence of the DCM who hosted a large reception for them. Embassy officers are always to arrive early at official functions. The rule is to be at a function at least 15 minutes before the official start time in order to assist the ambassador or other officers in receiving visitors. I was the first officer to arrive, and I seated myself in the living room waiting to greet early arrivals. I heard a door open and close behind me. I turned around and saw Ambassador Young coming out of a room, the bathroom I assumed, wearing nothing but a towel draped around his middle. Oops! I quickly jerked my head back around hoping and praying that he had not noticed me. I was very quiet so I thought there was a chance that he had not glanced into the living room. Of course there I was big as sin, but hope springs eternal.

Guests began arriving and I tried to forget the incident. Ambassador Young joined the party and while I knew that at some point I had to greet him, I kept putting it off. I dreaded going up to him after seeing him almost naked. I gaily chatted with everybody else while delaying greeting him. Suddenly I felt someone take my hand. I turned and looked into the face of Ambassador Young. I was surprised, and I didn't know what to say.

Still holding my hand he said, "When I was little we used to play a game: you peep at me, I peep at you. I told my wife, 'Some lady out there owes me a look!' "

We both howled with laughter, and our office photographer captured the moment.

Author with Ambassador Andrew Young, Tanzania 1980

The People One Meets

If stupidity got us into this mess, then why can't it get us out?
- Will Rogers

We had American speakers come to Tanzania frequently to lecture on economics, politics, democracy and other topics that we wanted to share with the Tanzanians. We also had American professors teaching at the University of Dar-es-Salaam, who had been awarded Fulbright Fellowships, and occasionally we had an American student at the university, also under the Fulbright program. There is one group which I will never forget. ..try as I might.

Once we had a group of American teachers, all women, from a Midwest state which shall remain nameless in order to protect the guilty. They were on a government grant, but basically had nothing to do with USIA. Several of them came to our office to tell us what they were in Tanzania for, and to get information. Almost overnight I found myself being house mother to this group. They were staying at the local YWCA and had the bare basics. Some teachers asked if they could come to my residence to do their laundry. Naturally, nobody had any soap powder, fabric softener or dryer sheets, so they used mine. After a few days one of them came to my office to ask me if she could get an abortion in Tanzania. I had no idea. I asked and was told that abortions were illegal in Tanzania, but they were legal in Kenya. I reluctantly gave her the information.

She wanted to know how she could get to Kenya. I told her it would be easier to get to the moon because the border between Kenya and Tanzania was closed.

She would have to fly to the Seychelles and overnight or fly to Zambia and overnight. I also said that no USIS staff member could help her. I sat there looking at her as she fumed, and I tried not to be judgmental. I felt sorry for her dilemma. She left my office without saying another word.

A few days later the sister of one of the teachers committed suicide. It fell upon me to deliver the devastating news. She was grief-stricken, and I invited her to move into my residence for a few days of solitude. I also made arrangements for her to call her family in the U.S.

Meanwhile, rumors were flying around town that this was a wild group of teachers. It was said that several had spent nights away from the YWCA, and none of them knew anybody in the country. I was told that one member of the group had gone out one night and returned the next morning with her blouse worn inside out. The rumors even reached the ears of Ambassador James Spain who called me into his office one day to talk about the teachers. I was shocked to learn that he had heard the same rumors I had.

He said, "Charlene, I would like for you to speak to the teachers about their behavior. Their behavior is reflecting negatively on all American women in Dar-es-Salaam, and I want it to stop immediately."

He added, "You can also tell them that if it does not stop, I will terminate their stay in Tanzania."

Oh, boy, I had to deliver that message. I felt distinctly uncomfortable telling the women this, but the ambassador said if I didn't speak to them, that he would speak to them, and it would not be pleasant.

In retrospect I think I should have let him speak to them, but I took a deep breath and agreed to deliver his message. I invited the group of teachers to our office and I delivered the ambassador's message. The guilty ones hung their heads in shame. All of them seemed angry with me. I was more embarrassed than they were; however, we heard no more rumors. They completed their project and left the country.

We had a U.S. professor who began showing signs of having a mental breakdown during his year at the university. He became uncommunicative, and when he was semi-lucid, he said strange things. Finally, we decided that he was going to cause problems if he continued at the university, and we made plans to send him back to the U.S. I was asked to accompany him on the two long flights to the U.S. I thought of flying with him for 12 hours to London, enduring a layover of several hours, and then an eight hour flight to the U.S., and another change of planes to reach his city. I declined the offer. My boss left it to me to tell the professor that he would be going home. I approached the subject as delicately as was possible. I explained that university officials and our office were concerned about his behavior, and that often when one was out of one's comfort zone, the mind can play tricks and on and on I went. No matter how I couched it, the bottom line was that he was going home and now.

When I told him that he would be accompanied by somebody, he said, "Somebody is going to lose some teeth."

I certainly didn't want to be the one to lose teeth, and I had nightmares thinking about spending hours in a flying boxcar with an out of control man. I advised Kent that a Marine should travel with him.

The professor was brought in early from the university the evening of his departure, and my task was to keep him occupied at my residence until it was time to leave for the airport. I didn't like this idea at all. I had no idea how he would act since he was not truly convinced that he needed to leave. I had prepared dinner, and we ate. I then had to make small talk for hours. I don't know if he said a word. Finally, the driver arrived to take him to Kent's house where the nurse joined him, and they were off to the airport. In the end, our embassy nurse and a Marine flew with the professor. The nurse had medicine in case he needed to be sedated, and they were met by embassy personnel in London where they had to change planes. The professor had been given a mild sedative before boarding the plane, and he behaved after one challenge to the Marine.

Another problem in Dar was Americans who wanted to take photographs. Americans don't leave home without their cameras. Cameras are an extension of their body. They want a picture of everything they see when abroad. Some countries are xenophobic and the sight of cameras makes them even more so. So many Americans were arrested in Dar for innocently taking photos that the only pictures I have of the country are of my house and driveway. They put the fear of taking pictures in me. The authorities always said that an American was taking pictures of some military installation when it was simply a bridge or a statue; there was little else to take photos of in the capital city. Maybe Americans should never leave home. They are away from family and friends and often they are not prepared for hardships.

They are so excited about going to a foreign country, and sometimes that foreign country is too foreign for them. Tanzania was such a place. There are other countries, such as Haiti, where some Americans want to kick up their heels. Some countries are not the kinds of places where one should kick up one's heels. Haiti was such a place.

Welcome To Liberia

Africa is a rubber ball; the harder you dash
it to the ground the higher it will rise.
*- Melvin B. Tolson, **Libretto for the Republic of Liberia***

The Tanzanian newspaper headline blared: BLOODY COUP IN LIBERIA! It was April, 1980, a few months after my assignment to Liberia as Information Officer had been announced. My assignment in Tanzania would end in September, 1980. With my heart sinking, I read about the military coup of April 12, 1980 in Monrovia, the date seared upon the hearts of all Liberians. That is the day that Army Master Sergeant Samuel K. Doe, a sixth grade dropout, led a coup against Liberian President William Tolbert. President Tolbert was disemboweled in front of his wife, who was not injured. A week later Doe invited the international press to the execution of 13 high level ministers of government, all Americo-Liberians, the elite of the country. These men, barely clothed, were marched through the streets of Monrovia, before jeering crowds, to the beach. They were tied to posts and shot. Most Americo-Liberians, the educated group that had governed since the founding of Liberia, fled the country. The "country people" - the people who had been denied education, who served the rulers - were now in charge.

Kent, my boss in Dar, tried to convince me to remain in Tanzania for one more year.

He said, "Surely, you don't want to go to Liberia where they are killing people and the country is in an uproar."

I replied, "I don't care what they are doing there, I am leaving here."

I then told Kent how miserable I had been during my two years in Tanzania. I said I loved my work, but living there had been no fun. He was surprised that I felt the way I did. He had had no idea, and I was glad that he didn't know how I felt. That meant I had masked it well. Finally he understood that I was leaving Tanzania even if I was now going into the bowels of hell. It was going to be a welcome change from Dar.

I left Tanzania at the end of September and spent my six weeks of home leave in Indiana. Of course I would have preferred to visit other countries enroute home, and visit other cities in the U.S., but Mother expected me to come home, and to home I went, even if somewhat grudgingly. Several months before my departure from Tanzania, I began having pains in my abdomen. I always felt that if I could put my hand inside and hold the area where the pain came from, that it would stop. As soon as I got home I made an appointment to see our family doctor. He joked as usual and decided that I simply had a nervous stomach, and gave me a prescription. He said it would take some time for the medication to work. I didn't want to alarm Mother, so when the pains began I would tell her that I was going to take a nap and I would writhe in agony until the pain subsided.

I didn't want to go out often with friends. I was content just curling up in the living room with Mother and watching TV. I was tired of being a diplomat. I wanted to be a "normal" person for a change. Mother's friends made over me, and her pastor always introduced me to the congregation as an "ambassador." I was the hometown girl who had made it big.

After six boring weeks I went to Washington and began my medical examinations. FSOs have to have a complete physical examination every two years or when finishing or beginning an assignment. I was medically cleared to leave for Liberia. On one of my last evenings in Washington I had dinner with a friend from my East Pakistan days. Beverly picked me up and took me to her home for dinner. During the evening she commented that I had not finished my glass of wine, and she knew I loved good wines. I told her that for some reason I didn't feel well. Nothing hurt me; I just felt unwell. I was glad to get back to the hotel and to bed. A few hours later I woke up in agony. My abdomen was on fire. I knew that I would have to go to the hospital. Somehow I managed to pack my suitcases. I don't know how long that took, but it seemed like hours. When I finally finished and locked the suitcases, I grabbed my purse and stumbled down to the desk.

The desk clerk took one look at me and asked, "Do you want an ambulance?"

"No," I gasped, "please call a taxi."

The George Washington University Hospital was three blocks down the street, but it might as well have been miles away. I could barely stand, let alone walk. The taxi took me to the emergency room entrance. While I waited to be seen I twisted and turned in my chair. It was impossible to be still. The pain felt as if I was being stabbed in the abdomen over and over. When the doctors examined me they found my blood pressure extremely high, and they said that told them I was in a lot of pain. They said the problem was either my pancreas or my gall bladder.

I had no knowledge of what either organ did, and truthfully at that point I didn't much care. I just wanted the pain to stop. They gave me something to ease the pain, wrote a note for me to give to State Department doctors, and sent me back to the hotel.

The next morning I returned to the medical unit and told them we had a problem. The doctor immediately ordered different tests, including one that would inject a dye into my system so they could see what organs were doing what. When I returned for them to take a look, they could see nothing because stones were coming out of my gall bladder and it was almost blocked. They said I had to have surgery.

I said, "You must be kidding. I'm on my way to Liberia."

"Oh, no, you're not," replied the doctor. "As of now your medical clearance is yanked."

I was distraught. I sought a second opinion outside of the State Department, and the doctor told me that he was the last person to recommend surgery, but he said I had to have surgery or risk complications.

I had planned to spend my last two nights in the U.S. with a friend who lived in New York City, Pat Byrd. I went to New York that weekend as planned, and Pat took me to a restaurant named, "The Horn of Plenty." It was a soul food restaurant and I ate to my heart's content. I woke up early the next morning in agony. I told Pat I had to get to a hospital. I dressed before she did and I was almost out the door before she caught up with me. On the street as she tried to hail a taxi, she told me to stop leaning on a mailbox or the taxi drivers would think I was drunk and would not stop. I cursed New York taxi drivers. Finally we got a taxi and got to a hospital. They didn't know what was wrong with me, but gave me something that stopped the pain. I left later that day for Washington. On Monday I returned to the medical unit at the State Department and told the doctor about my episode in New York. He apologized profusely that he had not given me something to prevent the pain, and told me to avoid eating fatty foods.

I decided to have the surgery in Washington because most of my friends were there. I did not want to return to Indianapolis for another boring six weeks. I moved to the Columbia Plaza, a complex of apartments where many FSOs stayed between assignments. It was across the street from the Department of State. Mother had flown from Indianapolis to be with me during the surgery. My surgeon was Jewish, and he asked me if Christmas was important to me because he wanted to operate the day after Christmas, and that meant I would have to check into the hospital on Christmas Day. I knew the sooner I had the surgery, the sooner I could get to Liberia. At the same time, the Cultural Affairs Officer in Monrovia was in another hospital in Washington. She has been medically evacuated a few days previously. On Christmas Eve Mother and I tried in vain to find a restaurant serving Christmas dinner. We ended up eating a Chinese meal. I felt sorry that Mother would be alone on Christmas Day. All of my friends in DC had gone home to be with their families. We were staying at Columbia Plaza, across the street from the State Department, where Foreign Service officers usually stayed when in Washington. The surgery went well. I was in the hospital for one week, and ordered to stay in Washington for six more weeks.

As soon as I was released from the hospital I began planning theatre and dinner outings. It was winter and Mother thought I should stay inside and let my body heal, while I felt that I should take advantage of being in

Washington, DC. Two weeks later Mother and I had words and she went home in disgust. After six weeks I was cleared to leave for Monrovia.

I decided that Mother might enjoy sharing some my adventures with me, and asked if she wanted to go to Liberia. We met at the airport in New York. She was such a glamorous woman; her nails were always beautiful, her various wigs always looked good, and she dressed well. I loved buying clothes for her that she either would not or could not afford to buy.

I arrived in Liberia with one suitcase missing. It arrived the next day, slit open, the top half of everything inside was missing. That included new clothing, credit cards and personal information. That was the first time I had had any items stolen in all my years of traveling abroad. I always boarded a plane with just my purse. I did not want to be burdened with carry-on bags and stuff. The only thing I ever wanted to carry onto a plane was a parachute, but since that was not practical, I only carried my purse. After that incident in Liberia, I began to carry anything that I did not want to lose. Once burned, twice shy.

Nothing was going to stop me from enjoying Liberia. I had a new lease on life and I felt great thanks to my surgery. I had two friends in Liberia, two women I had met at a conference in Kenya while I was stationed in Tanzania. One woman was Liberian and the other one was an American.

I had kept in touch with them during my two years in Tanzania and they were looking forward to having me in Liberia. I felt welcomed the moment my feet touched the ground. We were met by the PAO Frank Catanosa and taken to my residence, an elegant third floor walkup in Mamba Point, one block from the embassy. There was an empty elevator shaft inside the apartment. The owner had planned to install an elevator to open directly into each apartment, but he fled the country when the coup occurred. I had not totally recovered from my gall bladder surgery, and the walk up three flights of stairs had me gasping and in pain for several weeks. I placed a chair beside the door that I could collapse into when I got inside the apartment.

The Public Affairs Officer hosted a welcome reception for me to which he invited the Minister of Information, Col. Grey D. Allison and his wife, and other deputy ministers, and the press of Monrovia. I stood for hours in high heels greeting people. FSOs are not to sit at receptions or cocktail parties, but are to circulate and talk to people, not about ships and kings, but foreign policy things. At one point Mrs. Allison insisted that I sit with her to talk. I could have kissed her. I was so grateful to sit down. That was the last time I wore high heels to any event that required standing for any length of time.

I jumped right in learning the cast of characters. The new government was headed by Doe, a Khran; General Thomas Quiwonkpa, a Gio; Nicholas Podier, a Grebo; Thomas Weh Syen, a Kru; Nelson Toe, Harrison Dahn, Harrison Pennue, and a few others. This ragtag group called itself the People's Redemption Council, the PRC.

Doe was Chairman of the PRC, and Head of State; Weh-Syen was Vice-Chairman; Podier was named Speaker of the Interim-National Assembly. Gen. Thomas Quiwonkpa headed the military.

Liberians feel particularly close to Black Americans because their country was settled by freed American slaves with the first settlers arriving in 1822. In 1847 Liberia became the first independent country in Africa. Its flag, constitution, and even the names of some of its cities are all modeled on those of the United States.

When I arrived, the military government was preparing to celebrate the first anniversary of the coup, which occurred on April 12, 1980. Liberians, who tend to be superstitious, say that whatever happened on one date will happen on the same date the next year. There was tension in the air because April was fast approaching and rumors of an imminent coup could be heard everywhere. The U.S. had several military attaches at the embassy along with military trainers. To show our good will during the celebration (and also to give second thoughts to any who might have a coup in mind), the U.S. sent in a contingent of Green Berets who did parachute jumps along with the country's popular military commander, General Quiwonkpa. A U.S. Navy ship dropped in and several hundred American sailors strolled the streets of Monrovia. The Liberian public was invited to tour the Navy ship. Our ambassador hosted Doe and his Cabinet at a banquet on the Navy ship. There was a carnival atmosphere in the air and Liberians soon realized that with the show of U.S. force, there would be no coup that day.

Monrovia, the capital of Liberia, was a crumbling city in January, 1981. There were few sidewalks and fewer amenities, but there was such a genuine friendliness about the Liberians that made me love them. As the first black, female Information Attaché at the embassy, the press flocked to me. I was photographed and interviewed extensively.

I had expected to use my initial months as a period to learn the responsibilities of an Information Officer. I noticed that the PAO delegated many tasks to me that I was vaguely familiar with or had not done before. The CAO had seniority, but I was the one upon who serious tasks fell. My main task as IO was to publicize U.S. assistance in Liberia, including USAID and the Peace Corps; establish and broaden media contacts to assure effective programming of our programs; during that crucial transitional period, monitor the media for developments that particularly impacted U.S.-Liberia relations; and to assure Liberians of the continuing support of the U.S.' continuing support of their new government. I had five local employees in the press section.

The Ministry of Information became my second home. I went there frequently to take a tape of either the CBS Evening News or another national news program to show my colleagues.

My assistant and I lugged TV monitors and VCRs to accommodate a large crowd of Ministry of Information staffers who did not have access to U.S. news programs. The journalists were always amazed at the daring of U.S. reporters who shouted questions at the U.S. president or asked questions considered by the Liberians to be insensitive, and certainly would not have been tolerated by Head of State Doe. Whenever I walked through the front doors of the ministry, I was greeted with hugs from all of my colleagues. If I was in the office of one of the Deputy Ministers, and others heard I was in the building, they came directly to the minister's office to greet me. It was always like a homecoming.

One young man who worked at the ministry apparently misunderstood my hugs. One day he came to my office. He would not tell the receptionist why he wanted to see me. I told her to send him in. He came in, sat down and I asked how I could help him.

He replied, "I want to get to know you."

I asked what that meant.

He said with a sly smile, "I mean I want to get to know you, to really get to know you."

I then understood only too well what he meant. I ordered him out of my office. I called a friend at the Ministry of Information and told him the story. He was furious. He told me that my warmth and friendliness apparently gave the guy the wrong impression. He was going to see to it that the guy was fired.

I insisted that he not do that, and suggested that he simply explain to the young man how inappropriate his visit was, and let it go. I never saw the guy again, but I think the tongue lashing he got was preferable to finding himself without a job.

I became very fond of those journalists even though they wrote and said what the military government wanted them to. It was their job and we official Americans understood that. If the editor of an independent newspaper let something slip through that made Doe unhappy, the journalists at that newspaper were often arrested and jailed for as long as one month. A career as a journalist in Liberia was risky and dangerous. Liberia's Constitution, modeled after our own, enshrined press freedom, even though it was limited by ruling governments.

During the long rule of President William Tubman (1944-1971), he used the carrot by subsidizing independent newspapers. When the carrot was ineffective, he used the stick of imprisoning journalists under the charge of treason. Some Liberian newspapers tried to avoid political controversy, and jail, by practicing self-censorship. Under President William Tolbert, whose second term was cut short by the coup, discontent with the Americo-Liberian minority began finding its way into published pamphlets and newspaper columns.

Following the coup, journalists seemed emboldened enough to become more outspoken and more responsible to the people. That did not last long. As with most despots, Doe wanted to read or see nothing negative about him or his administration. Journalists and educated persons were always suspect to Doe and his cohorts. He made it clear from the beginning that only positive information about his regime would be acceptable.

Journalists who violated that and tried to print the truth or question or complain about some aspect of the government were imprisoned for as long as Doe liked. As he became more comfortable in his role as Head of State, his tolerance level was reduced to zero.

When I arrived there were two daily papers, a government newspaper and an independent newspaper. There were seven weekly papers, and three monthly magazines. Publishing was sporadic for most of them due to the shortage of newsprint and because there was little news that differed from what others were reporting. There was one television facility, ELTV, which operated as a commercial television station under the Ministry of Information, and government AM and FM radio stations. Another radio station was ELWA, funded by U.S. church groups. ELCM was a new Catholic FM station that operated only five hours daily.

Four months after my arrival, Frank returned to the U.S. leaving me in charge of three Americans and 11 Foreign Service Nations. I reported directly to the Chargé in the absence of an ambassador. Frank gave me an "excellent" performance rating before he left the post. He lauded my efforts of media coverage of the U.S. Green Berets and a Navy ship that participated in the first anniversary celebration of the revolution; briefing of foreign journalists and programming New York Times columnist Flora Lewis.

Later that year, Sergeant Nicholas Podier, Speaker of the Interim-National Assembly, celebrated his birthday by hosting a party at one of Monrovia's most lavish nightclubs. The Cultural Affairs Officer and I were invited by the man who planned the party. His job was to invite 80 of Podier's nearest and dearest friends. We attended the party, met Podier, danced, and had a great time. A few months later our office hosted an American jazz group that performed at a downtown theatre, and we invited Speaker Podier along with other members of the PRC, as a courtesy. Podier accepted the invitation and arrived at the theater with numerous bodyguards, but hurriedly left when the power went out for a few seconds at the beginning of the performance. He, of course, thought somebody was attempting to assassinate him. A few weeks later I received a telephone call from a military officer at the presidential mansion inviting me to present cultural awards at a ceremony along with Speaker Podier. I wondered why the Cultural Affairs Officer was not asked to present cultural awards, but I said I would be delighted to do so. Before we hung up I asked how I had been selected.

The officer replied, "Because we always see you in the newspapers."

When I hung up, I laughed and laughed. In the end, I handed out the awards alone because the Speaker was "indisposed" and unable to attend the event.

I inherited Henry, my houseman, from my boss. Henry had a dour expression, a keen sense of humor, and he was extremely competent in cleaning the apartment, washing and ironing my clothes, and he could cook simple dishes for me. Most importantly, he was totally trustworthy. Mother spent one month in Liberia and she thought Henry was the greatest. He told me that he had grown up in the same household as one of my main contacts, a man I'll call Gerald. In fact, it was Henry's father who took the boy into their home. That boy had become a member of Liberia's diplomatic service. It hurt Henry that when Gerald was invited to dinners or receptions at my residence, he never acknowledged Henry when he served him.

Henry was as polite to him as he was to other guests, and never showed what he must have felt in his heart. Everybody in the U.S. diplomatic community knew and liked Henry. He was an excellent bartender and server, and he was always asked to serve at functions hosted by the ambassador and other American officials.

I met and immediately loved the legendary Bai T. Moore, Minister for Cultural Affairs and Tourism, who is best known for his novel, "Murder in the Cassava Patch." This elderly gentleman was a prolific author, poet, folklorist and lover of Liberian culture. He wanted everyone to know and to enjoy Liberian culture. He invited a group of us from the American embassy to a village to witness the end of a coming out ceremony where boys had trained in the forest to become men and survivors. The Poro is a secret society for males in which boys enter at puberty and are taught traditions and survival skills in bush schools. Many years ago the training lasted for three to four years. The training has become shorter in modern times. The participants are forbidden to ever divulge what goes on during their training. Penalties for revealing their secrets have ranged from banishment from the society to death. The Sande society for young women, teaches them how to prepare herbs and roots to make love potions, poisons, and even ways to make a man impotent. There is another important feature of this society that is highly controversial, that I learned about after being invited to join.

That day as we awaited the arrival of the young men from the bush, the village was joyful. Beautiful old women stood in doorways smiling and waving as visitors poured into their village. The air vibrated with anticipation and anxiety.

I was seated next to Mrs. Moore who was clearly worried about her son surviving the training. She had told me earlier that all young men did not come out of the bush, that sometimes accidents happened. As I looked around at the gaiety I was struck by the richness of the culture. These Liberians knew from whence they came. They knew or in the case of the initiates, they learned, about their values and traditions, and the things necessary to prepare them for adult life. I realized that I had no rich traditions such as they had. I had no idea where my ancestors came from. It was a feeling of being totally isolated from everything and everyone around me. A white friend seated on the other side of me noticed that I had become somber. She asked what was wrong. I began trying to explain what I was feeling, but then I realized that she could never understand. She knew where her great-grandparents came from, whereas I had no clue. My people came to the U.S. in chains. I know not from where in Africa. I only know that my ancestors must have been strong, determined people to have survived that horrible, long voyage in shackles in the bowels of a ship, sick, scared, away from loved ones, and enduring the brutality of those with whips. Tears came to my eyes, but just then Mrs. Moore hunched me.

She said, "Here they come. Watch for my son."

As the young men ran through the village, looking straight ahead, there was applause and cheers that they had been successful. Mrs. Moore clutched my wrist and then we saw her son running and I heard her exhale. We gave each other a broad smile and we hugged.

The old Liberian ladies began dancing and singing in celebration. All the young men had safely returned from the bush school. They were now adult men.

The next week when I encountered Minister Moore I thanked him for inviting me to the ceremony. He then asked if I would like to participate in the Sande initiation for women. I said I would be delighted. He said he would send his wife and his sister with me. I wondered why he felt that I needed them along with me. I was thrilled with his invitation and I announced it to several female Liberian friends. Each one looked at me curiously, but didn't say anything. I didn't think too much about it. Later, I mentioned my excitement about the ceremony to a male friend.

He looked at me with astonishment and asked, "You are going to have a clitoridectomy?"

I looked at him as if he were crazy.

He said, "Yes, that's what they do in the Sande society. Didn't you know that?"

I replied, "I know Minister Moore has not lost his mind. Maybe that's why he said he would send his wife and sister with me, so they can explain to the society trainers that I am not to have a clitoridectomy!"

I wondered why my two female friends had not told me. It took a man to tell me. I relaxed knowing that I would be under the wings of Minister Moore's wife and sister. Unfortunately, I left Liberia earlier than planned because I was asked to take over the reins of USIS in Swaziland which had become a disaster.

Master Sergeant Samuel K. Doe and the People's Redemption Council

1981 - 1982

The smaller the lizard the greater its chances of becoming a crocodile.
                                                        - Ethiopia

The People's Redemption Council (PRC) came to power by a bloody coup against the elected president. Samuel K. Doe, who took over as Head of State, was a sixth grade drop-out, barely spoke recognizable English, and he was one of the most educated members of the PRC. The most popular member of the PRC was General Thomas Quiwonkpa, commanding general of the armed forces. Gen. Quiwonkpa lived in the army barracks with his men, unlike his cohorts. The other members of the PRC took over homes belonging to wealthy Liberians who had fled the country, or they threw out home owners and moved in. Few of the soldiers could drive cars, but they sauntered down the streets ordering car owners out of their cars, and they drove off in them, or attempted to. They had not had access to cars, but they wanted to drive, and who was going to stop them? As a result, there were numerous accidents and deaths among the PRC members. Finally Doe ordered the Council members to have drivers because he was losing men every day. Small men with big guns are the most dangerous. As the Head of State Doe was in over his head, but he quickly cemented his reputation as a dictator, and began ridding himself of the baggage he brought into power with him, his fellow conspirators and murderers. The jockeying for power began. Doe saw attempted coups everywhere among his cohorts, and began eliminating them.

I met the Deputy Head of State, Weh-Syen, when I accompanied the Chargé d'Affairs, Julius Walker, and the Director of the U.S. Agency for International Development (USAID) to see homes built by the U.S. military for Liberian soldiers. Previously, the Liberian Armed Forces had been small, poorly trained and held in low esteem by the populace. After the coup, Doe doubled the salaries of all soldiers and requested increased military assistance from the United States in order to improve the quality of the military. The U.S. responded favorably and generously, and launched several construction projects designed to provide better housing for the military. New homes were a top priority. One year after the coup, on its anniversary, Doe told the nation why he overthrew President Tolbert. He said he and other soldiers were sitting in his little military hut as rain poured in on them. The huts had no doors, dirt floors, and they were always hot. The soldiers talked about President Tolbert living comfortably in the presidential mansion, and they decided that they wanted to live as he did. It was as simple as that. Therefore, building decent housing was imperative.

Weh-Syen, a short, thin, humorless, swaggering man, was extremely insulting to Chargé Walker the day we toured the new barracks. Weh-Syen raved that the houses were hot and too small. The Chargé said air-conditioning was never an option, and pointed out that while the houses were small, they were well built and no rain would come in. Weh-Syen strutted about criticizing everything, and lacking any iota of diplomacy.

It was immediately apparent that we were dealing with an uneducated, ignorant man, but it was difficult to ignore some of the things he said. Chargé Walker was furious with the manner in which Weh-Syen treated us. I was afraid that at any moment the Chargé would say the wrong thing to Weh-Syen who was accompanied by armed soldiers, or worse yet, hit him. I would not have been surprised if Weh-Syen had ordered his men to shoot us. He had had a taste of power and was enjoying it. I didn't think he knew when too much was excessive, or what the consequences of killing American diplomats would mean for his country. The USAID Director acted as mediator, and often stepped into the fray when words became more heated. When we parted ways, neither group was happy.

Two weeks later as I dressed for work one morning, I heard the newscaster report that Weh-Syen and four other officers of the PRC had been arrested for treason. What a shock that was to the nation. Weh-Syen and Doe were extremely close. Had he really plotted against Doe? The rumors began that Doe was getting rid of his fellow coup plotters. He was making certain that of all the equals, he would prevail as the most equal of them all. Within days the trial was held before a military tribunal that was closed to the public. All five men were sentenced to death. From his prison window Weh-Syen proclaimed his innocence.

He yelled to passersby from his cell, "If I die, I die for nothing!"

The families and friends of the men sentenced to die gathered in protest outside the prison daily. The girlfriends of some of the condemned men were pregnant, and many of them stood outside the prison weeping and shouting. Some of the men had several girlfriends pregnant.

In the days before the executions Doe ordered that guns be removed from all the soldiers at the prison who were members of Wey Syen's ethnic group, the Kru. Doe feared the armed Kru soldiers might try to free Wey-Syen. How insulting that must have been to those soldiers. Another insult was to the families of the condemned. Execution dates are never announced. In trials of treason, after the executions, the bodies of the condemned were not returned to their families. It was said the bodies were dumped into the ocean. That was the final insult, and the most hurtful to the families, as planned by the Head of State. Some of my journalist friends who had been imprisoned at various times said they were told by prison guards that Doe always visited his condemned cohorts in prison, and personally tortured them before they were executed. On the evening that the execution of Wey Syen and the other condemned men was carried out, one of our embassy officers drove by the prison enroute to another part of the city. He said the area was full of screaming and crying family members of the condemned men. Later, when the officer returned home, the area around the prison was quiet. The executions were over. It was August 14, 1981.

Black is a Wonderful Thing. . .most Times

The struggle is my life.

- Nelson Mandela

Some of my white, fellow American diplomats felt free to express their intense dislike of Monrovia. I found it highly insulting. At the rare events I attended at which only Americans were present they griped about the uneducated people, the filthy streets, the old and crumbling buildings, the lack of sidewalks, the beggars, and the lack of everything they wanted. On the other hand, none of what they complained about bothered me. I wished that Liberia could afford to clean up and repair its streets; I regretted seeing beggars in any country, and we all were aware that Liberia lacked many of the conveniences we were accustomed to in the U.S.

Finally, one evening at a dinner where Americans were complaining about Liberia, I announced that henceforth I did not want to hear one negative word about Liberia. People looked shocked at my announcement. I had had enough of their complaints. I said it never mattered to me what a country looked like, that the most important thing was how the people treated me. My colleagues knew from all the newspaper articles about me that Liberians loved me, and the feeling was definitely mutual. Liberians treat all strangers as if they were friends. Everyone at that dinner table had been warmly welcomed by any Liberians they had met, and yet there were the continual put-downs of the country. My announcement worked; I never heard another negative word about Liberia from any Americans at the embassy.

My point was that we all knew we were coming to a "hardship post" per diplomatic language. We received a hardship allowance that increased our salaries which is the reason most diplomats go to such posts. The hardship differential is based on the amount of exposure to diseases and unsanitary conditions, political violence, lack of good medical facilities, the climate, and the lack of various cultural activities. We know that hardship posts do not have the comforts of home, and that is why we receive extra pay. Currently approximately 25 countries qualify for danger pay. Danger pay is based on the level of violence within the country, the number of civilian deaths, and the involvement of U.S. forces.

I learned something else about being in Africa. I first noticed in Haiti that as I walked or drove around the country I felt unusually comfortable. In Tanzania I experienced a sensation of total relaxation, despite not being happy in the country. Finally, in Liberia I realized what it was: for the first time in my life I was in countries where black people were in the majority, and as a black person I was a part of that majority. When people stared at me it was because they knew I was an American, a black American, and I was more one of them than not. Then I understood how white Americans in the U.S. felt, and how they could deny that racism existed. Their expectations were never unfulfilled. When they walked into a bank or a store in the U.S. nobody looked at them as if they were going to rob the place. When they applied for a loan, they were fairly certain they would get it. When they wanted to rent or to purchase a house, they gave not one thought to the notion that they might be refused because of their race.

They never walked into an establishment where they were not welcomed or wondered if the service would be lacking because of their race. When I walked into a restaurant or any business in a black African country nobody looked at me as if I did not belong there. I was one of them. For my white colleagues it was the first time in most of their lives that they were in the minority and they did not like it. The few whites who enjoyed being in Africa were rare. It is unfortunate that many white American diplomats dislike working in Africa. Africa needs people who want to be there; those who don't want to be there can and do leave negative impressions on the people, and the phrase, "ugly Americans" becomes very real.

I learned something else about blackness while in Africa. I realized that servants in black countries always err on the side of whiteness. For example, in Tanzania my housekeeper knew that if anybody from the embassy came to the house and said they were there to do work or to remove something for repairs, if I had not told her in advance, she was to call me before letting them in. One afternoon I came home from the office and was told that a Mr. Smith was waiting for me in the living room. I had no idea who Mr. Smith was. I walked into the living room and there sat a white man I had never seen before, sipping a glass of lemonade so generously given to him. He was a salesman of some sort, or so he said, and I showed him out. I lectured the housekeeper about letting anybody into the house. That man could have robbed me, learned the layout of the house, or planted something in the house. I was furious that Alice had allowed in a total stranger simply because he was white.

Meanwhile a close relative of Doe apparently developed a crush on me. I had seen Gaba, not his real name, at several social events. One Saturday evening as I relaxed at home the guard rang me from downstairs to say that Mr. Gaba was there to see me. I thought: what a nerve, but then I thought about my journalist friends, male and female, who dropped in all the time and I had no problems with that. I did have a problem with Gaba since he was not a journalist friend and I didn't care for the way he leered at me the few times I had seen him. I told the guard he could come up. I was not happy with Mr. Gaba. He came in and I immediately asked why he had dropped by without being invited. He apologized and I showed him into the living room. I sat on a sofa and he sat in a chair with his back to the door. Every few seconds he would jerk his head around as if expecting somebody to be behind him. I immediately realized that he thought I had a male visitor there who might be hiding and could possibly harm him. I began to enjoy his discomfort. I thought if he was uncomfortable enough that he would leave. After a few minutes of small talk he asked me to give him a tour of my apartment. I showed him the huge kitchen, the small "viewing room" as I called a room where I had several televisions (U.S., Liberian, and special office TV), the two guest bedrooms, and then the master bedroom. In my bedroom the bathroom door was not completely shut and it was dark inside the bathroom. Gaba kept looking at the door. I was amused watching him yank his head from one side of the room to the bathroom door as if he expected someone to pop out. I knew that he wanted to open that door, but he could not bring himself to do it. I stood there with a small smile on my face, as if daring him to touch the door.

I almost invited him to open it, in order to allay his concerns, but decided to let him sweat. We went back into the living room where he continued that jerking his head around looking for somebody and soon he left.

The next day I told one of the political officers that there might be an international incident if Gaba ever came to my residence again. I wanted it known at the embassy that I was not going to tolerate any foolishness from that man, notwithstanding the fact that he was a close relative of the head of state.

A few weeks later Senator Hayakawa came to Monrovia. Of course I had written his arrival and departure statements, questions and answers, speeches, and toasts, and they had been sent to Washington for the Senator's approval. The Liberian government hosted a luncheon for the Senator at the Ministry of Foreign Affairs where he would deliver my toast. I arrived at the Ministry, and Deputy Chief of Mission Ed Perkins and I were looking for our name cards at the table. Suddenly I found myself next to Gaba who was also searching the name cards. He found mine before I did, removed it, and switched it to the place setting next to his. I could feel myself swelling with anger. I think I was about to roar, after all, I have been accused of growling at times. Ed had seen Gaba making the switch, and then he saw my face. Ed smoothly reached over, took my name card, and put it back where it had been. He said something softly to Gaba about protocol. I was vibrating with anger.

As we seated ourselves Ed leaned over and whispered, "He's just a Renaissance man."

I snapped, "He's just an ass!"

A few weeks later I was at a social event and I noticed Gaba with his white wife. He, of course, ignored me. At one point I walked over to the couple. I could see sweat break out on Gaba's face. He had no idea what I was going to say to him or to his wife. I introduced myself to her and said I had been looking forward to meeting her, gave him a contemptuous smile and walked away. He never bothered me again.

I was happily seeing a Liberian man who was much younger than me and because of the age difference I refused to go out in public with him. I was concerned that people would gossip about me. He insisted that nobody would care. He would come over to my apartment some evenings, and most weekends, often after I returned from an official engagement, and we played Scrabble, sipped wine, listened to music, and had a very enjoyable time.

One Saturday evening he finally convinced me to go out to dinner with him. We went to a Chinese restaurant. Shortly after we arrived, in came a party of six people from the embassy, led by the ambassador's special assistant. They naturally stopped at my table. Had I had my faculties about me I would simply have introduced my friend to them as a journalist which was true. I often took journalists to lunch or to dinner and never felt that anybody would think I was on a personal date. Had he not been a special friend, I would have introduced him, but I was embarrassed at being out with this young man, and I felt guilty. We all said hello, and they stood waiting for introductions, and I sat looking around. I don't know what my friend was doing. Had he jumped up and introduced himself, I would have probably just crawled under the table.

Had I behaved normally nothing would have been suspected. We sat and they stood. Finally, they moved on to their table. I was miserable the rest of the evening.

That Monday when I went to the embassy, the ambassador's special assistant smiled coyly at me and asked, "Did you enjoy your dinner Saturday night?"

"No," I replied truthfully and kept moving.

I realized that in order to overcome the guilt feelings about the age difference that I would have to stop seeing my friend. I told him that I was ending our relationship and why. He did not like my reasoning, but he accepted it. The next day his brother came to see me to ask why I was ending the relationship. I thought he was out of his mind. He was a good friend, but I did not understand why he was questioning me about my decision to stop seeing his brother. But I explained my feelings to him. He asked me to reconsider my decision. I refused. When he left he said his wife would be coming to see me.

I mentioned this to another Liberian friend, and she said, "Oh, yes, when you break up with somebody here in Liberia, the whole family gets involved and comes to talk to you to see what can be done to get the parties back together."

I said, "You must be kidding. Why?"

She said that was the custom and I might as well get used to it.

A few days later the brother's wife came to see me. She began by apologizing that it took her so long to come to talk to me. It had been about a week since I broke up with her brother-in-law. She began by asking me outright why I ended the relationship. I tried to explain about the age difference, and it went right over her head. Perhaps Americans are the only people concerned with age differences.

She would not accept that as a valid reason. I was totally out of my element in trying to explain to two people who were basically strangers to me, why I had stopped seeing someone. I suppose I was fortunate that the rest of his family were upcountry. He and I remained friends, but we had no more Scrabble evenings.

I had a radio program on ELBC, fondly called by Liberians, "ELTheySay." I was invited to read poetry to music. Each week I spent a lot of time selecting the right piece of music for certain poems that had to do with Africa or African-Americans. I was always surprised that one of the political officers at our embassy listened to each program and commented on them. I was careful not to do any poems about coups, or governments, or murders, or uprisings since Liberia was just recovering from a coup. That made it a bit difficult because so many black poets write about that which concerns them and their countries, and often that is killing, police states, dictators, hate, and anger. At first the program was on the FM station weekly. Then it became twice weekly and then every night. The station director then put the program on the AM station, but I continued recording once a week. I didn't have time to record more often. I think all of the journalists listened to my program.

One of the deputy ministers of Information said, "I probably shouldn't say this, but you sound so sexy."

One year after I left Liberia, I was told the radio station was still playing my poetry readings.

A Dangerous Welcome

Courage is not the absence of fear, but rather the judgment
that something else is more important than fear.
- Ambrose Redmoon

As our caravan of three embassy cars rolled through the dark, empty streets of downtown Monrovia, I wondered if this would be the last night of my life. Liberia was under marshal law and a curfew had been declared by Head of State Doe. Doe had declared that no one was allowed on the city streets from midnight to 6:00 a.m., and here was our small caravan of cars moving through downtown Monrovia shortly before five o'clock in the morning. Two weeks earlier the Chargé d'Affairs Edward J. Perkins, had announced the arrival of our new ambassador, William Lacy Swing, and said all senior officers would greet him at Liberia's Robertsfield International Airport. As the Acting Public Affairs Officer for the U.S. Information Agency I was to be in the welcoming party. Against my will and better judgment, I now found myself in the second car of the small caravan praying that I would not only meet the ambassador but that I would live long enough to see the next African dawn.

At a Country Team Meeting (composed of the heads of all U.S. agencies represented at the embassy) Chargé Perkins had announced, "Our new ambassador will be arriving in two weeks and all heads of agencies, and any family members who want to go, will meet him at the airport. We should be at the airport by 5: 30 a.m."

We were stunned at this announcement since Liberia was under a curfew, and a curfew violation meant death. It was a one hour drive from Monrovia to the airport. The soldiers were ordered to shoot first. No questions would be asked or answered. No one was to be on the streets during curfew.

The Chargé continued, "I will get a special pass from the Ministry of Foreign Affairs to permit embassy cars to be on the streets."

I quickly spoke up, "Most of the soldiers can't read."

People chuckled uncomfortably.

The Chargé replied, "The soldiers will know what they mean."

I seriously doubted it. Somebody else mentioned that once we were safely past the Presidential Mansion, we still had to pass the Military Barracks where the road would be blocked. Our military attaches who were actively advising the fledgling government, piped up and said that would be no problem because their "friend," Captain Somebody, would be waiting there to allow us to pass immediately. Yeh, right, I thought. After the meeting some officers expressed doubts as to the safety of a caravan of American embassy cars breaking curfew to go to the airport. There was no question but that we would go. An ambassador is the ruling force at every embassy. He represents the president of the United States. When he walks into a room, we all stand as a sign of respect. I used to chuckle when I was in Washington because whenever the USIA Director walked into a conference room, all the Foreign Service Officers sprang to their feet while the Civil Service staff looked at us in amazement. There was no question that we would be at the airport to welcome our new ambassador.

Some thought the ambassador would tell us not to travel to the airport until curfew was lifted, that he would just tool around the airport like an ordinary man until we felt it was safe enough to get on the road, i.e., when the curfew lifted at 6 a.m. Alas, that was not going to happen. The only question that I had, which I kept to myself, but which was probably glaringly obvious to the Chargé was: Will we make it to the airport? I sensed nervousness among those of us who were obliged to go to the airport, but only I had the audacity to say anything to the Chargé. During the next two weeks I kept reminding him about the risks we were taking in breaking the curfew. He appeared to dismiss my concerns, yet something I said must have gotten through to him because a few days before the ambassador's arrival he announced that female dependents would not go to the airport, but female officers would. I felt sick. Well, I thought, at least he recognized the danger. As the Acting Public Affairs Officer it was my job to have a photographer at the airport to photograph the arrival of the second most important person in the country, the U.S. Ambassador. I got the best photographer in town, Sando Moore, son of the Minister of Culture, Bai T. Moore, who spent the night at my residence in order to leave with us at 4:30 a.m. He apparently felt that he would be safe with American diplomats because there was no hesitation on his part. In the dark that morning he and I drove the two blocks to the embassy, and joined the other officers in official embassy cars. We were in the second car of the three-car caravan. In the lead car were Chargé Perkins, the Embassy Counselor, Al Jazynka, and their driver. In my car were the Political Officer, the Special Assistant to Ambassador Swing, the photographer, our driver, and me, Acting Director of USIS.

In the third car were the Acting Director of USAID, Edward Anderson; the Acting Director of the Peace Corps, Beverlee Bruce, other agency heads and their driver. I thought to myself, most of us are Acting Heads of our agencies, so if we are killed, they will still have the Heads of agencies. We're like the pawns. Such thoughts are not good ones to have before attempting a dangerous venture of breaking curfew. Why does one think of such things when one is scared? It's like being on a plane for several hours and suddenly wondering what is keeping the plane up in the air. That is not the time to ponder such questions. The military attaches were to join the caravan after we passed the Presidential Mansion since they lived on the outskirts of Monrovia.

As we drove I thought of all the problems we could encounter. The lead car was a long, black American automobile with American flags flying from the front fenders, flags that could easily be mistaken for Liberian flags. The Liberian flag is modeled on the American flag. I was concerned that the soldiers at the Presidential Mansion would at first think it was a Liberian official's car, and then realizing that it was not, might think we were pretending to be Doe officials, and they might open fire with their semi-automatic weapons. Plus, most of the soldiers could not read. I could only close my eyes and pray as we drove through the empty streets. When the caravan reached the Presidential Mansion, we stopped. Liberian soldiers quickly surrounded each car, weapons aimed at us. The soldier standing next to our driver's door rapped sharply on the window for the driver to roll it down. The driver was petrified and didn't move. Again the soldier rapped on the window with his gun. The driver didn't move.

I could see the soldier becoming more agitated. I was seated behind the driver, and I leaned forward and ordered him to lower the window. He did so, and handed the soldier the pass that he only glanced at. I was still leaning forward and my eyes wandered to the pass. To my horror the soldier held it upside down. He could not read it.

My mind shrieked, "I knew it! I knew it!"

I prayed that a bit of sanity would prevail in the midst of controlled chaos. Our soldiers and those at the third car kept their eyes on the soldiers at the lead car. We knew if anything went wrong at the lead car we were all as good as gone. Liberian soldiers are quick on the trigger. Everything and everybody is suspect. Whenever I visited the Presidential Mansion I was painfully aware of armed soldiers every few feet. I always felt that if somebody let loose a loud fart, bullets would be flying all around the place. Finally the soldiers at the lead car stepped back and motioned for all three cars to continue. There was a huge collective sigh of relief. As the sun made its rise into the sky, our spirits also soared.

We arrived at the airport in time to collect ourselves before the plane landed. Ambassador Swing was the first one off the plane and he fairly danced down the metal steps. He was handsome, elegant, and unlike the waiting party of embassy officials, looked as if he had had a good night's sleep on the long flight over the Atlantic. We might have looked neat, but every one of us felt as disheveled as if we had been tossed about in a cement mixer. But we kept smiling as the ambassador worked his way down the receiving line, beaming at each member of his Country Team.

Little did he know that we were all smiling with relief because we had survived the night drive to the airport in the midst of curfew. It was a trip none of us would ever want to make again, but, of course, we would if need be. After all, we serve at the pleasure of the ambassador.

Doe's Official Working Visit to the United States

Nothing in the world is more dangerous than a
sincere ignorance and conscientious stupidity.
- Dr. M.L. King, Jr.

The butcher of Liberia, Head of State Doe, wanted an invitation to visit the United States. Russia and Libya were courting him, and while he trusted the U.S. more than the other two, he was trying to get the most for the least. He felt that an invitation from President Ronald Reagan would make him more legitimate in the eyes of his countrymen and other African leaders, and might even help to dispel memories of his violent entry into the world of statesmen. It took some doing, but finally the embassy was able to wrangle an invitation for an "official working visit" to the U.S. as opposed to "a state visit." There would be no White House dinner and the visit would be very low-keyed. That mattered not to Doe. As far as he was concerned, he had been invited to the U.S. by President Reagan and he was going to be received by the U.S. President. The ambassador invited me to join him, the DCM, and my boss at a meeting with Doe's people involved in planning the trip. Before the meeting the DCM and the ambassador discussed their concerns that Doe would wear his military uniform during his visit, and they wanted to discourage that, but didn't know how to broach such a delicate subject.

I knew all of the officers who were in Doe's planning group, and I had no compunction about asking how the Head of State would dress during his visit.

Inquiring minds wanted to know, and I felt that I was less bound by diplomatic protocol than the ambassador and the DCM. During a lull in the meeting, I casually inquired as to what the Head of State would wear during his visit. His staffers immediately said he would wear his military uniform. That gave the ambassador and the DCM the opportunity to tell them Americans would view his military dress negatively, and it would cause people to revisit the way Doe had come into power. Doe's staffers were not happy with this, but it was out and on the table. We emphasized the importance of this visit to Liberia, the reaction of Americans to the military coup, and said this was an opportunity for Doe to portray himself as he wanted Americans to remember him. His staffers understood, but would they be able to convey the message to Doe? I did not envy them. The visit was due to take place in the fall of 1982. The ambassador invited me to accompany him and the Doe party on their flight to the U.S. What an honor that was. I had been dealt a plum opportunity.

An embassy officer asked me, "How do you think your Public Affairs Officer feels about you going to the U.S. with the ambassador and Doe instead of him?"

I had not given it a thought, but now the thought of him stewing caused me to break into a wide grin. He always seemed amazed that I was so loved by the Liberians, and that the ambassador and DCM often asked my advice.

The Doe visit to the U.S. was scheduled for October, 1982. In July our ambassador went to Tunisia on vacation, and I went home to Indiana on vacation. Two weeks later I received word that the Doe visit had been moved up due to something more pressing on President Reagan's calendar.

Doe had been given the choice of going to the U.S. almost immediately or of waiting another year. As any dictator knows, tomorrow is not promised to him, so he chose to go immediately. I rushed to Washington from Indiana. We cabled the embassy to ask if I should return to Liberia. They replied telling me to remain in Washington. This change in plans was a blow to me since I had looked forward to arriving in grand style with the Head of State and his entourage. The ambassador cut short his vacation and flew back to Liberia to accompany the Doe party to Washington.

Doe arrived in Washington with a sizeable number of Liberian journalists and I accompanied them to all events. I was with them to make sure that they were at events on time; that they got photos of their Head of State at every opportunity, and that the American press did not trample them. By and large, the Liberian journalists were shy and retiring even though they had seen videos of aggressive American journalists shouting questions at the U.S. president, and pushing to get up closer to get answers to their questions. They laughed as they watched displays of irreverence by journalist that would never be permitted in Liberia. I told the Liberians they had to be aggressive or they would go home with no photos.

President Reagan had agreed to meet with the Liberian journalists. At the White House press briefing I made sure the Liberian journalists were right down front and ready to ask questions of President Reagan. I had explained the meaning of background and deep background to them, but I asked Larry Speakes, White House Deputy Press Secretary, to explain again. In Liberia there were no press briefings on or off background, deep or otherwise. If the press got word of even a rumor, they were off running and printing it.

It was important for the Liberian journalists to understand that any information they learned from President Reagan not be printed since it was on "deep background." That meant that they could not even attribute the news to a "government official." Larry Speakes briefed the journalists. When he finished he turned to leave without saying one word about deep background. He left the podium and began walking out of the room. As I glared at his back I silently screamed his name. It was as if I had screamed it out loud because he suddenly stopped, returned to the podium and defined deep background and background. Mental telepathy worked in that instance.

President Reagan then came out and answered a few questions. Afterwards, we then adjourned to the Rose Garden where President Reagan and Head of State Doe shook hands and posed for photos. This was Doe's first public appearance and I watched as he posed in his elegantly embroidered Liberian gown and matching headdress. He had listened to us and did not wear his military uniform. As they shook hands, President Reagan welcomed

"Chairman Moe" and blundered right on unaware of his faux pas. The ambassador and I cringed. I felt that Reagan could have taken the time to learn Doe's name, but then I remembered that he had memory issues. The Liberian journalists were in awe of being in the presence of an American president.

Doe's next public appearance was at the Pentagon. I arrived before he and his party did. A military attaché who had served in Liberia welcomed me and escorted me onto the parade grounds. The band struck up a fanfare when Doe arrived. He then inspected the troops.

Our military attaches in Liberia had worked with the Pentagon to put on a dazzling display which our military does extremely well. Doe was visibly impressed with the fanfare at the Pentagon. U.S. military personnel are impressive in their dress uniforms, and with their precision in walking and marching. I felt so proud, as I always do when I see such a display. I could only imagine Doe's regret at not wearing his military uniform. Since he had elevated himself from Sargeant to General, his uniform would have been splendiferous.

In the evening the Liberian ambassador held a reception for Doe to which all African ambassadors were invited, as well as high ranking State Department officials, and prominent Americans well versed in African affairs. When I was introduced to Doe, I told him I was the Press Attaché at the U.S. embassy in Monrovia. I don't think he heard or understood anything I said. His mind seemed elsewhere. He was out of his element. As I watched him stealthily, it became obvious that he wanted the evening to end as soon as possible. He sat as if on the edge of a pin that was about to prick him at any moment. He seemed stiff and unsure of himself, as well he should have been. He was surrounded by diplomats and people of knowledge who had ascended to their positions, whereas he, a grade school dropout, had seized power and had the blood of many on his hands. He represented the oldest black republic in the world, an honor he had neither earned nor had bestowed upon him by the people of Liberia.

Author being introduced to Liberian Head of State,
Samuel K. Doe, by U.S. Ambassador William Lacy Swing,
during Doe's official visit to the U.S. - 1982

American government officials were nervous about the American media interviewing Doe. Those of us from our embassy in Monrovia tried to protect Doe from the media and vice-versa.

We knew that one of the first questions asked of him by a U.S. journalist would be about the violent coup that brought him into power, and we knew that he would walk away from any venue where that question arose. He was incapable of deflecting unpleasant questions diplomatically and would behave badly as a spoiled kid might. In Liberia if a journalist asked a question he didn't like, Doe threw him in jail and closed the newspaper office. Doe was educationally and emotionally challenged, and operated with a quick response of shoot and /or leave. The picture of Doe stomping off a TV set before millions of people caused nightmares for this Information Officer and others with vested interests in seeing that his trip was successful. We knew that Doe would look like the idiot that he was to the American people, and our embassy wanted him to look like a statesman since we were asking our government to pour millions of dollars into Liberia. The U.S. had taken Liberia for granted for many years even though we had vital interests there.

We had been happy to let Presidents Tubman and Tolbert and the other Americo-Liberians live pompously while the poor got poorer, but we were not concerned until Doe came into power. The Cold War was in full swing, and Russia and the U.S. were courting Liberia, something the U.S. had never envisioned doing. Both countries poured money into Liberia. For awhile Doe was even courted by Libya which really frightened the U.S. Among the U.S. interests in Liberia were a huge Voice of America facility; rubber plantations owned by U.S. companies, and the Omega radio navigation used by military planes and ships, among other interests. If Liberia's leader behaved in the U.S. like the brute that he was, it would reflect negatively on those trying to help the Liberian nation, regardless of the reasons.

At the end of the reception I left with the Liberian press, along with most of the other diplomats. We Americans had no idea that at some point during the evening, a *Washington Post* reporter spoke to Doe and arranged to interview him after the reception. The next morning the front page of *The Washington Post's* Style section featured a photo of Doe, a picture of some of the former ministers tied to stakes just before their execution, and a story on Doe that began with the violent coup. Doe was furious. He began canceling appointments. The Voice of America (VOA), a part of USIA got shafted immediately. Doe refused to keep an appointment to present a warrior jacket to the VOA. He wanted to cancel other appointments, and our ambassador had to sit down with Doe and explain to him how a statesman behaves. Doe did not seem to understand or care that his behavior as a visiting head of state reflected not only on him, but also on the country and the people he represented. Our ambassador would be called upon often to reiterate this lesson during Doe's two-week visit to the U.S. Fortunately for Doe, he was accompanied by an American ambassador who was a skilled diplomat, but whose patience must have been tested during those two weeks.

A few days later I flew back to Liberia taking hundreds of photos that our professional photographers had taken. It was only when I was on the plane that I remembered the photos were in my checked baggage. I knew if that suitcase was lost, my career was over. What a stupid thing to have done. I should have hand-carried those photos and kept them close to my body at all times. All of Liberia awaited those photos.

The Liberian press had not sent any photos back, and the entire country wanted to see how the Head of State had been greeted in the U.S. Fortunately, my luggage arrived safely and my office immediately assembled a display of photos in windows outside our office where they were seen by hundreds of Liberians.

Leaving Liberia

All is never said.

- *Togo*

A few weeks after returning from the Doe visit to the U.S., I received a telephone call from my career counselor saying that the African Area Director wanted me to go to Swaziland in Southern Africa as the Public Affairs Officer. It was quite an honor for the Area Director to suggest my name for such a position. I would be the head of USIS. This is what all USIA officers aspire to: to be the head of your own office. I was excited but fearful and reluctant to leave the place I loved, and where my career was flourishing. I knew nothing about Swaziland, only that it was in Southern Africa and that it was a kingdom. I was not scheduled to leave Monrovia for another six months, and I wanted my six more months, but this was an opportunity to head my own post. Yet I hesitated. Perhaps it was time to leave. I was exasperated with the PAO who let incoming cables lay unanswered for weeks, as did outgoing cables that the Cultural Affairs Officer and I wrote. They lay on his desk buried under reports buried under other cables. If the ambassador sneezed, the PAO would grab his briefcase and head for the embassy. When I think of him, I think of a Dagwood Bumstead character with briefcase in hand, instead of a sandwich, flying out of the office. He spent more time at the embassy than at our office which

I found frustrating. I agreed to accept the assignment in Swaziland, even though I had misgivings.

I looked forward to being my own boss, only answering to the ambassador. I told a few friends that I would be leaving. Everybody seemed happy for me. Inside I grieved that they had not liked me as much as I liked them, or else why would they be so happy at my departure. It was pity party time. Suddenly it was two weeks before I was due to leave and the roof blew off. The Ministry of Information hosted a luncheon for me at a restaurant. As I dressed for the luncheon, I was listening to one of my friends on the radio and he dedicated a song to me by the Commodores, "Three Times a Lady." I began crying. Present at the luncheon were all of my media friends who worked for the Ministry of Information, including the Minister of Information and the deputy ministers. I was in tears at the accolades and admiration expressed. I could only murmur my thanks.

The *Daily Observer* newspaper printed a huge photo of me on its front page, and the headline of the story was, "Charlene Leaves For Swaziland." I had a terrible cold when the photo was taken and I looked awful to put it mildly. My eyes seemed barely opened. My sore nose seemed bulbous from all the blowing, and my hair looked like a rat's nest. Instead of asking the editor, Kenneth Best, why he used that photo, I asked why he used just my first name in the headline.

He chuckled and said, "Everybody in Liberia knows Charlene."

Other newspaper articles bade me farewell, and quoted the Minister of Information, Col. Grey D. Allison, as saying that I had strengthened Liberian-US relations.

In an uncommon public tribute, Col. Allison was quoted in the Liberian press as thanking me for "invaluable assistance to the Liberian government and people during her tenure."

Author receiving a gift upon her departure from Liberia from
the Liberian Minister of Information, Col. Gray D. Allison,
at a dinner in her honor at his residence - October, 1982

He added that I had opened a "new dimension" in U.S.-Liberian friendship. This in effect established a benchmark, a standard against which future USIA officers would be measured. Col. Allison and his wife hosted a dinner for me at their home where I was presented with an album filled with messages and photos. Around midnight the Minister took ten of us to a new, hot nightspot where we danced until 5 a.m. Another evening the top three female journalists in the country hosted a dinner dance for me. It went on all night. Ambassador Swing arrived late after another engagement, and he danced with us 'till the wee hours. I was becoming very weary and getting very little sleep. I was trying to wrap up my work, leave notes for my successor, and pack my personal belongings. My cold hung on, but the parties continued. At one point I marveled that I had thought nobody would miss me and that I would just tip-toe away.

Ambassador Swing held a farewell dinner at the residence and all of my friends and contacts were invited. Despite my tears, coughing and stopped up nose, I was elated. I was surrounded by all of my favorite people – Liberian journalists, and Deputy Chief of Mission Ed Perkins, and Ambassador William Lacy Swing. The ambassador turned off the air-conditioning because I was cold, but then everybody else sweltered. He wouldn't hear of cutting it on again because I would be cold. Every time someone began a farewell speech my tears welled up. I cried almost constantly. After dinner I sat on a sofa and about five people squeezed on it with me. Others sat on the floor at my feet. I heard the ambassador tell those sitting on the floor around me that there were chairs, but they refused and continued to sit close to me. I loved my Liberians. I felt completely at home there. Nobody questioned why a black woman was talking about "constructive engagement" which was code for maintaining apartheid in South Africa. They understood that my position required that nonsense be spoken on occasion. They understood that no black American could spout such garbage and mean it. I loved them for it. Now I was leaving the nest for the wild beyond. This was supposed to be a happy period. I was going on to something bigger and grander. I was going to be my own boss and run my own post, tiny though it would be. Somehow I knew deep inside that this would be the last time that I would feel such love and warmth in another country, or encounter a people as gentle, as loving and as welcoming as Liberians. They have a passion and fervor for life that is infectious.

The articles and the farewells continued. There were luncheons, dinners and parties. I drew the line when some wanted to host breakfasts for me. Friends and colleagues began making plans to accompany me to the airport. I never want anyone to see me off because I cry when goodbyes are in order. Plus, in Liberia the road to the airport is curvy and treacherous and many have lost their lives going to or from Robertsfield. I did not want that to happen. I finally convinced friends that it was important to me that they not go to the airport. I was already operating on my last nerve, and with a throng of people at the airport saying goodbye I would have had to be carried onto the plane.

Departure day arrived. As I began getting dressed to leave for the airport visitors began arriving. My Liberian friends who would have gone to the airport came to say goodbye. I could hardly get dressed. Henry kept knocking on my bedroom door telling me that somebody else had arrived.

Everybody in the U.S. diplomatic community knew and liked Henry, my houseman. He was an excellent bartender and server. They all wanted to use his services at their events. Our ambassador wanted Henry to work fulltime in his residence after I left Liberia. Henry and I talked and he said he would be happy to help out at the ambassador's residence, but he did not want to work there fulltime because the ambassador entertained so often.

When I told the ambassador's special assistant she said, "That's fine. As long as Henry can help us out from time to time. We just don't want to lose him."

Henry stayed on to work for my successor who wrote to me, "Henry is the best mother we (she and her daughter) ever had!"

My last visitor was a young, black embassy communicator who came with his two-year-old daughter.

He held her up and said, "Look at Charlene and remember her. She is your role model."

The little one looked at me with big, beautiful eyes, and she seemed to understand what her father had said.

I took her hand and said, "You will make all of us proud one day."

I hugged them both and stepped into the car. At last it was just the driver, George, and me. Just the way I wanted it.

As I rode through the streets of Monrovia for the last time, I thought back to the day I arrived in Liberia. I had looked forward to working in Liberia and it did not disappoint. I said a prayer that the country and its people would someday have a just leader who would not enrich himself at their expense. They deserved so much better. Little did I know that the situation would go from bad to worse to maniacal during a civil war that would keep the country in disarray for years. Neither did I know that my Liberian friends soon would be choosing sides; that some would be against the others; that some would be killed, or that I would be asked to return to head USIS in Liberia and would decide to turn it down because of my closeness to the people and the country. May God bless Liberia, a country raped repeatedly by its own people in the name of greed. It was October, 1982.

In the Lion's Den: Welcome to Southern Africa
October, 1982 — July 31, 1983

The world is white no longer, and it will never be white again.
- James Baldwin

My introduction to Southern Africa began at the airport in Paris, France, and it wasn't pleasant. It was October 14, 1982. My mother was accompanying me to Swaziland. I invited her to come because of her concern that I would be living in a mud hut. She had seen a *Sixty Minutes* program on Swazi royalty. The royal kraals were built of mud. Mother thought that if the king and queens of Swaziland lived in mud huts, that her daughter would live in the same or worse. She had not yet learned that being a diplomat has its rewards. We were enroute to my new assignment in Swaziland as Public Affairs Officer, spokeswoman for the United States Embassy, and First Secretary of the United States Embassy (my diplomatic title). I had stopped over for a briefing at our office in Paris. Much material used by our offices in Africa came from Paris and officers assigned to Africa generally stopped in Paris for a briefing. My office had booked us on the most direct route to Swaziland which was via South African Airways. We were in for an 18-hour flight to Johannesburg, South Africa, where we would spend the night, and fly to Mbabane, Swaziland, the next afternoon.

The flight would be long because few black African countries allowed South African planes to land for refueling due to the law of apartheid existing in South Africa. Because of that, we had to fly out of the way to refuel in Cape Verde. I was going to spend one day at our office in Johannesburg before flying to Mbabane, Swaziland. I looked forward to being in South Africa with a great deal of fear and foreboding. I had read much about the mistreatment of blacks in South Africa, and nothing made me think that I would not receive the same treatment.

At the Paris airport Mother and I were standing in a long line that slowly snaked its way to the check-in desk when I noticed a beefy, white family of four, two adults and two children, standing several yards across the way staring at us. Afrikaners I thought. They seemed to be discussing us. I could not imagine why, and I idly wondered why they were not getting in line since the line was growing longer. Suddenly the woman went to the head of the line and spoke to one of the two clerks taking tickets. She turned and gestured at Mother and me. The clerk leaned over the desk, looked at Mother and me, and shook her head negatively. By this time Mother and I were extremely curious. I wondered what the woman could be saying about us since she didn't know us or anything about us. I decided that I would ignore her. I had just turned away when suddenly the woman was standing beside me.

I turned to face her and she announced in an unmistakable South African accent, "We are going to get in front of you."

I knew I had not heard her correctly.

I said, "Excuse me?"

She repeated haughtily and rather impatiently, "We're going to get in front of you."

I knew I didn't hear what I had heard. I glanced at Mother whose face wore a quizzical expression. I wondered who was crazy here, me or this woman so bold as to declare that she and her family were going to get in front of us.

She repeated it, "Did you hear me? We're going to get in front of you."

I found my tongue, "No, you're not."

She replied, "Oh, going to be difficult are you?"

I said, "If being difficult means not letting you get in front of us, then YES I'm going to be very difficult!"

I could hear my voice rising. I tried to remember that I was a diplomat, and that Mother was with me.

This adventure had begun on Thursday when Mother met me in Washington. We flew out of Dulles Airport to Paris, France, where I was to have a day of orientation at our office in Paris. We arrived in Paris on a Friday morning. Our embassy in Paris had made our hotel reservations. When we arrived at the small hotel in Paris, I was told that we had one bed. I asked why. That was the only room available and it had a double bed. I called our embassy from the front desk and spoke to the person who had made the reservation. He saw nothing wrong with one bed for two women. I asked if he would have the same attitude had it been two men. Silence from the other end. We were sleepy and tired and went to our room. It was a small room behind the desk. I am sure that it was the room for the bonne, the maid. Mother sat in a chair as I undressed and got into bed. I kept telling her to get in, but she knew how I disliked sleeping with someone else, so she sat in the chair.

I woke up a few hours later, showered and went to the USIS office. I told them about the one bed, and I asked them to call the Hilton to get us a room which they did. I arrived back at the hotel and happily told Mother that we were moving to the Hilton. She was delighted. We checked out of the hotel and took a taxi to the Hilton where we were shown to a lovely room with two beds. The next day I took Mother on a tour of Paris and that evening we went to see the Folies Bergeres, the famous French music hall show. Sunday morning we went to Mass and strolled back to the hotel. We finished packing and left for the airport.

Now I glared at the brazen Afrikaner. I could not believe she had such nerve. I wondered if I needed to shake myself to wake up. I also wanted to shake the hell out of her. We had not yet arrived in South Africa, and we were tasting their apartheid already. She turned on her heel and rejoined her family. There was much talking and looking at us. I scowled at them in an attempt to discourage any more contact with us. After much discussion with her family, the woman came towards us again. I turned to face her head on. She had probably never been exposed to a free, angry, black American woman. If not, then she was in for a treat. She could tell that we were not South Africans by our speech and our dress. Her attempts to intimidate and indoctrinate us were not setting well with me. As she walked toward us, Mother and I glared at her. Directly in front of us was a burly, white male, apparently South African, and the woman asked him if she and her family could get in front of him. He permitted them to. She was determined not to stand in a line with two black women ahead of her. When we reached the desk I told the clerk what had happened.

She apologized and said, "I'm so sorry. The woman came to the desk to tell me that she and her family were going to get in front of you because they did not want to get at the end of the long line. I told her that she could not do that in France. We do not permit that."

I was amazed at the nerve of the South African woman. On the plane the family was seated not far from us. I thought about walking by and pouring hot coffee down the woman's back. I thought about banging her head with my shoe. I thought of all kinds of terrible things to do to her, but then I thought about Mother who was already nervous about spending any time in South Africa. What would happen to her if I got arrested? I prayed and a calm came over me. I thanked God that Mother was with me. I don't know what I might have done or said had she not been there.

Before we landed at the Johannesburg airport we were given disembarkation forms. One question was, "Are you carrying any drugs?" Mother had a small kit full of prescribed medicines for her heart, blood pressure and other ailments. I wondered if the South African authorities meant prescription drugs, or did they really expect somebody to confess to carrying illegal drugs? I was in a quandary. We were now in the lion's den and the wrong answer would keep us there. I decided to check the "Yes" box. We went through Customs and as the official read the form, his eyes popped.

He stared at us in disbelief and asked, "You're carrying drugs?!"

Oops, wrong answer. My heart dropped to my knees.

I hastened to explain that they were all prescribed medications for my mother, and I showed him the bottles. We passed. Reservations had been made for us at one of the few integrated hotels in the city of Johannesburg. We checked in and finally relaxed after our long flight and the stress of being in this unsavory country. I had been given directions on how to walk the few blocks to the USIS office from our hotel the next day. The next morning I called the office to tell them I was on the way. What I didn't say, but what I wanted to say was: If I have not arrived in a few minutes, start looking for me. I left Mother and went out onto the streets of Johannesburg. I tried to blend in, but there was no way I could. I saw a number of trains arriving and disgorging blacks who were rushing to their jobs. I soon realized I was lost. I tried to retrace my steps and got even more lost. I stopped three different black people to ask for directions, but they did not understand English. I began sweating.

A white South African man saw me standing still, looking puzzled, and asked if he could help. I did not want to be seen talking to a white man on the street. I thought that was forbidden. I ignored him and turned away. He persisted, and finally in order to get him away from me, I told him where I was trying to go. He said it was nearby, and he would walk me there. I asked him to just tell me how to get there, but he insisted on walking with me. I felt faint. We walked about two blocks. I have no idea what he said because I was watching for the police to arrive. When we arrived at USIS, I thanked him and hurried inside. Afterwards a staff member walked me back to the hotel. The next morning we flew to Mbabane, Swaziland.

The Kingdom of Swaziland

People of the same blood eat from the same pot.

- Lesotho

As we left our Royal Swazi jet upon arriving in Mbabane, Swaziland, we were met by a photographer and the departing Public Affairs Officer who was overlapping with me for a few days. We were driven to the PAO residence, an ivy-covered, brick dwelling, which consisted of three bedrooms, four bathrooms, a den, living room, dining room, kitchen, family room, a 35 ft. room for entertaining, large entrance halls, and two fireplaces, one in the entrance hall. It was October and spring was in bloom. The purple blossoms of jacaranda trees decorated the grounds of my residence. The staff consisted of a housekeeper and two gardeners to care for the flowers and grounds. I had flowers in all the bathrooms, hallways, bedrooms, living room, etc. What a treat that was. My housekeeper, Esther, was pleasant, not lovable, but correct. The living room furniture and drapery reeked of smoke from the large fireplace that was lit daily to warm the living room. There were no fireplaces in the bedrooms where they were needed most.

The Kingdom of Swaziland conjures up notions of tininess, prettiness, delicateness and a magical quality about the country. Swaziland had few of those attributes. The capital city, Mbabane, is nestled comfortably between majestic mountains known as Sheba's Breasts. South Africa surrounds the country on three sides, and Mozambique is on the fourth side. The culture is steeped in skullduggery ranging from the royal family to the common folk.

When shaking hands with Swazis their left hand grasps their right wrist to show that the left hand is not reaching for a weapon while the right hand is engaged in the handshake. While some embassy officials adopted this handshake, I did not because of the absolute deceit lurking behind the custom. Swaziland is a true monarchy, operating with parallel western-style and traditional governments.

The King of Swaziland, King Sobuza II, died shortly before I arrived in the kingdom. He was also known as The Ngwenyama, the Lion. Sobuza ruled for 60 years. He ruled jointly with the Queen Mother, The Ndlovukazi, the She Elephant. The king approved all decisions affecting the traditional society. When King Sobuza died, the position of The Authorized Person was created. The Authorized Person made decisions with the advice of a tiny group of traditional advisors known as the Liqoqo. In traditional and modern society, decisions are reached by consensus. In theory this results in a non-confrontational society; however, if alcohol is involved the Swazis are the most confrontational people one would ever meet. The country has one of the highest rates of alcoholism in Africa. It is a traditional society that views with suspicion non-Swazi ideas such as the competitiveness of free enterprise, and democracy. Such attitudes led to the prohibition of open political activities and extensive control over labor unions. The South African influence was strong in the kingdom and not always in harmony with U.S. interests.

I found that most Swazis read South African newspapers and got their international news from South Africa, news which was filtered for a black audience. The political sector of the government operated in a complicated manner of royal and family relationships.

When King Sobuza ruled the country it was simply an extension of his family. Some say he had 81 wives; others say the number is larger and unknown. Nearly every person in the kingdom is a Dlamini - the name of the royal family - or is married to one. The king's wealth consisted of cattle, as is the case in many agrarian societies.

Shortly before my predecessor left the country, noted Swazi anthropologist, Thoko Ginindza, contacted me after seeing me on Swazi television. The former PAO was amazed and said he had been inviting her to events for three years and she never came, and yet she called to meet me. Mother and I liked Thoko immediately. One Sunday she took us to visit her family kraal in the countryside. We sat on the ground and tried to communicate with her grandmother and her uncle. It was quite an educational experience for Mother. I watched her as she took in everything around her. The uncle was bare-chested and Swazi skins covered his front and rear. The grandmother spoke to us in SiSwati and she told Thoko that Mother and I were trying to pretend that we didn't speak it. Thoko tried to explain that we were Americans, but that didn't make a bit of difference to her. She could not grasp the concept that we were from another country across the ocean.

When we left the family kraal, Thoko's uncle gave us a live chicken. Thoko explained that it was a welcome present. We returned home with the trussed chicken in the trunk of the car. Once at home he was put in the garage and the next day I gave it to Esther. I could not bring myself to kill and eat the chicken.

Back in the U.S., I didn't eat chicken until I no longer had to accompany Aunt Bess to the chicken market on Saturday to pick out a live chicken and watch her wring its neck in the backyard for Sunday dinner.

She then dunked it in a huge pot of hot water. Oh, the smell. There was no way I was going to eat anything that smelled like that! Then she cut it open and pulled out the innards. Yuk. I would only eat ground beef and Mother had to learn 100 ways to fix it. To her credit, she did.

My predecessor had basically neglected the office while he enjoyed his hobby of acting in a local theater group. I began working 12 hour days, for almost seven days a week. I attended Mass on Saturday evenings so that I could spend all day Sunday at the office. Several Swazis asked me if I left my car at the office and walked home. I said no, that when they saw my car at the office it meant that I was there. I had had no idea of the work that a one-officer post required. We had the same amount of cables and reports to write that the largest post had. The problem was there was only one officer – me. Be that as it may, I was up to the task. The office staff consisted of a Swazi librarian, a Swazi driver-deliveryman, and a British woman, Susan, who informed me that she ran the office. The cleaning woman also acted as receptionist. I had no secretary or press assistant. The previous PAO spent a lot of time with his theatre group, and allowed Susan to oversee the office and terrorize the staff. She was usually in her office entertaining visitors, drinking tea or chatting on the telephone. She told me with great delight that the Swazis were "drunkards" and "stupid." I asked why she remained in the country feeling the way she did. Oh, she claimed that she had great friends among the Swazis.

She had never written a cable about anything, she proudly proclaimed, and there was strong inference that she was not going to begin now. The office was in shambles. The files were a mess. I work hard and I expect others to do the same.

I was in the office every day by 6:30 am and I went home around 6:30 pm. I didn't expect anyone else in the office to put in 12 hours a day. I simply wanted them to do their work during the work hours. I didn't have an Information Assistant which I needed badly. I continued to remind Susan of her work requirements and what I expected of her. She seemed a bit taken aback. She was not helpful; in fact, her inability to produce work made more work for me. I would assign something with a deadline – we always had deadlines – and if the deadline was not met by her, it meant that I then had to do the task she was supposed to have done, and I had less time to get it done. I was working too hard to put up with nonsense. Eventually it became necessary to fire Susan. Within minutes of her departure the news was all over town, and Swazis began calling to congratulate me for firing her. She didn't take it lying down. She went to the ambassador. She contacted our embassy in South Africa to appeal to them to force me to rehire her. They all reminded her that I was the head of USIS in Mbabane and the decision to hire or to fire her was mine and mine alone. She called our office in Washington, but nothing could be done without my approval, and I was not having her back under any circumstances. I hired two new FSNs and an American part-time secretary. With Susan's departure, the atmosphere in the office changed. The staff was more relaxed and not on edge every minute.

New staff meant training them. I continued laboring under the burden of lack of qualified staff, little or no mission support, and months of 12 hour work days. The Swazi press began clamoring for interviews.

I had begun using program opportunities such as American participants, videotapes and assorted visitors to promote U.S. interests and to develop my widening circle of contacts. My first public appearance was a television interview by an American expatriate living in Swaziland and highly critical of USIS. It took place in my residence with Mother looking on. He was a hostile questioner, but I maintained my poise and explained fully and authoritatively the agency's mission and my role as PAO. After the interview aired a number of my contacts spoke favorably of the interview and most expressed annoyance at the questioner.

I was surprised to learn that in the three years of USIS operation in Mbabane, the Fulbright Scholarship program had never been in effect. When I arrived the Fulbright application deadline was close at hand, but I engaged the necessary cooperation from the agency and Swazi officials, thus ensuring post participation for the first time. As I established more exchange programs interest by the Swazi populace as a whole was very gratifying. The press picked up on this and sought interviews which resulted in university professors coming into the office to ask how we could help them to get more training or how we could help their students get advanced degrees. One candidate nominated by my office was selected to participate in the Hubert H. Humphrey Program, and three out of four candidates proposed for the Fulbright program were awarded scholarships.

During the first few months I selected six American specialists to visit and speak to selected audiences. They were warmly received by the Swazi community and given full coverage by the Swazi media. Everything our cultural center did was followed closely by the media and printed or broadcast to an interested audience.

Working in Swaziland was going to be a challenge. The country had a legacy of a colonial mentality. The traditional role relegated to women was not liberating. The people were suspicions of the U.S. and its policy toward South Africa. It was a nation steeped in tradition and extremely reluctant to enter the twentieth century. The Swazis were accustomed to nodding and winking at the white South Africans, especially the South African men who came to Swaziland on weekends looking for hot women. I resented it seemingly more than the Swazis.

Ambassador Klunker

"I'll bet when you get down on them rusty knees and get to
worrying God, he just goes in his privy house and slams the door.
That's what he's thinking about you and your prayers."

- Zora Neale Hurston

I worked with some brilliant, wonderful, gracious and outstanding
ambassadors, and then I got a clunker, the man designated to be the U.S.
Ambassador to the Kingdom of Swaziland, Robert H. Phinney. I met him
in Washington, D.C. shortly after he had stumbled through his Senate
Confirmation Hearings. He had not studied the massive notebooks prepared
by skilled foreign service officers detailing U.S. – Swaziland relations. He
knew next to nothing about the delicate balance Swaziland had to maintain
being surrounded by South Africa on three sides, or the differences between
a kingdom and a democracy, and he knew little about official U.S. policy in
southern Africa. During the hearings he demonstrated his lack of knowledge.
He was a disaster; however, the Senate, in its wisdom, decreed that he could
go to Swaziland as an ambassador only if he had a Deputy Chief of Mission
(DCM) in the embassy. They apparently realized that he was not capable of
administering an embassy without someone to guide him. Swaziland had never
before had an ambassador and a DCM because it is such a small post. A low-level
political officer was assigned as DCM. There was also concern in Washington as
to how the Swazis might react to having a U.S. ambassador who was a laughing

stock in his own country. The July 1982 issue of the Washingtonian Magazine carried an article on, "Best and Worst Ambassadors." The magazine called him, "Mr. Klunker." The article said he knew nothing about Africa, and detailed how he had flubbed his responses to questions from U.S. Senators during the Confirmation Hearings.

When I met him at a meeting at the State Department with the Swaziland desk officer, Ambassador Klunker asked me some silly questions, and he seemed to be very uncomfortable. The outgoing country officer was a black male, and I noticed that Ambassador Klunker never addressed him during the meeting. Later I learned Ambassador Klunker blamed the black desk officer for not "preparing him" for the Senate Hearings, even though it was Klunker's duty to study the exhaustive briefing books prepared by the desk officer. At this meeting he learned that his Public Affairs Officer and embassy spokesperson was a black female. He kept a pained expression on his red, wrinkled face. When the meeting ended, the new country officer, a white female, walked me to the elevator.

Her final words to me were, "Try to get to know the ambassador on a personal level."

I thought that was an odd thing to say. I had gotten negative vibes from him, and I could tell that there would be no "personal level" in our relationship. Much later I realized the country officer knew that it was going to be difficult, if not impossible, for a black officer to work with the man, that he would never accept me as a representative of the United States government. From the moment of my arrival in Swaziland Ambassador Klunker made life difficult, excruciatingly difficult, I should emphasize.

The first out of body experience concerned the movie, "Roots," and high level contacts. One Sunday Thoko invited me to the home of her aunt and uncle. On the way I learned that her uncle was the Prime Minister of Swaziland, Prince Mabandla Dlamini. We had a wonderful time with the prince and his family. The Prime Minister asked if my office had a copy of the movie, "Roots," which we did. He said he and his family would like to see it, and I promised to take it over soon.

A few days later I mentioned to Ambassador Klunker that I had met the Prime Minister.

He snarled, "What business do you have hobnobbing with the Prime Minister?"

No need to be diplomatic with a black officer. Just curl your lip and ask who the hell does she think she is meeting with the Prime Minister. No ambassador had ever spoken to me in such a manner. He addressed me as he probably would not speak to a guttersnipe.

I swallowed and calmly replied, "Thoko Ginindza invited me to visit her aunt and uncle. On the way to their house she happened to mention that her uncle is the Prime Minister."

In any other country, a PAO would be applauded for making such a high level contact that could benefit the embassy as a whole. Ambassador Klunker was livid. When I added that the Prime Minister wanted me to show "Roots" to his family, he almost had a stroke.

He thundered, "You will not show 'Roots' to anybody!"

I responded, "Excuse me?"

He said, "That movie doesn't show the U.S. in the best light. It makes white Americans seem cruel."

And? I wanted to ask.

He added, "And besides, my black friends said 'Roots' does not represent black history."

I nearly choked. I knew in my heart that he did not have any "black friends." I pointed out that the book and the movie had been hailed by blacks and whites. At the time it was shown, it was the most watched TV program in history. I said every country I had served in, USIS had shown "Roots" time and time again. I said it was the story of one man's roots, and historians felt it was an accurate depiction of slaves brought from Africa. I also pointed out that a major part of American history was the history of black people. Ambassador Klunker said a driver could deliver the film to the Prime Minister's residence. I said that would be a major insult to the Prime Minister. He repeated that I was not to take the film to the Prime Minister's home.

Klunker said he wanted to be "the only contact with the Prime Minister to prevent any misunderstandings from happening through something said."

I left his office seething.

The following day Ambassador Klunker came to my office to "explain." He said he had had second thoughts and felt more harm would be done if I didn't take the film to the Prime Minister's residence.

He said I should go this time, but thereafter I was "never to go to the Prime Minister's home, or have any contact with him."

He also said embassy officers should not have contacts above the Permanent Secretary level. He then immediately changed his mind and said no contacts above the Deputy Minister level. I learned later that this mandate only applied to the two black officers who headed their agencies in Mbabane. I told him that my integrity and professionalism were being challenged, and that was a new experience for me. He asked about my previous posts. I said at other posts the ambassadors encouraged us to have contacts at the highest level.

This ambassador is going to be a pisscutter! I'm ready for it, but what will it do to my career?

Ambassador Klunker had not yet been able to present his credentials because he arrived in Swaziland during the mourning period for King Sobuza, and no new ambassadors were being accredited during that period. Therefore, for all intents and purposes the U.S. ambassador was not in the country and could have no contact with government officials. Therefore, he was jealous and critical of those of us who did have high level government contacts.

A few days after our conversation about "Roots," Klunker summoned me to his office.

He began, "I wonder if I made myself clear that you are not to have any contacts at the Prime Minister level?"

"Quite clear."

"Do you have any questions about my decision?"

"Just one. What do I say if I am invited to a party at the Prime Minister's home?"

"You say you are not qualified to meet on that level. That's the ambassador's job."

"That's what you want me to say if I am invited to a party at the Prime Minister's?"

He looked confused, "Well, you'll think of something."

He then asked, "Are you comfortable with my decision?"

I replied, "I don't have to be comfortable with it. I will follow your orders."

Back in my office I called the Deputy Director of the African Area at USIA, Washington and told him the difficulty I was encountering in working with this ambassador. He said he or the Director would contact State re "this stupidity." The next day a cable arrived from the Director that he was coming to Swaziland after a conference in Zimbabwe and wanted an appointment with the ambassador.

I had not planned to unpack my belongings since I didn't know how long I could put up with such an ignorant, racist ambassador, but I decided I would feel better with my paintings and carvings around me, and I unpacked.

My Director arrived and spent two hours with Ambassador Klunker. He told me later that Klunker was embarrassed that the Director came. Klunker had the nerve to say that the "handbook said I could supervise mission contacts." The Director said Klunker would relax once he presented his credentials. He said Klunker felt threatened by me and Melina, the black officer from another agency.

He said he tried to tell Klunker what my job was, but "it goes in one ear and out the other." He also told Klunker that he was getting quite a reputation in Washington.

First, there was a problem with the black desk officer, and now he had a problem with the two black female officers here. He said Klunker feels that all career FS officers resent him because he's a political appointee.

I resent him because he's dumb!

A few months later, Chris Matthews, then special assistant to Rep. Tip O'Neill, now moderator of "Hard Ball," came to Swaziland to speak on U.S. politics. He brought his wife, Kathleen, a TV news anchor in Washington, D.C., and their new baby. Chris had been a Peace Corps Volunteer in Swaziland in the '60s, and he was excited about being back in the country after a long absence. He spoke at the university, and I made an appointment for him to meet with the Secretary to the Prime Minister who was a personal contact of mine. The Secretary to the Prime Minister does not type or take notes. It's a considerably elevated position. I accompanied them to the meeting, and at the end, the Secretary asked if they would like to meet the Prime Minister. I knew he was doing this as a special favor to me, and I was thrilled for them. Chris and Kathleen were delighted. The Secretary opened the door for the Matthews to go into the Prime Minister's chamber. I remain seated.

He said, "Charlene, aren't you coming?"

I said nothing. I was thinking. I knew if I went in the ambassador would say that I was insubordinate because he had forbidden me to meet with the Prime Minister. On the other hand if I didn't go in, he would say that I embarrassed him.

I smiled and said, "I'm sorry, but the ambassador has said I am not to have any contact with the Prime Minister."

After we left the Prime Minister's office, I explained to Chris and Kathleen why I had not gone into the Prime Minister's office. They were shocked. Chris asked if he could tell the ambassador that I did NOT go into the Prime Minister's office.

I gleefully said, "Please do!"

When they paid their final call on the ambassador Chris enthusiastically told him that because of me they had the pleasure of meeting the Prime Minister. The Klunker glared at me. Chris hastened to assure him that I did not go into the Prime Minister's office due to his order forbidding me to have any contact with him. Klunker's face turned flaming red. I nearly guffawed. As soon as Chris and Kathleen left the country I was summoned back to Ambassador Klunker's office. He pulled open a desk drawer as usual. Some of us suspected that he turned on a tape recorder whenever he met with certain officers.

He thundered, "Why didn't you go into the Prime Minister's office?"

I said innocently, "Didn't you order me to have no contact with the Prime Minister?"

He said, "You should have gone in!"

I smiled smugly and repeated his orders. He was humiliated because I didn't go in, and he knew that would get around the halls in Washington making him look like the jerk that he was. Too bad. If I were going to be damned either way, I would choose the way that would benefit me the most. I kept smiling and acting innocent until he gave up in disgust.

Cultures Collide

I'm sick and tired of being sick and tired.

-Fannie Lou Hamer

When King Sobuza II died in August, 1982, two months before my arrival in Swaziland, one of his many wives, Queen Mother Dzeliwe was appointed regent. In Swaziland the king is not allowed to select his successor. The Liqoqo, the Supreme Council of State, decides which wife of the king will be the She-Elephant/Queen Mother. The son of that queen will be the next king. In deciding on who will be king, a lot depends on the mother. She must have only one son and she must be of sterling character. Once the king is appointed, he can only marry a woman after she becomes pregnant, proof that she can bear his heirs.

Friday, February 25, 1983, was the opening of Parliament. Queen Mother Dzeliwe would be making her first public appearance at the ceremony. She now ruled the country with the advice and consent of the Liqoqo, the Supreme Council of State, until that Council chose a male heir. On Tuesday I mentioned to the DCM that I would be going to the opening of Parliament. Shortly thereafter I had a telephone call from the ambassador asking me to come to the embassy. The DCM was also present. The Klunker opened the meeting by saying he hoped we could work together closely in the future, and said he had some ideas about the Prime Minister and the U.S. image in Swaziland. Then he got to the real reason I had been summoned.

He said he had wanted the DCM to attend the opening of Parliament, but the office of Foreign Affairs said there was limited seating and only the ambassador could attend. I said nothing.

He asked, "How are you getting to attend?"

I replied that the Swaziland Broadcasting Service issued two press passes for my press assistant and me. He then asked why was I going. I explained that it was a part of my function as the Public Affairs Officer to attend such events and to report on them.

He is so dumb! Dumb! Dumb! And so transparent! He has no clue as to what my job is. The DCM is almost as dumb! They probably thought I got my passes through the Prime Minister or some other high level official that I should have no contact with.

The meeting ended with the Klunker saying he hoped we can meet daily when I return from home leave.

Daily? It's time for a transfer! I will not be meeting daily with an idiot ambassador who has no clue that he's an idiot!

My press aide, Enoch, and I sat in lofty seats at Parliament awaiting the appearance of the Queen. One minister after another arrived draped in the traditional animal skins around the waist, with a Swazi scarf fixed over the chest, leaving one shoulder bare, and some ministers carried spears and shields of animal skins bearing the Swazi emblem. Some carried knobkerries, a combination cane/weapon. All of these accoutrements were reminders that they came from a nation of warriors and warriors they remained.

Lesser royals, princesses, princes and handmaidens arrived. When the chamber was full, Her Majesty Dzeliwe, Queen Regent and She Elephant, entered to songs praising her. Weighty goatskins made up her skirt. What looked like bullets encircled her waist, and surrounded her elaborate beehive hairdo, the signature hair-do of Swazi women. The queen was a large, hefty woman. She carried a staff, was barefoot, and bracelets encircled her ample ankles. She sat on the edge of a chair on the dais surrounded by the Authorized Person, the Police commissioner, the Army commander and two female guards. A young girl sat at her feet, as is the custom. The royal family feels that only a youngster is innocent of the traditional royal family intrigues and poisonings. The same youngster also cooked for the queen. It was rumored that poisoning was the preferred way of dispatching enemies within the royal family. The

Queen seemed shy, and she sweated profusely. From time to time she wiped her face. She was unaccustomed to being in the limelight. The She Elephant was always in the shadow of The Ngwenyama (Lion) and King of Swaziland, Sobhuza II, who ruled for more than 60 years before his death. The Queen's robust figure bore the heavy skins gracefully. In this modern day, many Swazi women used material of black toweling or other black material as skirts, rather than the heavy, and often smelly, skins. The Queen wore the real thing. She was a figure from yesteryear, and I felt as if I had been transported back in time to the days of Shaka Zulu, the fierce warrior of the Zulus who waged war in Southern Africa in the early years. I was accustomed to seeing the ministers in three piece suits, but today was a special occasion, and they had dressed according to tradition.

The Minister of Education read the Queen's speech in English and it was then translated into SiSwati. When he finished the Queen's speech, more praise songs were sung to her as she left the chamber. Parliament was now officially opened. It was an exciting time, and both Enoch and I were thrilled at what we had just seen. It is rare that one sees the She Elephant. We strolled through the gardens of Parliament smiling and shaking hands, and then I felt movement. It felt as if the ground was shaking. I asked Enoch what was happening. He said the food was coming. I was puzzled. Suddenly there were huge platters of enormous chunks of meat being passed around. The meat was heaped on trays the size of a door that took two people to carry - one at the front and the other at the rear. There was much pushing and shoving. People were snatching and grabbing the meat. Enoch leaped in and using both hands grabbed two huge chunks of meat. There were no napkins in sight. Enoch turned and tried to hand me one of the chunks of meat. I stared at it. Again he offered it, and remembering my Peace Corps training of never insulting a host country national, I took the chunk of meat in my bare hand. We walked toward the exit and my car. When we were out of sight of the guests, I handed Enoch the meat, which he happily wolfed down. The stately attendees at the opening of Parliament all but fought for a chunk of the meat, grabbed it, and gobbled it. Cultures definitely collided that day in the gardens of Parliament.

Worry and Revelation

*When you're a black woman, you seldom get to do just
what you want to do; you always do what you have to do.*
                                                    - Dorothy I. Height

When one is far away from home, illnesses of older family members is
even more serious than when you are with them. To get to the U.S. from
Swaziland, I had a two hour flight on Royal Swazi Airlines to Johannesburg,
South Africa. There was a layover of several hours. I then took Pan American
for an 12 hr. flight to New York City or Washington, DC, and then waited for
a plane going to Indianapolis. The overseas portion took 18 hours flying time.
The entire trip could be done in about 24 hours if all the stars were aligned.

On January 24, 1983 Daddy Doug Jackson, my other father, called
from Indianapolis to tell me that Mother was in the hospital and had been
for one week due to a nose bleed. She could not have visitors and her doctor
would not return his calls. He and his wife, Mama Gladys, felt that I should
know. Of course Mother did not want me to know because she was always
concerned about worrying me. The Jacksons told me that Uncle Rabbit had
had colon surgery and was released from the hospital three days ago. He had
been recuperating at Aunt Bess'. When she took him in for a check-up, they
immediately placed him in intensive care.

*Oh, Lord, my family is falling apart! Those are my only three remaining
family members.*

235

The next day I called Aunt Bess. She didn't know what was going on with Mother either. I told her not to worry, that I would try to get my Washington office to get some information. There was no point in my calling Mother's doctor because he and I had a long history of animosity. Meanwhile, I was jittery and nervous not knowing what was going on. Both Mother and Uncle Rabbit were in the hospital and only 80 yr. old Aunt Bess to try to look after both. I cabled my personnel officer to move up my home leave to mid-February. I hated to go home during the winter, but I needed to get there as soon as possible. On January 31st I called Aunt Bess who told me that Mother had been released from the hospital, and that I was never to let Mother know that I knew she had been in the hospital.

African–Aamerican History Month

After distress, solace.
- Swahili Proverb

Frustration was mine. I had a staff that lacked initiative or drive; content to sit on their butts until you hand them something specific to do. Even then there are faults in any work that requires thinking. Perhaps they have never been challenged before. I'm trying to get the staff excited about African-American History Month. It has never been celebrated here before.

It's February 2nd, ten days before opening night and I am still too busy to focus on the month. The agency is burying me under paperwork and deadlines for reports and cables. Thoko, bless her, has arranged for the Deputy Prime Minister to deliver the keynote speech which she and I agreed to write. I then had to call the DCM for him to explain to the ambassador that I did not call the Deputy Prime Minister. Thoko arranged it entirely. Our driver is out sick, and I'm the only one in the office who can drive. So now I am the messenger along with everything else.

Ambassador Klunker. Political appointee. Spoil-sport. Idiot.

As I continued preparing for the opening event one newspaper did an article and said the public was invited. I was now concerned that 200 people would show up. I told *The Times* they had to do a retraction which they did. Someone lent us a piano and I had a singer. Thoko arranged for a bartender and a caterer.

I was delighted to find an American gospel singer, Tanya, to perform at the celebration, and I located a team of male dancers to do the exciting and vigorous Sibaca dance. A few days before opening night one of King Sobuza's sons, Prince Pikka, came to visit me. I was delighted to meet a member of the royal family, and I used his visit as an opportunity to invite him to our opening night program.

The evening arrived and I welcomed the guests. As the program began, I took a seat near the back of the room. A friend, Melina, who headed another U.S. government agency had arrived earlier and was seated across the aisle from me. Melina had a tremendous sense of humor. She could talk out of the side of her mouth like a gun moll, and was forever saying something hilarious about somebody when we were in situations that forbade laughing.

Tanya stepped upon the stage. Her song was to set the tone for the evening, to put the audience in a spiritual and reverential mood. I settled in my chair, prepared to enjoy the evening. Tanya began singing and began hitting higher and higher notes. As she did, her voice began to crack. I happened to glance over at Melina who was watching Tanya with a big smile on her face. When Tanya tried to hit another high note, Melina doubled over. I stared at her in sheer amazement. I hardly heard Tanya. I hoped Melina would not burst out laughing, although it seemed that she would at any moment. She straightened up, and again Tanya tried to hit a high note and tore it all to pieces. Melina was clutching her stomach, and trying to suppress her mirth. What had been a broad smile on her face was now a broad grin. Finally, thankfully, Tanya ended the song.

I don't know how long Melina would have been able to control her laughter. Afterwards I asked Melina why she was so tickled.

She simply asked, "Did you hear Tanya?"

Nothing more needed to be said.

All invited guests came, including Prince Pikka. The Deputy Prime Minister's speech was absolutely dynamic. I thought to myself: Thoko and I wrote a tremendous speech. We are good! Following the program we had a reception in the Library. I was talking to a small group of people when I heard loud voices. I turned to the group beside me just in time to see one journalist throw his drink in the face of another journalist who reacted by hitting the other one. Immediately Charles, a big, American USAID officer, grabbed both of them by the scruff, hauled them outside, and sent them on their way. I thanked my lucky stars that the ambassador had left minutes before the fight; otherwise I am positive I would have been blamed for it. The other Swazi guests were not perturbed by the disturbance. One journalist from the Swazi Broadcasting office apologized to me and said he would take it up with their boss.

When the Swazis get drunk they don't care what they do or say. I found that extremely disconcerting. A Peace Corps volunteer working in a hospital told me that during payday weekends they see terrible injuries from fights and car accidents. The embassy advises official Americans to try to stay off the road leading down into the valley on payday weekends. It's going to be a long three years.

A few months later Tanya invited Melina, her daughter, Mallory, and me to her church. O.C. Smith, a well-known American singer, now a minister and was going to visit her church. We dignitaries arrived to the welcome of parishioners who waited outside to greet us. They knew who Melina and I were because our pictures were often in the newspapers or we were on television. We were greeted by Tanya and the minister and ushered to our seats of honor, right down front. The service began. Neither Melina nor I had any idea that Tanya was going to sing until she stepped to the microphone. We dared not look at each other, but I glimpsed Melina's daughter lean forward and slyly look at both of us. With the first note, I felt my stomach begin to heave with laughter. Tanya then tried to hit a high note and missed it by a mile. I heard Mallory chuckle. Melina's shoulders started shaking. I looked down at the floor, and found it so fascinating that I continued on down as if searching for something, anything to prevent myself from looking at Tanya or Mallory or Melina. Mallory's chuckle was becoming louder. I kept hunching Melina. She said later that she knew I wanted her to make Mallory leave, but she was fighting hard to not laugh out loud. I wanted Mallory to leave before all three of us brought down the house by screaming with laughter. I was frantic. Here we were two senior U.S. diplomats in this tiny kingdom, representing the people and government of the United States, and we were about to totally lose control and guffaw, in a church no less. We were going to be the talk of the kingdom and the Klunker would probably have both of us expelled from the country. I could see myself totally out of control, rolling around on the floor, laughing loudly and gleefully, and no doubt peeing in the process.

I couldn't leave the church because we were right down front, and I knew if I got up to leave, I would start laughing halfway down the aisle.

Why is it that the harder you try to contain laughter, the more you laugh? It was either the longest song known to man, or Tanya made up all those verses. When she finally ended, tears were pouring down our faces. Parishioners must have thought we were really touched by that song. It indeed had touched our funny bones. Then and there, I promised the Lord and myself that no matter where I was, if Tanya ever got up to sing, I would immediately leave the premises.

The Klunker, the Kingdom, and the Dreaded Cotton Mouth

Any woman who has a great deal to offer the world is in trouble.
And if she's a black woman, she's in deep trouble.
                                        - Hazel Scott

I decided it was only fair to give the Deputy Chief of Mission (DCM) his own special name since *The Washingtonian* had given the Klunker his name. Hereafter, DCM stands for the Dreaded Cotton Mouth. He reminded me of a snake in the way he lurked behind the Klunker, watching, gossiping, goading, instigating and making no attempt to teach the Klunker the finer points of being an ambassador. On the other hand, he probably didn't know either. The Klunker obviously thought his reason for being in Mbabane was to challenge, provoke and crack the whip on the two black officers. Mastah misses his slaves.

On February 14th the *Times of Swaziland* headline read: "COUP AVERTED." The story said the Prime Minister wanted to replace the Justice and Foreign Ministers. When the Liqoqo rebelled, the Prime Minister rescinded his order. A few days later a journalist friend came to my office with a bombshell: two members of the Liqoqo had been arrested and were scheduled to go on trial the next day. They were accused of making "seditious" statements about the Royal Swaziland Police Force. One of the accused was a prince and the other was a chief. The Prime Minister has come in for a share of blame. Some said he was too soft; others say he is too tough on corruption, and too influential with the Queen Regent.

There were reports that the Prime Minister had been arrested for treason. This kingdom was rife with rumors. South African news broadcasted that the Prime Minister had been ousted. That evening Prince Mabandla was interviewed on Swazi television and he said he knew nothing about being removed from his position. Confusion reigned as to whether the Prime Minister was in or out of office. The next evening Swazi Broadcasting announced that he was out and played a tape of the Governor of Lobamba stating that he was out. The Prime Minister had to move out of his residence immediately. All of his official cars were taken away, and they used rental trucks. Their whereabouts were secret until a week later when a South African newspaper reported that Prince Mabandla, the former Prime Minister, and his family had fled to South Africa where they sought asylum.

I was anxious to get home to see about Mother and Uncle Rabbit and that worry stayed on my mind. Meanwhile, I had to push and pull my office staff who had become accustomed to doing little or nothing which was why the post was in such a rut, and why I was asked to take over.

Aunt Bess wrote and said, "You're the boss. You're supposed to be taking it easy."

My career counselor said it usually took one year to get a moribund office back on its feet and my 12 hour days should pay off in a few more months. I hoped that I would not be there for a few more months, but I worked doggedly as if I would be there for life. I wanted USIS programs to succeed, and to be of use to the mission. The Country Team met once a week and as we went around the table reporting on new developments, Melina and I had little to report.

Ambassador Klunker looked at us with shifty eyes as if demanding that we come up with some news of the kingdom. Nothing could have made me open my mouth to share anything with Klunker and the Dreaded Cotton Mouth. I had tried to work with them, and had been rebuffed. Now I was on my way out, I prayed, and they had ceased to exist as far as I was concerned.

One morning I woke up around 3 a.m. and had to go to the bathroom. I know that in Africa one should never walk around in the dark because you never know what you might run into. I went into the bathroom next to my bedroom and sat down on the toilet. As my eyes wandered over the tub I noticed something different about the tub. I turned on the light and there coming out of the tub drain were lots and lots of black baby snakes- black mambas, no doubt. My mind screamed LYE! I wanted lye to get them back into the drain. I ran through the house, into the kitchen and out to the back porch and grabbed a gallon of bleach. I poured it into the tub and the snakes began going back down. I then ran the hot, hot water for several minutes to be sure they stayed down there, and then I closed the tub drain. That morning when I got to my office I called the embassy to send someone over to check the outside drain. They discovered that a black mamba had given birth in the drain and the baby snakes were emerging in my tub. Thereafter, every night all tub and sink drains were closed tightly. I often shuddered when I thought what would have happened if I had not gotten up at that time. What if those snakes had gotten out of the tub and into my bedroom and I had gotten out of bed and stepped into a nest of snakes? I am convinced that my mind would have snapped.

My mental and physical health suffered greatly. I didn't mind the hard work and being at the office for 12-14 hour days, but the constant aggravation by the Klunker and the Dreaded Cotton Mouth were becoming too much. I began having chest pains. They frightened me, but I didn't see a doctor.

From day one I had negative vibes about being in Swaziland. My relations with Ambassador Klunker worsened. He was a total embarrassment to me, and should have been to other embassy officers also. Several Swazis noticed that when the ambassador attended cocktail parties or dinners, he would enter the room and stand alone, or head for the British or the Israeli ambassador. They asked me why. I had no answer for them, but I suspected that it was because he had no use for black people and only felt comfortable with other whites. I realized that I had to leave Swaziland or risk ruining my career.

At one point a State Department official visited Swaziland and came to my office to speak to me. He had been briefed by my office in Washington about the difficulties I was having with this ambassador. He told me that I should not worry about my career because they were prepared to place a memo in my file stating that in Swaziland I had had to deal with a "very difficult ambassador." That was all well and good, but I could not continue the day after day quizzing and constant challenges from an ignorant man. Everyone said he had been appointed as ambassador due to his in-laws' contributions to President George H.W. Bush's campaign. While he was a shoe salesman he met and married Sally Gerber, the Gerber baby food heiress.

Many of us felt that Mrs. Phinney should have been the ambassador. Americans and Swazis took to her immediately because she was warm and friendly, everything that her husband was not.

Since this is a one person post, when the PAO goes on vacation someone from the embassy oversees my office. The ambassador has declared that everybody at the embassy and other missions are entirely too busy and nobody is available to take over for me. That's great cooperation. My director called the ambassador and told him that I would be leaving for home leave as scheduled and the USIS staff would be on their own during the six weeks that I am away.

Yuk! Yuk! I looked forward to leaving this post even if it's only for six weeks. Hopefully, I can convince my office to allow me to transfer to another post or to return to Washington. I have begun to hate this place.

On April 12 I was in the office at 6:15 am. I left at 10:30 to get to the airport for a 12:45 flight to Jo'burg. At the airport a South African security guard searched my carry-on bag over my protests of diplomatic immunity. To white South Africans black people are like something unpleasant on the bottom of their shoes. They don't care how they treat us. My Pan Am flight left at 8 pm for an 18 hr. flight to New York City. Shortly before we arrived at Robertsfield International Airport in Liberia at 3 am, we ran into a storm. That 747 plane rocked and dropped and I almost prayed out loud I was so scared. We landed safely, thanks be to God. I had left the southern part of Africa and was now on the western part with a time difference, cultural difference and where I could breathe without fear of being insulted or made to disappear.

After arriving at the JFK airport in New York, I took a shuttle to LaGuardia where I waited for Mother's flight. She arrived safely and we checked into a hotel. The weather was cold and rainy. We stood in line at "Tickets" to get half-priced tickets to some Broadway plays. For the next few days we saw "Dreamgirls," "Evita," and "Porgy and Bess." After a few days in New York Mother and I went to Washington, and she stayed for a few days before leaving for Indiana. I had a few days of temporary duty at my agency in Washington and I used the time to request a transfer out of Swaziland. The Area office is supportive. My personnel officer is less supportive, but she realizes that no matter what she says, I am going to leave Swaziland, by hook or by crook. At this time, I don't care which as long as I get out.

I left Washington for Indiana where I could start enjoying my home leave. A few days later I received news that the transfer had been approved. Hallelujah! I agreed to return to Swaziland and remain until my replacement arrived. The Personnel office speculated that they would have an officer available in approximately two months. Two months in Swaziland with Ambassador Klunker was like a lifetime, but I knew the end was in sight. I invited Mother to return to Swaziland with me so that she could enjoy the mineral springs in Manzini and the two doggies, Sheba and Sugarfoot.

My next encounter with South Africans occurred when Mother and I were returning to Swaziland after my home leave. We flew from New York to Johannesburg where we spent the night at a hotel near the airport that accommodated blacks and whites. I had arranged for my driver to pick us up the next day for a scenic, four-hour drive to Swaziland.

When we arrived at the South African border post of Oshoek, Mother and I got out of the car and went into a small Customs building. A white South African clerk sat behind a cubby-holed window filing her nails. I placed our two Diplomatic passports in the window. She leaned back in her chair and said something that I couldn't hear. She repeated it. I still didn't hear her. She was almost whispering.

Finally I managed to hear her say, "Hand me your passports."

I said, "There they are."

All she had to do was reach out and get them.

She responded, "Hand them to me."

I was not going to humor the woman. She was being ridiculous. The passports were placed in the window. All she had to do was to pick them up. I didn't see how I could "hand" them to her. I stood there. She sat there. Finally, I picked up the passports, and practically threw them through the cubbyhole. They landed on the floor beside her. She was furious, but there was no way she could tell me to pick them up since they lay on her side of the window. She stamped the passports and put them back in the window. Without looking at her, I snatched them up, and we left. Mother and I got back in the car, and as we began pulling away two South African border guards, one black and one white, stopped us. The black officer asked if they could inspect the trunk of my car. At first I said sure; I had nothing to hide. I knew they confiscated books and other things they didn't think blacks should have, but I was a diplomat and they could not confiscate anything of mine.

Then I remembered that as a diplomat I was also entitled to all rights and privileges thereof. I leaped out and met the two officers at the rear of the car. I motioned for the driver to leave the trunk closed.

I looked hard at the two South Africans, "Do you see the license plate on this car?"

They acknowledged they did.

"Is it a diplomatic plate?" I asked.

They acknowledged it was.

I said, "Then you may NOT inspect my trunk."

Not another word was said. I turned on my heel and got back into the car, as did the driver. The two border guards stood there looking foolish. If they wanted to create an international incident, I was ready.

I said to the driver, "Let's ride."

He did so with a broad smile on his face.

I know Mother's little heart must have been fluttering. She knew her daughter, and she was acutely aware that we were still in South Africa and that her daughter's mouth might keep us there. But she was game. She never said a word, and seemed very calm, but I knew she feared for both of us.

We arrived in Mbabane safely and at my residence the two dogs ran to greet Mother. They ignored me completely which pleased me greatly as I did not cotton to being welcomed by muddy paws. Apparently they were not happy that I had gone off for several weeks and left them behind. After a couple of hours they were ready to forgive me and I got wet, wet kisses from Sugarfoot and Sheba.

The Klunker had been notified of my transfer, and the moment that I was back in my office, he summoned me.

He began in his usual gruff manner, "Why are you leaving here?"

I'm fine, thank you. Yes, I had a wonderful home leave. It was very kind of you to let another officer handle USIS operations in my absence. None of that was asked or said. Why was I leaving Swaziland? He had only to listen to himself on tape to answer that question.

I smiled pleasantly and replied, "For personal reasons."

He rephrased the question several times, but my answer was always the same. I was not going to give him the satisfaction of hearing me say that I was leaving because of his antics. He knew exactly why I was leaving and he was embarrassed because Washington had approved my transfer request to get away from him and his silliness.

July 4th arrived. It was no holiday for me. At most of our embassies, the celebration is held at the ambassador's residence, and government officials and embassy heads of agencies are invited. I had always enjoyed our July 4th celebrations. In Swaziland, I did not look forward to anything that involved the Klunker.

8 am – Klunker called saying he wanted a photographer at his residence.

9 am – The Swazi Broadcasting Company called because they couldn't find the ambassador's residence to set up microphones for speeches.

9:01 am – An embassy staffer called saying they needed another Swazi flag.

9:10 am – I rush to my office to get a flag and take it to the Klunker's residence.

11 am – I am in the tub when another embassy staffer arrives asking for the damned podium.

Somehow we got through the ceremony with my mind intact and I left as soon as protocol permitted.

The Klunker continued being an ass. One month had gone by and I still had no replacement. I called my personnel officer asking about my replacement. She reminded me that I had agreed to remain in Swaziland until my replacement arrived. I grumbled, but concurred. I continued working as hard as ever, entertaining as usual, hiring staff and being responsive to The Klunker's demands. Furious that I was leaving the post because of him, Klunker knuckled down to really make my life miserable. Finally, before I completely snapped, I called the Deputy Director of the African Area in Washington, Kent Obee, who had been my PAO in Tanzania and knew me well.

I said, "Kent, If you don't get me out of here, I am going to kill this ambassador!"

He said, "Start packing. I'll have your (travel) orders cut immediately. "

I have never heard sweeter words. I was on my way home.

Some of my Swazi friends suspected or knew of the difficulties I had with Ambassador Klunker. They began planning events for my departure. The Klunker's secretary called me two weeks before I was due to leave to say that he wanted to have a farewell dinner for me.

I told her my last days were already booked. Himself then called me to state his desire to have a farewell dinner. I think it finally dawned on him how he would look to Swazis if he did not host a farewell event for a popular, departing head of a U.S. government agency. I read to him the list of events and dinners scheduled for me by friends during my final two weeks in the country. There was nothing he could say. There was no time available for him; he had waited too late, and he was not invited to any of my farewell events. I was positively gleeful.

I searched for a family to give my two dogs to. I wanted to keep them together because Sheba, the German Shepherd mix, had a calming influence on Sugarfoot, the Doberman girl. Sugarfoot was younger, but tended to be the domineering one. Sugarfoot wolfed down her food, and Sheba always left a little food in her bowl for Sugarfoot. They were sweet babies. My secretary wanted both dogs, but she had five children and I didn't know how the dogs would behave with children. Finally, I had to give them to her. I heard the dogs adjusted fine to the kids. I was relieved.

A few days before my departure there was a scheduled weekly meeting of the Country Team composed of all agency heads. I did not attend. I had scheduled a medical appointment to coincide with the Country Team meeting, and I notified the ambassador's secretary as I was leaving my office. Later I learned that Klunker had pastries and coffee brought in as a farewell to me. That was my way of thumbing my nose at him – at last I could do so. I was leaving the country and no longer under his rule. He had made my life hell for ten months. I had no further contact with him; no farewell call, no nothing. My departure orders were cabled to Mbabane.

The packers came from South Africa to pack up my effects. I left my American secretary in charge of the office. USIA Washington did not ask Klunker for help in running the office until my replacement arrived. Thoko Ginindza and her son, Martin Dlamini, drove Mother and me to the airport. We had a two hour flight to Johannesburg; a layover there; 6 ½ hrs. to Monrovia where we had a refueling stop, and then 8 hrs. to New York City. We went to LaGuardia airport for Mother's plane to Indy and my plane to Washington. It was July 31, 1983.

Oh, remember the advice the friend passed on to me when I left the U.S. for Africa for the first time? She said if an African can't eat it or screw it, he'll tear it up. She was right.

A few months later Klunker asked Washington to find him "a more acceptable country." I wondered what "a more acceptable country" meant. My desk officer in the African Area office said it meant Klunker wanted to be assigned to a non-black country. I wondered what other country would want him. Apparently none did; he resigned and left Swaziland.

My friendship with Thoko continued and we visited during the years that she and her son studied in the U.S. She completed her Ph.D., and Martin did undergraduate work at Howard University. Thanks to Thoko, I met and enjoyed the friendship of the great Dr. Hilda Kuper, the official biographer of King Sobuza II. Thoko died a few years later. I will always treasure her friendship.

Washington, D.C.
1983-1987

There are roads out of the secret places within us along
which we all must move as we go to touch others.
                                                - Romare Bearden

Back to the real world of Washington, DC. I had never worked in our office in Washington. We went right into training and then overseas. I looked forward to seeing what we did in the U.S. I stayed at a hotel for almost a week while I cleaned my studio condo which was vacant. I wanted two or three weeks vacation, but the Area Office said I was needed immediately, and the most I could take would be one week. That was not nearly long enough. I arrived exhausted, with nerves wound up tight, and I needed to rest. But my new job awaited me. My air freight arrived and I took some items out of storage – sofa-bed, vacuum cleaner, coffee table and a small bookcase. I let the bed out every night or slept on top of the sofa.

On August 8th I reported to work as Chief, Grants Division, Africa Branch. Certain jobs are only for FSOs, usually supervising Civil Service employees. I wanted to work in the Foreign Service Press Center in New York, to work with my first PAO, Frank Gomez. But the Africa Area Office wanted me to be in the Grants division. Our Associate Director said the Africa Branch was in bad shape administratively. I learned that my office handled international visitors who came for one month of traveling throughout the

U.S. and meeting with their counterparts. Some of the programs were for individuals, and others were for groups of ten or more.

Overseas we nominated individuals who we felt would be in high level positions someday in their country, and we wanted to acquaint them with the U.S. They become alumni and there is always a connection between our country and theirs.

As I was leaving her office, she added, "Apparently we're happier to have you than you are to be with us."

She said she had heard that I wanted to go to the Foreign Press Center. I smiled and skedaddled out of her office, and back to my own. I then met the cast of characters: Eleanor, program officer, extremely competent; Jack (syn), program officer, brash, loud, drinks at lunchtime; Carrie, program officer, in her 70s, should have been retired; Ellie, program officer who had been demoted several grades; Angela, program office, kicked out of the Foreign Service, a free spirit; Janice, clerk, competent, but doesn't listen carefully. There was a lot to learn in that office. How do bosses learn? By doing? By screwing up?

One day Jack sailed into my office, tossed a piece of paper on my desk and said, "Sign this."

I asked, "What is it?"

He replied, "It's for my promotion."

I thought he was insane. FSOs have to go through several panels before we can get promoted, and here he was handing me a piece of paper to sign. I didn't think he deserved a promotion, and so I pushed the paper aside.

A few days later the clerk came in with a paper and as she handed it to me, she said, "I'm due a promotion."

She is due a promotion? I wondered what kind of language that was. I then called Eleanor in to ask questions about those two. She explained that with Civil Service there are yearly promotions, and when CS employees meet the criteria, they are almost automatically given a promotion.

"Oh, no!" I exclaimed. "That's not going to happen. They are going to have to show me something more than I've seen so far. They are doing their jobs, but barely at that."

When they realized that I was not going to automatically give them a promotion after working with them for one month, Janice found another job at a higher salary. Then we were without a clerk. I began the laborious process of interviewing. Jack let the word get out that he "might" leave our office since I would not sign for his promotion. My boss and I thought that would be a wonderful idea. I don't think too many other offices wanted him. Finally he found an office that would take him. When they called me for a reference, I said simply that he was a hard worker and was a shaker and a mover. I did not add that he would "shake" up the office, and his supervisor would wish/pray/try to "move" him on. I was positively giddy when he left.

Ellie always had a coke an on her desk. I assumed she drank a lot of cokes. One day I was looking for something on her desk while she was out to lunch, and I got a whiff of beer. It was coming from her coke can. I picked it up and smelled it. Some of the program officers were watching me and they laughed.

I asked if they knew she had beer in her coke cans. They all said sure, and they thought I knew. I poured out the beer and when Ellie returned from lunch I called her in and told her she could not have beer at work. She, of course, denied having beer in her can. I did not believe her since I had smelled the beer in her can and had seen it when I poured it out. She kept denying it, but I let her know that drinking on the job would not be tolerated. She was about to be in for another demotion.

I hired a clerk for our office, a young, black woman who seemed intelligent and anxious to establish a career. She had never worked for government before and I was pleased with her ability to express herself and with her demeanor in general. I told her of the opportunities for study that the government helped pay for and other benefits for anyone who wanted to move beyond being a clerk. She did her work very well at the beginning, but as she became more comfortable in the office I noticed that she had begun flirting with a young intern in our office. She began neglecting her work and spending a lot of time hanging around his desk. It was very noticeable. I finally had to speak to her about completing her work before chatting with friends. She pouted for a few days and continued flirting and neglecting her work. I was accustomed to working with people who were all about moving up in their careers, and I was not quite sure how to react to this change in Donna. I spoke to her again, and I began documenting our conversations and her shortcomings. Program officers began complaining about her work. She rushed through her work and it was sloppy and half done.

I spoke to her again and to my utter amazement she said, "I'm black and you're black, and you're supposed to be helping me."

I said, "Donna, what do you think I'm trying to do? I hired you when no one else would. I gave you a chance and you repay me by half doing your work which embarrasses this office and me. All work going out of this office reflects on me."

She stomped out of my office and left me marveling at her seeming lack of concern for her job. A few days later I sent her up to the office of the Director of USIA to deliver a memo. That afternoon I received a call from the Director's secretary, a friend of mine.

She said, "Charlene, when your secretary brought up that memo, she immediately began talking against you and saying some terrible things."

I was horrified.

She continued, "She asked if I knew you and I said yes, you were a friend of mine. I think she realized she had spoken to the wrong person."

I called Donna in and asked what had she said and why. She sat there with a knowing smile and did not respond. A few days later I received a call from Personnel. It seemed that Donna had gone to Personnel to complain about me wanting her to do her work properly.

The officer told me that he had said to Donna, "You certainly have a lot to say about Ms. Duline. I'm going to ask her to complete a performance report and let's see what she has to say about you."

Donna had not expected that kind of a response. I did a report on her and I showed it to her before sending it to Personnel.

She was unhappy with it, but I had documentation and memos from all of the program officers as to her work.

A few days later the personnel officer called and said they were going to fire Donna, that she was not the kind of person they wanted at USIA with her lack of ethics and professionalism. I asked him not to fire her.

He said, "I'm sorry, Charlene, you are out of it now. We are going to fire her."

I felt sorry for her, as I do for all underdogs. I called her into my office and told her what she had created for herself. I told her she was going to be fired and I advised her to resign, if Personnel would let her. I explained that if she were fired, she would probably never be able to get another job with the U.S. government, and that it would be in her best interests to quit, which she did. She was the first of my experiences in working with low level clerks who hated their jobs, but didn't want to bother going to a school to learn anything meaningful, and spent their time resenting their supervisors because they made more money due to the fact that they were educated, intelligent and totally professional.

One day I received a call from one of the Equal Employment Opportunity counselors asking if I was interested in applying for long-term study at a university. The Jefferson Fellowship was awarded by USIA to one or two FSOs each year. It was a sabbatical for us. In previous years, the officer took classes, but was not permitted to study for an advanced degree because the agency didn't want the officer to feel any pressure.

It was to be a relaxing year at a university at which time the officer could exchange ideas with colleagues and professors. This was the first year that the officer could work towards obtaining an advanced degree.

I applied and a few months later I was notified that I had been awarded a Jefferson Fellowship. The counselor said I could select any university in the U.S. to attend for one year. I thought it would be heavenly to attend the University of Hawaii, but I had just recently unpacked over 300 boxes of household effects and I was not anxious to do that again any time soon. I decided that I would study African and Latin American Affairs. I chose to study for a degree, but the agency was adamant that they didn't want me to be under any pressure. I selected a university in the Washington area, Johns Hopkins University, the School for Advanced International Studies (SAIS). After two years as a Branch Chief I was now off to relax for a year, or so I thought.

I began classes at SAIS in August, 1985. There were diplomats from China, Jamaica, St. Lucia and students from many other countries in my classes. I had selected my classes carefully so that I would be free on Fridays. Well, there was so much homework and so many books, magazines and articles to read, that I was at the library seven days a week. Fridays were like any other day. There were not only no long weekends, there were NO weekends. I had no time for television or even to talk on the phone with friends. I wondered what had I gotten myself into. I had been away from university life for many years. I didn't want to embarrass my agency by flunking a course. One professor, a former FSO, advised that I not kill myself trying to get As in every course. He told me to relax, try to have fun, and settle for Bs.

I did not listen to that. I wanted all As and I earned them. The first semester I took extensive notes. I read everything assigned. Of course I didn't remember it, but I read it. My life had changed drastically. I often thought: And this is a reward for good work? This was not at all what I had bargained for. At the end of the first semester one of the students, Denise Harrison, asked if I was enjoying SAIS. I said I wasn't because of all the reading.

She surprised me by saying, "You aren't trying to read all of that material are you?"

I replied, "Well, yeah, I am."

She said, "They don't expect you to read all those books. Besides, you can't remember it all anyway. They expect you to read the first and last paragraphs of each chapter and skim the articles. They assume that you are familiar with the work of the authors and know basically what they are saying."

I said, "I'm not familiar with anything. And why would they assign all of that stuff to be read if we aren't expected to read it??

Denise looked at me helplessly. I was hopeless, but I took her advice for the second semester. I also treated myself to my first computer, an Apple. I figured if the agency could spend around $15,000 or more on me that I could spend $1800 for a computer. In retrospect, I am sort of sorry that I opted to obtain a degree. I would have enjoyed my stay at SAIS a lot more had I not felt under pressure.

I graduated in May, 1986, from SAIS with a M.S. degree in International Public Policy. SAIS had its own graduation and speaker, completely different from the one at the main campus in Maryland. We did not wear caps and gowns, but wore elegant dresses and suits and as our names were called we marched up to the stage to be handed our diplomas by our guest speaker, Rev. Jesse Jackson.

I hugged him and he said, "Congratulations. I know it was rough."

I smiled and thought: You have no idea.

After the ceremony, we and our guests drank champagne and nibbled on huge, sweet strawberries, a tribute to elegance and gracious living that they didn't have on the main campus of Johns Hopkins University.

Twenty-five Years Later. . .a Small Bridge to One World

"Let there be peace on earth . . ."

-Sy Miller and Jill Jackson

We rocked, we sang, we cried, we hugged, we hooted and hollered. We were 4,000 returned Peace Corps volunteers celebrating the 25th anniversary of the U.S. Peace Corps in a huge, billowing, white tent on the Mall in Washington, D.C, September 18 – 21, 1986. I was assigned to Washington, and utterly thrilled to be among the thousands of volunteers who had served their country. Now I was a diplomat, but that paled in comparison to having been a Peace Corps volunteer. Inside the tent the environment was warm and protective. It was as if we were enveloped in a gigantic hug. The heart-rending moments were frequent and each one was magical and emotional. We saw fellow volunteers we had not seen in over 20 years and we met some of the newer volunteers. We shut out the world as we celebrated a president's dream and the people who made it happen. For this one weekend we celebrated volunteers who answered the clarion call of John F. Kennedy, and those whose vision made it possible.

Never before had so many young and old Americans marched off to foreign lands armed only with weapons of idealism, energy, and strong hands and backs to help the host peoples to dig, to build, and to grow in democracy and freedom. Our theme for the weekend was what we firmly believed in, peace on earth, and at the end of every event we sang our anthem, "Let There Be Peace on Earth."

Peace was the reason we journeyed to foreign lands to live and work with the people of those countries. We survived the training camp in the rain forest of Puerto Rico, climbed up mountains, rappelled down dams, and struggled with ourselves as we were challenged to do much more than we ever thought we could.

"... and let it begin with me."

President Corazon Aquino of the Philippines was our keynote speaker. We were honored and thrilled because she, the widow of an assassinated Philippines leader, symbolized much that we volunteers represented: peace, democracy, truth and justice. The air in the tent vibrated with love and hope. When President Aquino walked onto the stage wearing her trademark yellow, we gave her a thunderous welcome. When we finally settled town, President Aquino noticed the volunteers who had served in her country. Hundreds of them sat front and center wearing brilliant yellow tee shirts with "Philippines" emblazoned on the front. She beamed as she saluted them, and they rose as one body to roar their welcome.

"Let there be peace on earth, the peace that was meant to be."

When Sarge Shriver took the stage, we went wild again. Here was the "father" of the Peace Corps. He told us that the Peace Corps had 400 volunteers overseas before Congress had allocated any money. What faith! What vision!

He said, "Returned volunteers represent the promise, not the power of America."

He praised volunteers "for their moral vision, (and) a decent respect for the opinions of all mankind."

He added, "We should remember with affection and respect that the host nations gambled with us. Their leaders had the courage to trust what we were saying. That proves that Peace Corps has always been a two-way street."

He concluded by saying, "Volunteers stay just as you are, be servants of peace. Work at home as you have worked abroad. Teach those who are ignorant. Care for those who are sick. Serve. Serve. Serve. That's the challenge."

"With God as our father, brothers all are we…"

One of the most emotional events of the weekend was the Commemorative Walk from the Lincoln Memorial to Arlington National Cemetery to the JFK gravesite, and on to the amphitheater for a memorial service. Some 4,000 of us lined up to march across Memorial Bridge. The nations were in alphabetical order, and waving high over each group was the flag of the country where we served. In some groups, as in my Peru grouping, some host country nationals who had worked with the Peace Corps, marched with us. Amidst a sea of vivid colors each group moved out singing the national anthem of their country. As far as the eye could see there was the bright yellow of the Philippine volunteers; the kaleidoscopic prints of those who served in Africa; the multi-colored saris, sarongs, wraps, ethnic dresses and robes, and various unique hats and canes from almost every country in the world. It was a sight to behold. Few of the citizenry were out that early Sunday morning which was unfortunate. They would have felt as we did, that they had been transported to a special place, and that they were sharing a special moment with special people marching into history.

We spanned the entire bridge. As the first group entered the amphitheater, the last group departed from the Lincoln Memorial.

"Let me walk with my brother in perfect harmony."

At Arlington Cemetery the only sounds were of moving feet. A solemnity fell over us. We now honored our founder, President John F. Kennedy. Sargent Shriver, Loret Ruppe, the then Peace Corps Director, and two returned volunteers who were present at Kennedy's speech in Ann Arbor, laid a wreath at his gravesite. The wreath said simply, "Thank you." Each of us paused at President Kennedy's gravesite for a silent reflection, and we continued on to the amphitheater for the memorial service honoring the 199 volunteers who died while serving 1961-1986 and their families who were present. We listened to eloquent speakers—Bill Moyers, former Peace Corps Deputy Director;

Father Hesbergh from Notre Dame who left his sick bed to be there, and Gordon Radley, RPCV Malawi, the brother of Lawrence Radley, who with David Crozier, were the first PCVs to die in service. Radley spoke for the Memorial Families.

Each family was introduced and presented with a yellow commemorative rose by Loret Ruppe and Sargent Shriver. It was a majestic memorial of praise, hope and peace. I turned to whisper to a colleague and my eyes met the tear-filled eyes of a family member of a deceased volunteer. Suddenly my tears were unleashed, cleansing, refreshing, sharing and caring tears. I wanted to hug and thank each family for the gift of their loved one. The families honored us with their presence. The service was tender, loving, and meaningful.

The ceremony ended with us standing, holding hands, crying, swaying and singing our anthem, "Let There Be Peace on Earth." We vowed to continue to work harder for the cause we represented and believed in for 25 years: world peace.

"Let peace begin with me, let this be the moment now..."

For three days we were grouped together in a common cause once again. We searched for, and found, familiar faces. We were one. There was a palpable contentment in the air. Each one of us was a link to a familiar past when we were all we had, and for that weekend we were all we needed. Now we gathered in a huge tent, sitting on the ground to be closer to each other, and to enjoy this unique moment. We, the pioneer volunteers, trained in the rainforest of Puerto Rico, learned rock climbing, "drown-proofing," and developed an appreciation for skills we never knew we had. We showered in wooden structures, shook scorpions out of our clothes, and squatted in outhouses.

"With every step I take, let this be my solemn vow"

At the International Festival that closed out the weekend, we ate food from Latin America, Africa, and Korea. We listened to Indian musicians, and a Caribbean steel band. We were entranced by dancers from the South

Pacific, West Africa, the Philippines and El Salvador. For that weekend we were once again part of a brave, new world. I sat with two old friends who had served with me, friends of 25 years whom I respected and loved. Together we had toughened our bodies and minds, scolded and cajoled each other, and survived the best two years of our lives. The people we lived with and worked with would never forget Americans or the volunteers who came to serve them. Nor would we ever forget them.

For two years we lived as the poorest peasant did; ate what they ate; abhorred injustices to them by the rich, and tried to make things better for their children. They looked to us with hope. What we did was a drop in the bucket, but in many countries throughout the world, people know that Americans care about them.

"To take each moment and live each moment in peace eternally"

We were the "Kennedy Kids" as some called us. We were the ones far from home during the Cuban Missile Crisis. We were the ones who grieved in our villages when our president was assassinated, not knowing what was happening in our country because we were far away serving others. We were the ones determined to change the world, and in our own little way, we did. Now we celebrated the human spirit that enabled us to do so much with so little.

"Let there be peace on earth and let it begin with me."

Back to the Real World

When you are looking for obstacles, you can't find opportunities.
- J.C. Bell

Returning to USIA, I needed a one year assignment because I had been in Washington for three years and at the end of the fourth year I was expected to be back overseas. I was assigned to the Office of American Republics (Latin America and the Caribbean) as the Deputy Policy Officer. It was my first time working in an office composed almost entirely of FSOs and it was certainly different. Some of the officers indicated that they were above all the other FSOs, and some were fairly decent to work with. My direct supervisor, the Policy Officer, was a wonderful, gentle man. I often had to call upon him to calm an officer who was stressed by the demands made by the office director. We had several secretaries and only one was white, Lisa. Lisa was almost always angry about something, especially at lunch time when she couldn't get into the conference room to watch a soap opera because a meeting was taking place in there. She was a tiny terror, cursed out loud, and slammed things around on her desk. I laughed at her and with her. One day my boss asked me how I got Lisa to do my work so quickly.

He said, "When I give her something to do, it takes her forever to get it done."

I said, "I simply compliment her on her work. She does it fast; it's always perfect, and I tell her."

I wanted to work in this office because I wanted to return to Haiti, and being in this area office should have given me the best opportunity for a position in the Caribbean. I was offered the post of Country Cultural Affairs Officer (CAO) in Brazil. At first the idea appealed to me, even though I knew black officers had a difficult time living and working in Brazil. One black officer was always being stopped while driving and asked for identification. If was as if a black woman was not supposed to drive an American car. I knew I could handle the racism in Brazil, but when I learned that the CAO often flew into a city and out the same day, I refused the assignment. I knew that when I flew into a city I was not going to fly out the same day. I needed several days if not weeks to get my nerves back together to fly out. That settled that. It was tempting, but I would have been a nervous wreck all the time. The next offer was Panama. I hesitated, but then it was close to home, and was, according to all reports, a little paradise. I accepted the assignment.

I began language and area studies at the Foreign Service Institute. The purpose of weekly area studies was to introduce us to the culture of the countries we were assigned to. Dr. Hugo Pineda, a Chilean, spoke to a group of Foreign Service officers and spouses going to Central and South America. I was the only black in the group. Pineda was a professor at American University.

He prefaced his remarks with, "What I'm going to say now may be very painful to some in this room."

He need not have worried. It was only painful to me. He said he would begin with "blancoismo, whiteness."

Pineda told our group that in Latin America it is "perfectly all right to rape a black woman because it is no crime." My hackles began rising. He told my white colleagues that they could not invite a black friend to lunch at a restaurant because it is not accepted in the Latin society. I almost choked. I remembered that during my Peace Corps days I traveled with a white friend throughout Latin America and we felt totally welcomed everyplace we went. We even joined a white, male Peace Corps volunteer for dinner one evening in Chile, the home of Pineda.

He rambled on saying that Latin men prefer "sexy, black mistresses, but they want their wives and mothers of their children to be as white as possible."

Thus, he said, there was a joke in Latin countries that a man should always look for the "grandmother in the kitchen" to see what color she is.

I might as well have been invisible.

At one point he said "Until recently Costa Rica and Chile did not allow blacks into those countries."

I wondered how recent that was. In 1963 I spent five days in Chile. I wondered if he meant those countries didn't allow blacks to visit or to immigrate. I waited patiently for him to end so that I could ask questions. I was later sorry that I had not interrupted him. When Pineda spoke about "machismoism," the virility and masculinity that Latin men pride themselves on, he expressed some regrets that we would be exposed to that. I heard no regrets when he talked about "blancoismo." When Pineda finished, he dashed out the door, not taking any questions. I was crushed. I had a lot to say to him and to my colleagues.

I was outraged at his speech. I was also shocked that the Foreign Service Institute would have such a person speaking to officers going to Latin America, or that they would tolerate such an insensitive person. Surely my class was not the first to which he had made such disgusting remarks. The next day I wrote a letter to the director of the institute, Edward Marasciuio. In my letter I asked that Pineda be told of my response to his remarks, and I strongly suggested that a person more sensitive be chosen the next time the topic of "blancoism" was on the agenda. The reply was a weak apology. Apparently something was said to Pineda because a few weeks later I ran into him as he waited for an elevator. I walked up to him and began rebuking him for his previous remarks.

He said, "Oh, you're the one who complained. You're about to make me lose my job."

Just then the elevator arrived and as he stepped on I yelled, "You should lose your job!"

A few days later I overheard the spouse of an officer going to Panama saying, "Can you imagine somebody complaining about Dr. Pineda's remarks?"

I spoke right up and said, "I complained because I found his remarks about blacks insulting and not true."

I discussed this issue with several black and white friends and their reactions were the same as mine: outrage. I also told some of the Spanish instructors about it. They were sympathetic, but they did not seem surprised.

The language classes were intense, and grueling. Classes were six hours a day, and we had at least three hours of homework each evening. At lunch time most of us dashed to the language lab to listen to tapes in Spanish. I listened to Spanish newscasts and I was always amazed when I managed to understand a story told in rapid fire Spanish.

And then it was time for the packers to pack up my furniture to go into storage and to pack my other belongings for shipment to Panama. It was in January and there was snow on the ground. The packers took three days to pack. I always packed my clothes myself. I had always had excellent packers, but I was particularly concerned about these packers because when they left my apartment building it was dark, and the truck had no lights. I was concerned that my effects would be spilled all over the Beltway because they had no lights. I stood outside in the cold watching the last of my boxes go into the huge truck and wondered if I would ever see them again. The next day I left for Noriega's Panama.

Welcome to Panama
January, 1988 — March 1, 1989

If all else fails, immortality can always be assured by spectacular error.
- John Kenneth Galbraith

Agregada Cultural de la Embajada Americana de Panama was my title, Cultural Affairs Officer, of the Embassy of the United States of America to the Republic of Panama. The instant I was named to the post, the country erupted. The U.S. wanted General Manuel Antonio Noriega, army commander and supreme ruler of the country to step down. Not to worry, said I, if the U.S. wants Noriega to go, he's as good as gone. After all, we had rid Haiti of Duvalier and the Philippines of Marcos.

Shortly before I left for Panama, the State Department warned American citizens against travel to Panama due to "deliberate harassment." That warning didn't apply to U.S. diplomats. We then suspended all U.S. military and economic aid to Panama "until democracy is restored." I began to wonder about countries I was assigned to. Haiti, of course, was my perfect post, as one's first post tends to be. A few days after I arrived in Tanzania the country went to war with Uganda, and rid Africa of Idi Amin. As soon as I was assigned to Liberia, there was a coup. After being named to Swaziland, the death of King Sobuza occurred. Now, just before leaving for Panama, my government is warning all Americans, *except diplomats,* against going there. What is wrong with that picture?

266

The Panamanian embassy told the USIA courier that the diplomatic visa issued to me was the last that would be issued to an American diplomat. Into this mix I came boldly on January 13, 1988, as the Cultural Affairs Officer.

Before I arrived in Panama, protestors broke out all of the windows of the USIS office. The office was relocated closer to the embassy. The protesters also festooned the embassy with red paint while government troops stood by. The Panamanian government offered to remove the paint from the building but the U.S. refused the offer and allowed the paint to remain. The embassy said there was no need to remove the paint because it would simply happen again. The Panamanian government responded derisively in the newspaper that the U.S. reply was akin to somebody saying they would not take a bath because they would just get dirty again.

My plane arrived at 8:30 pm and I was met at the airport by my assistant cultural affairs officer. She drove as if we were being pursued. Death seemed to wait at every corner. All of the stop lights had been destroyed during the rioting in August the year before, and there were few stop signs. Everybody drove fast. My assistant bragged that everybody said she drove like the Panamanians. That was certainly no comfort to me and we had many near crashes.

I spent my first night in Panama in a hotel and the next day I was picked up by our office driver and taken to my new office. We always arrive at a post exhausted from packing, moving, getting last minute things in order, briefings by various people in the agency, farewell activities, and then we arrive to continue the hectic pace. I met my staff, and the PAO who barely had time to greet me before dashing out of the office.

I attended a briefing at the embassy, a luncheon at the El Cortigo restaurant with the Deputy Chief of Mission, political officer, assistant cultural affairs officer and six international visitors going to the U.S. for a 30 day program. I was taken to one of the U.S. military bases to do some basic food shopping. When I returned to my office my assistant and my secretary gifted me with an exquisite floral arrangement of birds of paradise. My assistant, Teresita Appin, had retired, but graciously agreed to remain for one week to brief me. She was a delightful, older, elegant woman.

After work I took my suitcases to my new apartment, and my first impression was that the apartment was gigantic. I immediately left to attend a "roast" hosted by the West Indian community at the Officers' Club at Albrook Air Force Base. I was not sure why my hostess thought I would enjoy the roast since I knew none of the people and I was too tired to be my usual scintillating self. I suppose she wanted me to meet members of the West Indian community. Later I was able to enjoy their wonderful hospitality. When I arrived back at my apartment it was 10:30 p.m. I had been handed a set of about 15 keys. I had no clue as to which one opened the iron grill in front of my door, or which opened the two locks on the door. At first I tried to be quiet, but after about ten minutes of trying different keys, I sort of hoped that I would wake up the entire building. Maybe somebody would come to help me find the damned key. It must have taken at least 20 minutes to get inside my apartment. I noticed that there were only two apartments to a floor.

The apartment was huge. The back of it was on the third floor.

Because it was built on rocks, the "front" was on the equivalent of the eighth floor and faced the ocean. One entered the living room from a small hall. Glass doors and windows gave an excellent view of the ocean, and the thunder of the mighty waves could be heard throughout the apartment. To the right of the living room was a study. To the left were a large, formal dining room, a large kitchen, laundry room, and maid's room and bath. Between the living room and the dining room was a hallway that lead to three bedrooms and two bathrooms. The master bathroom contained a double sink, tub, enclosed shower, bidet and toilet separate in their own compartments, and a walk-in linen closet. It was almost the size of my living room in Washington.

The first weekend an embassy car took several of us new arrivals to the Commissary and PX Exchange on two of our military bases. It felt good to be surrounded by American military men and their families. The bases resembled small town American cities and it was soothing to my ears to hear English spoken. I was surprised to see Panamanians shopping in the Commissary and I learned that some Panamanians were members of the U.S. military, and others had special privileges that allowed them to shop on our bases. The Commissary did not carry alcohol and we had to go to another base for wines and liquors. Once my car arrived I was able to drive to the bases, have lunch, and shop leisurely. Shopping was an all day event and I spent more money than intended because I did not want to make the trip to the bases every Saturday which undoubtedly was the busiest day of the week.

I began going on Sundays after Mass when the streets and the stores were less congested. I risked my neck every time I drove in Panama because no street lights were working and every driver was hell-bent on driving fast as if he were the only driver on the streets. And during the rainy season which seemed to be most of the time when I was there, I hurried to get home before the streets flooded which they did quickly. There was no place to pull over, and I had to continue on my way. I was always afraid that my brakes would get flooded and I would be in one heck of a pickle. I had a very unpleasant incident once when I was trying to make a right turn onto a busy one-way street. The traffic was heavy and I kept inching out but nobody slowed down. The driver behind me began honking for me to move out. When I didn't, he started pushing my car with his car. At the first bump, I jumped out of my car to see what damage he had done. I wanted to confront him, but I immediately decided that he must be unbalanced and that I'd better get back in my car. His car windows were tinted and I could not see the person behind the wheel. He pushed my car further out into the street. I was terrified. Again he pushed my car further. A bus driver approaching saw what was happening and he slowed down and put his hand out the window to slow down other drivers. I was weak with relief. I made the turn and since I was going to turn left at the next corner, I got all the way over to the left side of the street, and just as I was making the left hand turn, that foolish driver, now beside me, zoomed ahead and we both turned at the same time. I had to jam on my brakes to prevent a collision. He drove like the hounds were behind him and did not stop at the next corner. That was quite an experience.

There were two levels of underground parking in my apartment building. At one point my boss' wife happened to mention that a fer-de-lance snake had been found in one garage. She asked which building I lived in. When I said I lived in the Sonesta, she suddenly could not remember which building the snake was in. I knew then that it was my building. I looked up information about the fer-de-lance and learned that it, unlike other snakes, will chase a person, and its bite is deadly. For the next 14 months I tip-toed into the garage, hoping and praying that I would see that damned snake before it saw me. The thought of being chased by a snake was more than terrifying.

When I arrived in Panama I quickly began a search for a maid. The first maid I tried was from Colombia. She wanted to stay out late, while I felt that she should be inside my residence by 11:00 p.m. She wanted me to pay for her three meals a day, and told me that she ate steak. She lasted for five days. The next one, Marta, came three days each week. She was gone by the time I came home in the evenings, and I only saw her on Saturdays.

During my first few days in Panama my office received bomb threats daily, and we ran from our third floor offices in a bank building, down the street and into the embassy where we remained until our offices were swept for bombs. I was impressed by the Marines guarding the embassy. They were in full battle dress and carried huge, automatic weapons. By contrast, the USIS office had *one, unarmed* guard at the front door who monitored those approaching our office via closed circuit TV.

There was one way in and the same way out of our office. There was something wrong with that scenario I thought. I was told that our security measures were not complete. I'll say.

A few weeks later, the opposition, the Civil Crusade, began gearing up for another round with Noriega. They wanted him to step down as the head of Panama. The opposition was known as the "rabiblancos" (white asses) because the protestors, for the most part, were white Panamanians. The poorer and blacker Panamanians tended to favor Noriega who, they said, had created jobs for them and were more concerned about them. They were his people. The rabiblancos, in their pristine white, took to the streets banging pots and pans, waving white handkerchiefs, and demanding Noriega's resignation in an attempt to dismiss him as if he were a servant, one wag said. During the week the rabiblancos marched; on weekends they took time off to go to the beach, or to fly to Panama South (Florida) for a break and to shop. The riots ebbed and rose, and rose and ebbed. Noriega, known as "La Pina," the pineapple, because of his pockmarked face, ignored demands for his departure. Instead, he sent out the "Dobermen," his shock troops, to discourage marchers. The opposition gathered in parks and managed to march one or two blocks before the Dobermen began throwing tear gas. As this went on, high school and university students joined the clamor for Noriega to step down. He responded by teargasing the students and closing the schools and the university.

The front page of one newspaper had a cartoon of a peasant waving a newspaper at Noriega with the headline, "Noriega Paid by the CIA."

Noriega was replying, "What do you want? That I should work for free?"

NBC and ABC news crews practically camped out in our office. They wanted to see blood, preferably ours. El General was strangely quiet for awhile. I knew that when he did speak, it would be in tongues of fire. The U.S. suspended all military and economic aid. A Miami grand jury indicted Noriega for his involvement in money laundering for the Medellin drug cartel, and for allowing cartel members to live in Panama under his protection. At one point, members of M-19, the feared terrorists of Colombia, came to Panama to act as MEDIATORS between two quarreling groups. I was shocked that M-19 would ever be considered as mediators since they were known killers, and had killed many people in Colombia, including all of the justices of the Supreme Court of Colombia. There they were in Panama to mediate, and just one block from my residence. During the days that M-19 was in town, I drove past their hotel faster than usual.

There I was, seemingly in what was fast becoming my usual position of being in the midst of a prolonged political crisis which quickly worsened after my arrival. The U.S. imposed economic sanctions and ceased recognition of the Noriega government. In short order, both universities were closed for extended periods due to violent demonstrations by the students. This made regular contact with university officials nearly impossible and contact with government officials was forbidden. It was impossible to do business as usual with the closing of nearly all of my contact institutions, constant bomb threats, and daily demonstrations in the city. The Public Affairs Officer was new in his position and relied to a great extent on the seasoned Information Officer, Cynthia Farrell.

He jumped in and out of the office and never had time to sit down to discuss the post, our programming or talk about any essentials a newly arrived officer needed to know. Cynthia was under siege by the international media. Journalists called her day and night at her home, at the office, and to her credit, I never saw or heard her lose her temper. She was an outstanding officer. Cynthia had family in Panama, and I am certain that made a huge difference in her personal life.

Panama had a large U.S. embassy presence. There were officers from almost every U.S. government agency. As tension mounted between the U.S. and the Noriega regime, Panamanian newspapers and politicians began clamoring that the U.S. was seeking a reason to delay handing over the Panama Canal to Panama. That treaty had been negotiated under President Jimmy Carter.

We had a large academic exchange program which the Assistant CAO handled; however, the Soviet Union Bloc had the largest scholarship program in the region in Panama. They provided funding for 400-800 Panamanians to study in one of the Bloc countries. One of the U.S.'s main interests was in preparing Panamanians to operate the Panama Canal after December 31, 1999. It was paramount to have a stable political government in power along with a significant number of Panamanians who spoke and understood English. Our efforts were concentrated on strengthening the engineering faculty at the University of Panama, supporting efforts of other faculties toward the development of a democratic political system, and improving the quality of English teaching in the country.

Undergraduate scholarships had been established for Central America by Congress, as a result of the Kissinger Commission Report which recommended this as part of long-range policy plans toward Central America.

Other programming included individual and group International Visitors programs, American musicians teaching and performing in Panama, photo exhibits, and book programs. Five American officers served at USIS Panama.

Banana Republic

"Contrariwise," continued Tweedledee, "if it was so, it might be, and
if it were so, it would be; but as it isn't, it ain't. That's logic!"
- Lewis Carrol

General Noriega was fired! That was the hot news in March, 1988, two months after my arrival in the isthmus. I heard the news in Honduras where I was attending a workshop for all Cultural Affairs Officers in Central America. The President of Panama, Eric Arturo Delvalle, fired Noriega, or attempted to. Delvalle went on television (taped of course – no fool he) to remove Noriega from office. The general refused to be fired, and instead fired Delvalle who was already in hiding. Noriega appointed the Minister of Education, a frail, old man, Solis Palma, to be sworn in as president in the middle of the night. Members of the National Assembly, roused from their beds, dozed through the ceremony. The U.S. reacted as if it had been soundly slapped. And indeed it had been.

The workshop I was attending was in San Pedro Sula, the second city of Honduras, 110 miles from the capital city of Tegucigalpa. I rather expected a resort-type of place. The Director of the American Republics Office himself was coming to the conference, along with other top dogs from Washington. I looked forward to being able to breathe after being so cloistered in Panama City, living under a curfew imposed by the ambassador for our safety, and scared that I was going to have to make a run for the border at any moment.

I operated in a state of controlled hysteria, which threatened to become more and more uncontrolled.

My boss, the Public Affairs Officer, left a few days ahead of me in order to meet privately with the Director in Costa Rica. I met them at the airport in Costa Rica where I changed planes. After spending several hours at the airport waiting for the plane, I looked up and saw our Latin America Director surrounded by four subordinates sprinting through the terminal. I joined the caravan and we marched out to the airfield and boarded a small, nondescript plane. That means it was not the kind of plane that I want to remember. I swallowed hard, was tempted to end my career then and there, but I crawled onto the damned thing. I remembered that some of my staff members told me the name of the airline, SOSA, meant "Stay Off And Stay Alive." The mind is a wonderful thing in that I don't remember a thing about the flight except that we finally arrived in San Pedro Sula.

We arrived at twilight, and landed on a dusty field. We got off the plane and walked toward the terminal.

We looked at each other and one guy said what we all were thinking: "This looks like a banana republic."

Think of every old movie you have ever seen about a poor Latin or African country. It looked exactly like a movie set. When the dust settled, we saw an old, rusty building where several armed officers in khaki uniforms stood looking at us as they picked their teeth. Inside the dingy room were a couple of wooden benches, a couple of uniformed men, and a couple of ceiling fans that lazily moved stirring up dust. Our Director towered over the Honduran officials as they lazily perused our diplomatic passports, and looked sideways at us.

With one exception – me - my group consisted of white, arrogant males looking for all the world like they had flown in to save somebody or something, and they wanted to get these airport formalities over with as quickly as possible. I could not match them for their air of superiority and hauteur.

We were staying at the "best" hotel in town. The president of the country was even staying there. The hotel looked nice from the outside. The lobby was decent, and then I got to my room. It looked much like the airport had – grim, with green furniture, green bedspread and green drapes. We are talking dingy, ugly, dirty green. I was afraid to look into the corners of the room. My shower was broken and half of the tub's innards lay in the tub. I called the desk when I noticed this which was after I unpacked. They wanted to move me, but that never happened. The towels smelled awful. I itched the second day and wondered if I had fleas. I felt like shaking after bathing, rather than using those towels.

That night we attended a theatrical performance. The president of Honduras spoke to the audience before the main presentation. Our group numbering about 30 sat in the first two rows. The president's bodyguards were stationed below the stage and all across the front of it, facing us with their automatic weapons pointed at us.

Throughout the performance, Lou, a hilarious Italian-American FSO sitting next to me kept leaning over saying things like, "I hope that gun doesn't go off accidentally or it'll blow us through the roof!"

Or, "Do you notice the finger of this guy tightening on the trigger?"

Or, "Why do they need such big guns? That could take your head off!"

I wanted to choke Lou. It was funny, but also I could feel myself becoming more and more nervous – because I was thinking the SAME THING! Finally the president finished speaking and sat down, and the guards moved on.

The next day the news came that Gen. Noriega had fired the president of the country and replaced him. The former president was in hiding. The PAO flew back immediately to help handle the public affairs aspects of which there were many. Some Panamanians suspected that the former president was hiding in our ambassador's residence. The ambassador's bodyguards were doubled; they all were packing heat, and the U.S. and Panamanian press were covering him like a blanket.

Meanwhile back at the hotel I drank the water. There was never any question in my mind about whether the water was safe to drink. We drank the water in Panama. Me – who spent the first five years of life in the Foreign Service boiling water for 20 minutes and then filtering it, who kept a bottle of water in the bathroom for brushing my teeth, who used boiled water for ice cubes – me. The water, the hotel, the towels, the room and the plane ride had combined to make me sick, and I was ready to get back to Panama and deal with Noriega and his henchmen.

I managed to get back to Panama before the results of drinking Honduran water really kicked in, and then I was doubled up with cramps and diarrhea. I dragged myself into the office on Sunday to help the Information Officer field questions and visits from international journalists, especially the U.S. media.

Television networks sent crews and well known American TV reporters arrived; the written media sent reporters who practically camped out in our office.

Noriega's psychological war against the embassy went into overdrive. One newspaper accused some embassy officials of plotting to assassinate Noriega. This was intended to incite public reaction against the U.S. Opposition and independent newspapers were forcibly closed by Noriega. Meanwhile our office continued showing strong support for the suppressed media by issuing statements of support designed to irritate Noriega, and taking visiting congressional delegations to see the closed facilities, and notifying the international press of ill treatment of Panamanian journalists. When President Delvalle went into hiding, our office arranged for him to be interviewed by the opposition Panamanian media, the U.S. media, and by officers from the Southern Command Network (in Panama).

Land of the Wild Surmise
and Outrageous Conjecture

All the people like us are We, and everyone else is They.
- Rudyard Kipling

American officials had been trying to get rid of Noriega for some time. They used him, it was said, to help train the contras, even though there was evidence that Noriega was involved in drug dealings with other countries. We turned a blind eye because at that time it was in our best interests to do so. It was said that Elliott Abrams, the Assistant Secretary of State for Inter-American Affairs, and higher ups had agreed to quash a pending drug indictment of Noriega and would allow him to leave Panama quietly. It seems that Noriega agreed to this plan, but reneged when conflicting offers came from the Department of Defense, and the CIA. He thought he could do what he had always done: play both ends against the middle. Abrams had just come out of the Iran-contra affair smelling nothing like a rose. He and his small circle of old Latin American hands had total disdain for the countries they were responsible for. They seemed to view them as pawns on a gigantic chessboard to be moved about as they chose.

One diplomat called their attitude, "A combination of arrogance and ignorance."

That arrogance and ignorance was evident in some of Abrams' staff meetings that I attended as Deputy Policy Officer while in the Office of American Republics.

Usually the Policy Officer attended Abram's meetings, but he was unavailable one day and I attended. I remember that meeting with distaste. As usual I was the only black officer at the meeting. State Department officials involved with Inter-American Affairs sat around the table with Abrams at the head. Other agencies' representatives sat in chairs against the wall. The meeting began with loose talk about the "natives" in a Caribbean nation. Abrams then began discussing an upcoming meeting between then-Secretary of State George Shultz and the black leader of a Caribbean country. Abrams said the meeting would take place at a certain country club in that country. Someone laughingly said blacks were not allowed in that club. Everyone laughed except me and those who sat facing me. Not all of the men at the table were aware that a black officer was among them. Abrams, who faced me, gave me an apologetic smile. My face was a mask. He said times had changed in that country, and Shultz would meet with the country's president at that particular country club. His tone indicated that the frivolity should cease. As the meeting continued, I noticed some of the men craning their necks to see who sat behind them. Only when they saw me did they understand why Abrams had not continued with the banter about a black president not being allowed into a country club in his own country.

Meanwhile the U.S. government applied economic sanctions against Panama, and announced it would only recognize officials of the Delvalle government, and would not recognize or deal with any Noriega officials. As far as the U.S. was concerned, Delvalle was Panama's legitimate president. We froze Panama's assets in the U.S. and asked other countries not to pay any monies to Noriega.

The city was tense. Everybody wanted to know where Delvalle was hiding. Many Panamanians thought he was under the protection of U.S. military forces on one of our bases in Panama. He wasn't. The truth was that he, his wife, adult children, grandchildren, and maids were granted asylum by the U.S. government, and were ensconced at the U.S. Ambassador's residence. Some of Delvalle's supporters called for a strike against Noriega in an attempt to bring back Delvalle. The majority of the opposition hesitated. They said it took Delvalle two years to speak out against Noriega's excesses, so why should they risk their butts now for Delvalle. Americans were told to be cautious when on the streets of Panama.

The embassy had managed to get my Diplomatic Carnet, an identification card identifying the carrier as a diplomat in that particular country, before we stopped dealing with Noriega, but I was unable to get a diplomatic license plate for my car. For 14 months I drove around the city with expired Indiana tags on my car. Fortunately the license plate was on the back of the car, so by the time a soldier or policeman saw it, I was gone. The U.S. government held hostage money belonging to Panama in banks in the U.S. Panama needed the money to pay salaries and to keep the country running. Finally, Noriega was forced to close all banks in Panama because there was simply no money. *The New York Times* quoted Abrams as saying Noriega was hanging on "by his fingertips." But hanging on he was. The Panamanian economy was in shambles. Earlier the U.S. had suspended all economic and military aid to the country. We had no further use of Noriega.

The U.S. refused to pay the seven million dollars due from the Panama Canal Commission to Noriega's regime, and President Reagan announced that U.S. companies and individuals were prohibited from paying any monies to the current government in power. Panamanians, frustrated over the bank closings, businesses shutting down, and the crumbling economy, then directed their anger at the United States. Throughout the city there were huge billboards with photographs of our ambassador, his adult daughter, and the Deputy Chief of Mission (DCM) along with insulting messages, and pro-Noriega newspapers ridiculed the ambassador in cartoons.

One U.S. newspaper said U.S. Senators were "threatening." THEY were threatening? I was outraged. It was our butts on the line there, yet they were threatening. There was a lot of chest thumping from both governments. One Sunday The New York Times carried a lengthy article on the situation of American diplomats in Panama. They compared conditions that existed in Panama to those that existed in Iran when Americans were taken hostage, and said the conditions were exactly the same. The Washington Post carried stories saying American diplomats in Panama were sitting ducks, and the situation was ripe for us to be taken hostage. Nice of them to give Noriega ideas.

Meanwhile I sat in my office alternately drooling and foaming at the mouth, and trying hard to pretend that everything was normal. Noriega began tightening his power. He had already shut down several newspapers, and then he began closing the radio stations. More and more businesses shuttered their doors. Nobody had access to any money, except official Americans.

The chief of police said if stores remained closed the people had the right to break in to get food. The manager of my apartment building notified residents that we only had enough cooking gas for one or two days. I dashed out to the Post Exchange to buy a microwave oven, but they were out. I bought a toaster oven instead, and stocked up on foods that required no cooking.

The U.S. applied economic sanctions and refused to release money in the U.S. belonging to Panama, money Panama needed to pay salaries and to keep the country running. Panamanians were becoming more and more angry with the U.S. government. Several times when demonstrations against us were threatened, the PAO was concerned enough to send home all the local employees, but we Americans had to remain in the office. Throughout the city tires and garbage were set afire in protest against U.S. policy towards Panama. I was terrified of the drama unfolding – indeed, turbulescing - around me.

Panamanian retirees who had worked for the U.S. government could not cash their checks since the banks were closed. The bank was located in our building, and bank officials told them to return at 2:00 p.m. day. That infuriated the old men and some went home, got their machetes and returned. They were ready to do battle. They faced the Dobermen troops who stood by waiting to be unleashed. What a spectacle that would have been had they fired on those old people. The bank opened and they were allowed to cash their checks.

In early March U.S. SouthCom officials announced the start of regularly scheduled training activities.

The Foreign Minister of Panama called a news conference to protest that the exercises were being held without the authorization of the Panamanian government and in violation of the Panama Canal Treaty. SouthCom officials said this was a routine annual exercise that dates back to 1980, and was a continuing effort to train for the defense of the Panama Canal, and that the Panamanian Defense Forces were notified in advance. These word skirmishes were becoming a daily occurrence.

Tensions increased between the Noriega regime and the U.S. government. Embassy officials were told that Panama no longer would exonerate our household effects from taxes since we did not recognize the Noriega government. The embassy advised us to send our important photographs and documents out of the country, such as marriage licenses, divorce papers, birth certificates, etc. We were also told to pack a small bag and keep in the trunk of our cars. Bad times were about to get worse. Following their advice I packed a small bag with a change of clothing and bottled water in case we had to leave running. I carried extra money with me.

On March 15, 1988, the PAO was declared *persona non grata* and given 48 hours to leave the country.

The embassy issued a response that said, "The U.S. does not take orders from despots."

He did not leave and was given a bodyguard. The Noriega regime regarded the PAO as being too active in getting out news and interviews with President Delvalle for the media, and they wanted him out of the country. The U.S. ambassador went out with four bodyguards, and a backup car. The bodyguards were armed and ready for action.

The security alert for official Americans was raised: other than to work, only go out if absolutely necessary. The ambassador sent out a notice to all American personnel to be in their homes by 9:00 p.m. and to let someone know where they were at all times.

Early in the morning of March 16 there was an attempted coup against Noriega, and shooting was heard in the military cartel. For several hours nobody knew which side was winning. There was joy in our office that a coup attempt was going on. I could only think that at that moment people were dying, and I felt sad. People in the office laughed and began celebrating the end of Noriega. They were crushed when the international press arrived with the news that after the shooting ended Noriega came out onto his balcony smiling and blowing kisses at them. La Pina was still very much in charge. The Dobermen drove up and down Avenue Balboa (outside our office) and a major thoroughfare. They were ready to kick ass. NBC's evening news reported that U.S. troops in Panama could be ready for action in 30 minutes. Why would it take that long? That was not very comforting. And then, there was a deceptive calm. Everybody was on edge expecting something to happen. This was the first time I had ever worked in a country whose government we did not recognize. I wondered how long this could go on. I wondered how long I could go on.

One day Noriega's troops put down huge tacks and nails on the highways leading to our military bases. There were twelve U.S. military bases in Panama, and three minor U.S. military installations. It was an eye-opening experience for me to realize that even with all of those U.S. military bases, Noriega was still threatening Americans.

It was a message to Americans that we would not be able to flee to any of our bases. There were thousands of U.S. troops in Panama, representing the Army, Navy and the Air Force. I would have thought that a dictator of a country the size of Panama would have hesitated before awakening the giant, the giant being the U.S. military. Well, I've been wrong before. The Noriega regime began arresting U.S. soldiers and holding them for hours. They were specifically targeted. It was pure harassment. Everyone was under a terrible strain as we lurched from one incident to another, from one day to the next. Naturally crime increased drastically. Only the gringos and those who worked for them had money. Somehow we learned that the armed guards at our residences were not being paid. The embassy was alarmed since those guards were our first line of defense, and arranged with the owners of our buildings to pay the guards.

The New York Times quoted an embassy official as saying, "Noriega has not harmed a hair on an American head, but we are all terrified."

That was an understatement. Every morning when I drove out of my garage I passed the police who guarded the Minister of Justice who lived next door to me. They glared at me. On Sundays the Dobermen were across the street from the church I attended and they glared. The Dobermen were outside Catholic churches because several times the opposition staged demonstrations at Catholic churches. Catholic priests had been extremely vocal in calling for Noriega to step down. Most of the priests were from other countries and they reduced their calls for his ouster when Noriega hinted that they might be expelled from Panama.

One Sunday newspaper printed a list of 220 Panamanians with the headline that these were the people the U.S. embassy "planned to kill." The article said we had our lists, and they had their lists. Prior to this the same paper printed the U.S. military emergency evacuation plan in Spanish and English. They also printed a list of all American diplomats with our titles and the headline screamed, "U.S. EMBASSY HAS ENOUGH PERSONNEL FOR THREE EMBASSIES!" The article said we had 92 diplomats. Actually that number had been decreased a few years previously. The beat went on.

In one government newspaper Noriega told the Panamanians that they should express to American diplomats in person how unhappy they were at our government's antics. He promised that the next day the newspaper would publish our photos, names and addresses for Panamanians to come to our homes. We had no contingency plans in the event that he did publish our addresses. Communication was definitely lacking at that embassy. I had never felt so uninformed or in such danger. The Papal Nuncio and the British Ambassador met with Noriega and told him that if he printed our addresses some Americans would undoubtedly be killed, and the U.S. military would come down hard on Panama, which, of course, would not have helped the dead Americans. Fortunately for us, Noriega listened to them. The next day he published our photos and names, but not our addresses. We hung tough, but so did Noriega. He was sitting in the cat bird seat and we were out in the friggin' pea patch.

When President Reagan announced that no Americans in Panama could pay any money to the Noriega regime, the embassy was already three months behind in paying its electricity bill. Power was to have been cut off one week previously. It was not. Embassy officials, in their wisdom, said Noriega would not dare cut off our power. A few days later, at 10:00 am on a Sunday morning, Noriega's hit teams went to apartment buildings where American diplomats lived. They cut off power to most apartments, but not all. Perhaps their lists were incomplete. Five embassy families lived in my building, but power was only cut to two apartments. Mine was not cut. It was panic time since no contingency plans had been made. In most cases, wives and children moved to hotels while the husbands stayed in the hot, dark apartments to prevent break-ins. Embassy officials were unable to make decisions about what people should do. Families grumbled about the $58 per person per day allowed and $8 per person for food. That is not the per diem for Panama, mind you, but that was all the embassy wanted to spring for. Eight dollars for food would not pay for one meal at the Marriott Hotel where most families moved to.

On Monday morning the hit teams hit U.S. offices, including the embassy, and shut off electricity. In our office building they cut off power to all embassy offices except for USIS. Suddenly the embassy was talking about putting people in apartment hotels for a long time rather than pay the electricity bill. Wiser heads prevailed, and, as quiet as it was kept, the bill was finally paid. Between the Noriega regime and my government, such as it was, I felt as if I were in an insane asylum. We knew who was in charge in Panama. We didn't know who was in charge in the U.S.

As a result of the upheaval and stress, all U.S. diplomats were given a one time only Rest and Recreation leave (R&R). We had a choice of going to Curacao or to the U.S. Most of us chose to go to the U.S. We all needed that break. For me, never had home seemed so wonderful. I had planned for Mother to go to Panama with me and I had her ticket. I spent two weeks at home and it was almost time to return to Panama. A dear friend from Liberian days, Dorothy Anderson, called me a few days before our scheduled departure. She was alarmed when she learned that Mother was going back with me.

Dorothy's voice was full of concern when she said, "Charlene, I've been reading about what's going on in Panama. Are you sure that it's safe for Mrs. Parks to go to Panama with you?"

I hesitated before answering because the truth was no American in Panama was safe. Panama was extremely volatile.

Dorothy added, "What if something happens while you are at work and you can't get back home? Mrs. Parks will be alone. Think about it."

I knew she was right. When we hung up, I told Mother what Dorothy had said.

To my surprise Mother replied, "Well, I've been wondering about that, but if you want me to go, I'll go."

I almost cried. I needed her company. I needed a loving face there. But I knew Panama was a fluid situation. Diplomats are fond of calling a situation "fluid" when all hell is breaking loose and nobody knows who's on first base, and if things can get worse, they will.

I told Mother that perhaps she should stay at home, and she seemed relieved. I had been looking forward to having her accompany me back. I felt so alone in Panama. It was with a heavy heart that I left home and returned to Panama. I know Mother hated seeing me go back into the unknown. She knew what was going on in Panama even though I didn't discuss it with her. I had become aware that since I had joined the Foreign Service, Mother listened intently to world news. For the first time in my life, I was not ready to leave Indiana. Even with its flaws and bass-ackwards attitudes, it was where my family and friends were – people who loved me.

At the airport in Miami another passenger told me that Panama was not letting any American diplomats into the country. My spirits soared when I heard that. He said the previous week Panamanian airport authorities had turned away three American diplomats who had visas issued by the Panamanian ambassador in Washington who the Noriega regime no longer recognized. The only visas his regime now recognized were those issued by an official appointed by Noriega in Tampa, Florida. Throughout the flight I clutched my rosary and smoked while praying that the Panamanian authorities would not allow me back into the country. I was not thrilled with the idea of a return flight, but if I could leave Panama for good, I would bite the bullet, clutch the rosary tighter and puff on more cigarettes on the return flight. I was excited at the thought of getting out of Panama.

We landed and I got out my Diplomatic passport and proceeded to Customs. My ears were waiting for those blessed words telling me I would not be admitted. They immediately let me back into Panama without a whimper. I was crushed.

The office driver met me and drove me home where I found that Marva, my secretary, had remembered to turn on lights in the apartment, and she left me a welcome back pie in the fridge. I was back into the fray.

The Noriega regime had been publishing information that the U.S. was going to invade the country in July. Oh, that it were so, I wished. The regime called for the Dignity Battalions (volunteer fighters) to come to Panama City to train. They said that the U.S. Army hospital, Gorgas, had 5000 coffins ready for dead Americans.

The country was in ruins. I knew that it would be a long, long time before it recovered from the economic sanctions. The sanctions didn't touch Noriega. He still had his millions tucked away somewhere. He had been our good buddy a few years ago. Now he could laugh at Uncle Sam because we wanted to get rid of him.

He made it crystal clear that he would not go quietly or gently. My own opinion was that he should have been taken out long ago, before the poor and the hungry turned on us. We were all up the proverbial creek without the proverbial paddle. This post had always been a pisser, but now it was a complete pisser. We were trying to operate in the land of the wild surmise and the outrageous conjecture.

Two American diplomats were picked up and held for several hours. The government denied they had them in custody. Another American diplomat's car was sacked and burned by government troops. Noriega's regime denied responsibility. A number of U.S. soldiers were detained for no cause. The U.S. government refused to recognize the new president of Panama, and we continued trying to ignore strongman Noriega. We should have taken that show on the road.

I often felt as if I were in the Land of Oz. I sat at my desk trying to do cultural programming while around me people were trying to hold onto their very heads. Some were calling for strikes. Others were calling on Noriega to step down. U.S. senators were yapping and threatening. Most of our programming had been put on hold.

While the PAO was on vacation, the Information Officer and I decided to continue our work as if the world was not tumbling around us. I requested American speakers to visit Panama to talk about economics, or anything that used to be of interest. One speaker who came to Panama admitted that she was terrified of coming, but she said she trusted us and since we obviously felt she would be safe, she came. Oh, if she had only known the terror I felt.

The state of affairs was getting too hot for comfort. Suddenly the embassy would only let us cash checks up to $100 a week. I spent more than that every Saturday at the Commissary, not to mention the PX. All of us were over-buying since we knew that we might be shut in for days. There were continuous demonstrations and calls for demonstrations against the U.S. embassy. The bomb threats continued. Through the U.S. Southern Command Television network I watched daily U.S. national evening news to see what happened in Panama while I was at work. Panamanian TV was mum on protests. Noriega had closed some TV stations and the others showed things all rosy and glowing. I found myself thirsting for Africa where quick coups put everybody out of his misery, and the beat went on. Noriega was a past master at psychological warfare. Everybody's nerves were fraying.

One night U.S. troops at one of our bases began shooting. They said they thought they saw something or somebody. There were two hours of shooting. Panamanian newspapers ridiculed the U.S. army saying the soldiers were acting like the Keystone Cops, running around the base shooting at each other. The soldiers said they thought somebody had gotten onto the base that shouldn't have been there. Noriega laughed at their antics. He said they were scared of swaying palm trees. He might not have been far from wrong. Anything was possible in the land of the wild surmise.

At one point the local employees of the embassy and USIS went to speak to the Administrative Counselor at the embassy. They were concerned that the U.S. would abandon them as it did the Foreign Service National employees in Vietnam and they were slaughtered. The Counselor told them to have their passports and birth certificates in order, and he would get back to them. They were also concerned about showing U.S. embassy identification if stopped by the police or soldiers. They had many concerns, and rightly so. People were hungry. Shops were closed. Buses and taxis went on strike. Everybody was edgy and nervous. The U.S. offered Noriega a deal: leave Panama quietly and we would drop all drug charges against him. He wanted to name his replacement, have a say in Army matters, and in effect, have a "Panamanian solution." He rejected the U.S. deal and the U.S. removed all offers from the table.

Our embassy began discussing how best for us to get to our military bases in case we had to leave suddenly. Should we go in a convoy or individually?

Americans in my neighborhood were instructed to try to make it to Fort Clayton, and there were different routes to get there. Of course, I didn't know any of the routes. My Panamanian secretary and I decided that when matters came to a head, I would drive to within a mile of her house, remove my license plate, abandon my car, and walk to her house. I could be mistaken for a black Panamanian as long as I didn't open my mouth. She was my safety net. That was our secret.

All U.S. diplomatic license plates were going to expire in January and since we didn't recognize the reigning government, there would be no more license plates issued to American embassy personnel. All American diplomats would then be driving illegally, and there was a strong possibility that our cars would be confiscated. I ran that risk everyday since I had been driving with expired plates for months. I could not drive outside the city because there were car checks for proper documents. The embassy didn't dwell on unpleasant matters until everybody from the ambassador on down was going to be affected. Then they got very concerned.

They had no answers as usual. They would think about that tomorrow.

Life was interesting during those days. Our scholarship program was as large as ever and university students were beating down the door despite the pro-Noriega newspaper blasting USIS for "infiltrating" the university. One newspaper's headline read: "CIA-USIA infiltration at the University of Panama." I infiltrated it every chance I got. I helped students in international relations put on an international fair.

I was invited back to help judge an English speech contest. I sent books to help the university library. The director of the new Center of Latin Studies at the university met with me to ask for our help for a number of events. So much for infiltration.

Christmas arrived. There was little pomp. Official Americans were still under curfew orders, and nobody really wanted to be on the streets at night. I hosted a Christmas party, and while we tried to enjoy ourselves, everyone's mind was on what was going to happen to Panama. I invited some of my West Indian friends, members of my staff, and some of my Panamanian contacts.

We ate, drank and tried hard to be merry. What a year it had been, but it paled in comparison to what the following year would bring. I somehow knew this would be the last year for the Panama everyone had known. There was little hope. The Americans were to be the saviors, but we blew that.

One year earlier, shortly after I arrived, the ambassador had cabled the Department of State requesting permission to begin a drawdown of embassy staff. He requested a shortening of our tours in Panama for obvious reasons. He proposed keeping only "essential" personnel and sending everybody else home. When the PAO and I discussed whether I should stay or the Assistant CAO, I said she should remain because she was in the middle of selecting candidates for university scholarships. That was her bailiwick; she had been in Panama for several years, and knew the people involved. The CAO did not handle student applications. All U.S. agencies represented in Panama had to approve of the drawdown. Some agencies argued against the drawdown because they wanted their people to remain for various reasons.

There was also a problem of getting people in to replace some of those leaving. No additional American diplomats were being allowed to enter the country. In mid-February, 1989, we learned that the draw down at the embassy was finally going to happen. Only essential personnel would remain in Panama. The rest of us could leave as soon as possible. My belongings had barely been unpacked and they were about to be repacked and returned to the U.S. I was not sorry to leave Panama. I left behind uncertainty, increasing crime, lack of work, and more business closings. The most important thing was that I didn't have to leave running, and my household effects also got out safely. The Americans who left later were not as fortunate. Many of their belongings had been packed and were in a warehouse awaiting shipment to the U.S. They were destroyed when those buildings burned during the U.S. invasion of Panama on December 21, 1989.

The Night They Came for Me

I glory in conflict, that I may hereafter exult in victory.
- Frederick Douglass

The night the soldiers came for me was the night I expected during the 14 months I lived in Panama. I kept a suitcase in my car with a change of clothing and bottled water. I carried my passport and extra money with me daily. I knew we might have to leave quickly, but deep in the recesses of my mind was a thought that perhaps Noriega's men might come for me before I was ready to leave. The night of December 21, 1989, they came.

In December 1989, the U.S. had had enough of Noriega thumbing his nose at us. Noriega's soldiers harassed American diplomats and servicemen. Some U.S. soldiers were stopped, taken to jail and held for hours before the embassy learned about the incident. The ambassador had asked us to keep someone informed of where were going and when we should arrive in an attempt to learn immediately of any unlawful seizures of official Americans. Billboards and newspaper articles mocked our ambassador, his adult daughter, and the deputy chief of mission. The summer of '89 Noriega cocked his leg on Uncle Sam, rigged a presidential election and began killing those who opposed him. On the night of December 21, 1989, American troops invaded Panama searching for Noriega. On the same night some Panamanian soldiers wreaked their own revenge on Americans.

Don and Sara, Americans, were my next door neighbors. Don worked for an American company in Panama. I used to wonder how they would leave Panama if embassy people had to leave quickly. They were not official Americans, i.e., diplomats, so they would not be among those leaving the country first. I felt a lot of compassion for them because they were always so kind to me. They always told me that if I ever felt afraid to stay alone in my huge apartment, that I could come to their apartment.

It was a few days before Christmas, and they were celebrating the arrival earlier that day of their two teenagers, a girl and a boy. Nobody knew that Americans were invading Panama that night. Around 1:00 a.m. the family was awakened by loud banging on the iron grill in front of their apartment door. Don looked through the peephole and was alarmed by what he saw. There were several armed Panamanian soldiers at the door. He signaled to his wife to get the kids up and to get dressed. He wasn't sure what he was going to do, so he stalled for time by telling the soldiers his wife had to get dressed. Don whispered to his son to help his mother and sister drop to the balcony of the apartment below where they could hide. If they missed the balcony, they would land on the rocks below and be killed. They were seven floors up. The soldiers were becoming impatient, and again banged on the iron grill. When Don finally opened the wooden door, he left the iron gate locked. He tried to appear calm. As he talked to the soldiers, Sara went out the window and her son carefully dropped her onto the balcony below. Don told the soldiers that his wife was getting dressed, and he would open the door as soon as she was decent.

The soldiers had no way of knowing that their children were also in the apartment. As Don stalled for time, the soldiers went to the apartment next door, where I had lived. A Latin United Nations representative opened the door. Don heard the soldiers say they thought an American (me!) lived there. The man told them I had left several months ago.

Meanwhile, in their apartment, their daughter was too frightened to go over the balcony. The son went next. By now the soldiers were threatening to shoot their way in. The son went back up to their balcony to help his sister. He told his father to go ahead and he would get his sister down somehow. Don went over the balcony and joined his wife below. Still the daughter would not make the jump. Suddenly they heard the soldiers breaking down the gate. It was now too late for the teenagers to try to get to the balcony below. They huddled in a small flower box beneath the window in the den. One soldier went to the window as others searched the apartment. One soldier dangled his hand outside the window inches away from their heads. Fortunately he never looked down. When the soldiers left, the brother cajoled and finally managed to hoist his sister to the balcony above, and he quickly followed. They hid among huge plants on the 35-ft. balcony.

Sara and Don, hiding on the balcony below their apartment, heard the commotion in their apartment and thought the soldiers had taken their children. The soldiers searched the apartment for the couple, and were furious when they realized they had been cheated of their prey. They moved up to the next floor where an American man lived with his Panamanian wife and children. This was the apartment where Don and Sara's children were hiding on the terrace.

Had the soldiers gone out onto the terrace, they would have found the children for sure. The soldiers said they had to take the American man in for questioning. His wife begged them not to take him, but they insisted he would be returned after questioning. His bullet-riddled body was found the next day.

For the rest of the night Sara and Don huddled on the terrace not knowing where their children were. They thought the solders had taken them away. When dawn came after a long night, the couple timidly knocked on the door of their neighbors whose terrace sheltered them. They were Panamanians. Don said he knew he and Sara were taking a chance since they didn't know which side these people were on, but they had to find their children. The neighbors welcomed them with open arms. Sara sobbed that their children were missing. Two of the neighbors went up to Don and Sara's apartment and searched and called the kids. They weren't there. Sara tearfully asked them to check the rocks below for their bodies. They found nothing. Everyone was now convinced the soldiers had taken the children away.

Meanwhile, the woman upstairs whose husband had been taken away, went out onto her terrace and found the two frightened teenagers. She hugged them, took them inside and told them their parents were searching for them.

The kids had heard the men calling them, but they were afraid it was the soldiers. The family was finally reunited. Don was anxious to get his family to safety. He and some of the men went out onto the streets looking for U.S. soldiers. They didn't have to go far before finding some. Don told them about the Panamanian soldiers searching for them and taking away the other American.

The American soldiers went back to the building with Don, gathered up the family with one suitcase each, and took them to safety at a U.S. military base. On Christmas day they were flown out of Panama on an American military plane.

On New Year's Day Sara called me in Washington and told me what had happened to them. I shivered as I listened to her. I asked her how they were able to get over that balcony and drop to the floor below. She had no idea how they had done it. I wondered if I could have been so brave since I would have been alone. No one knows what he would do in such a situation. Fortunately I was spared that decision since most U.S. diplomats had left the country. I regarded my former neighbors in a new light, with definite respect for their survival skills. I thought how brave, how scared, and how blessed they had been, all at the same time. We will never know whether the soldiers had orders to kill Americans in retaliation for our invasion of Panama, or if these were renegade soldiers. Sara and Don had the angels on their side that night, for which we are all grateful.

Back in Washington, DC

All's well that ends.

- Anon

Back in Washington, DC. It seemed I had just left and I had – 14 months ago.

I had rented my condo. The rental agreement contained a Diplomatic Clause which stated that if I returned to Washington on government orders, the tenants had 30 days to vacate the apartment. My condo was managed by a retired Foreign Service couple who had gone into real estate. The couple living in my condo were outraged that I had returned and wanted my condo back. They went to an attorney who notified my agents that the laws of the District of Columbia superseded the Diplomat Clause. The DC law stated the tenants had 90 days to move out. I was incredulous not to mention upset, angry, and a heap of other things. The agents pleaded with me not to contact the tenants. I reluctantly agreed to let them handle matters. I was staying in temporary quarters that faced the building where my condo was located. Every morning when I got up and opened the drapes, I was looking at my building and yearning to get back into it. When my agents tried to cajole the tenants and offered other choice apartments they could move to, even with me helping to pay for their move, they refused.

Their constant cry was, "But we love this apartment!"

I said to the agent, "Tell them I love it too and that's why I bought it!"

294

On the 87th day they moved out. I had the unit re-carpeted, painted, and then arranged for my hundreds of boxes containing my household effects, to be delivered.

At USIA I was assigned to the Office of Private Sector Programs. I was the Program Officer for political and security affairs and liaison with the Office of European Affairs. I evaluated grant requests and project proposals from private sector organizations, and coordinated the implementation of those programs between our overseas posts and the private sector institutions, including selection of participants, conference speakers and seminar themes. I handled six long-term, highly political and competing non-profit organizations, each with different sets of relational, logistical and political problems and conundrums. The one year in that position was like juggling six balls and I am not a juggler. I was often called upon by the USIA Director or Deputy Director to sit in on meetings with disgruntled, political operatives representing one of my organizations whose unhappiness with aspects of their grants resulted in thinly-veiled threats of taking their complaints directly to key members of Congress. It was no wonder that only Foreign Service Officers handled these programs. Anybody else would have been terrified of those outside organizations who knew little of government structure and guidelines, and cared less about the limits they were held to.

I remember that one organization had an annual fundraiser. It was quite a gala affair to which I was invited since my office partially funded this organization. Each ambassador in Washington hosted a dinner for a certain number of guests who had paid mightily for the honor. My particular group began with dinner at the home of the Peruvian Ambassador. I met a key Democrat that evening and told him that I had been a Peace Corps volunteer in Peru.

Later, when he addressed the gathering I was surprised to hear him mention me and tell them that I had served as a volunteer in Peru and now I was a Foreign Service Officer, still representing the best of my country. Following the dinner, guests from all the embassies met for an evening of champagne and dancing at the Russian Embassy. I kept my invitation for years until the U.S. and Russian developed more cordial relations. I knew that at some point, probably during one of my security clearance updates, an FBI agent would ask me why I went into the Russian Embassy on such and such a date. It was quite an evening. I also was privileged to attend a seminar breakfast at Georgetown University which some of our foreign visitors participated in. The main speakers were former President Jimmy Carter, accompanied by Mrs. Rosalynn Carter, and Professor Madeleine Albright. I was very impressed by her and overjoyed when President Clinton appointed her as Secretary of State.

My next assignment was announced and it was Cultural Affairs Officer in Dakar, Senegal. While I was not thrilled with the cultural part since I prefer the Information side, I did look forward to going to a French speaking African post. When I told Mother of my new assignment, she asked me not to go. For some reason I did not question her. I knew she was not well. She had had surgery months earlier, and recovered nicely from it. I told her I would see what I could do to get out of the assignment. I spoke to my career counselor who was not happy. She pointed out that everybody's parents were aging and not well, and that Foreign Service Officers were expected to be in the field after two to three years back in the U.S.

Finally, my assignment was canceled and Mother was delighted. I had looked forward to it, as it was going to be my last overseas post. I planned to retire after Senegal. Now I needed another two year assignment in Washington. My former boss in the Office of International Visitors Programs asked me to come back. With one exception, the office staff was the same. It would be like going back home. I had forgotten the problems with clerical staff. At first I turned it down and then I thought about it. I would be my own boss basically. I would not be dealing with organizations with political antennae that often reached out and grabbed me, and I knew the cast of characters at the program agencies we dealt with. Most of the staff was happy with my return.

Almost immediately problems began. I interviewed one young, black woman for clerk, among others, including young, black males. I felt sorry for this particular woman because she was heavy, some called her fat. I felt that if I did not hire her, that nobody else would. Her former office gave her a glowing review and I took her. My heart rules my head. Almost immediately files were misplaced or lost. The program officers began complaining about her work. There were always major mistakes, and they had to make her do their work over and over. Meanwhile, the other clerk felt overburdened because the program officers then began giving her their work. Everybody was unhappy. I spoke to the clerk to ask what the problems were and why couldn't she file properly. She had no answer. Finally she felt that I was complaining too much and she went to the EEO office. Ah, yes, that is the favorite thing for people to do in Washington who are incompetent and/or ignorant of the rules.

The EEO officer who spoke to me knew how concerned I was about black clerks. We talked about this clerk's problems. She talked to the clerk at length and a few days later the officer called me.

She said, "Charlene, we have it! I now know what her problem is!"

"What?" I exclaimed.

She replied, "The problem is that she is legally blind!"

I was horrified. Nobody knew that. She had never told anyone in the agency that she could barely see. The EEO officer felt there were some health problems and sent her to a doctor who in turn sent her to an ophthalmologist who diagnosed her as being legally blind. I called her in and told her that she had been cheating herself. Had anybody known that, she would have had a job that did not include constantly trying to read and file and type. She thanked me for getting her help. She was removed from my office and given a job that she was more capable of handling. I was happy for her.

Interviews for another clerk began. And the selection process was the same rigmarole. I hired another young woman who turned out to be unpleasant to everyone in the office. I had a few months to go before retiring. Foreign Service Officers can retire after 20 years because of our demanding assignments at difficult posts, learning new languages and new cultures, and packing every two or three years. I received credit for Peace Corps service and I had thousands of hours of sick leave which contributed to my early retirement.

The agency began offering buyouts to Civil Service employees, but not to Foreign Service employees. I wanted a buyout desperately. I was ready to leave.

I hated leaving with a sour taste in my mouth, but I knew that as long as I worked in Washington, that sour taste would remain. When Foreign Service women got together the talk was always about the problems of working with clerical staff in Washington. They only have to show up at work to get promoted. We could not understand that it was all but automatic after one year. In the Foreign Service we have to almost storm heaven to get a promotion. Although I must confess that I received a number of promotions during my years.

One of my friends, also an FSO, said, "I'm glad one of us is being promoted. Every time I see the Promotion List your name is on it."

I had to laugh, but it was true. And after our hostages were released from Iran, President Carter gave all government employees a 9% raise and he gave Foreign Service Officers an 18% raise.

By 1994 I was tired of pushing, pulling, and cajoling resentful clerical staff while trying to manage an office. They were the typical problems of people being hired who had few skills and a complete lack of professionalism in the workplace. I planned to retire in January, 1995, when I could take the State Department Retirement Course which was one week of classes designed for those who wanted to work after retirement and three months for a job search, and being paid for those three months. January of 1995 seemed far off.

In an August issue of Essence magazine my horoscope read:

"YOUR YEAR AHEAD: January 1995 marks the beginning of a new cycle. Good riddance to tiresome folks and situations."

Later in August I had a call from the Foreign Service Personnel Office. I was told that 1994 would be the last year that USIA would participate in the State Department Retirement Course because it had become too expensive. The officer said that because I had registered so far in advance I had been given permission to take the course which began in the Fall. I could take the three month course and return to the agency to work for one month to fulfill my retirement requirement, and then I would be officially retired. I agreed to that stipulation. I was ecstatic. I could leave the agency in one month. I had a lot of annual leave to use or lose, so I began taking several days off each week. A few weeks later a new program officer joined my staff. I was the only one who knew that he was my successor. I asked my boss to keep secret my departure.

She was not happy and wanted to host a farewell function, but I insisted that I wanted to quietly slip away.

On my last day in the office, I wrote a farewell note to my staff on my computer, hit the Send key, picked up my purse and left the office, ostensibly for lunch. My heart sang. It was over. I had three months of paid vacation. I would return to the agency for one final month of work in another office, and then I would be happily retired. I sold my condo. The government-hired packers arrived to pack some 400 plus boxes of my personal effects to send to Indiana. I shipped my car, and I arrived in Indianapolis on May 1, 1995. What a journey it had been since I left the cornfields of Indiana in 1956 for freedom and control of my destiny. It had been quite a ride.

P*ostscript*

I am now retired. I have tried to serve my country and mankind. The people whose poverty I shared in Peru will always remember that Americans cared. It was the United Nation's mission of service to mankind that also spoke to my soul. Years later as a diplomat in the U.S. Foreign Service, the values that enabled me to be an effective Peace Corps volunteer and United Nations international secretary, enabled me to be an effective diplomat. My life has truly been one glorious experience after another.

I got settled in Indy, unpacked all 400 plus boxes with help every day from Mama Gladys Jackson, my "other mother" as I called her. She and Daddy Dougie Jackson, were the people I used to call when I had problems or needed to break unpleasant news to Mother. They were such wonderful, loving "other parents." Mother never thought I would retire to Indianapolis, and once she said, "I know you'll come back to see Gladys and Doug."

For my birthday in August, 1995, Mother gave me the gift of a precious, 2 yr. old black miniature poodle, named Ebony. Ebony and her mother belonged to a friend of mine and I thought she was precious. Mother bought her for me, and the moment she was put in my arms, she thought I was her mother. She was very special. Mother would come over and spend several

300

nights with us just to play with Ebony. She loved animals as did everybody in our family.

I had been back in Indiana only four months when Mother had a heart attack and died after an angioplasty procedure. My world was knocked from under me. I wanted to postpone her funeral. A funeral meant that Mother was definitely gone. I didn't want to acknowledge that. Mama Gladys stayed at my side and she pushed and pulled ever so gently to get me to make decisions and arrangements. I thought my grandmother's death was devastating, but when Mother left me, it was a terrible shock. I had planned for us to travel a bit to see some of the U.S. I wanted to give her a surprise birthday party in November. There were so many things I wanted to do for her. Our family was not the kind that talks about loving each other, and when she began to say it to me in the past few years, I disliked it. It didn't seem real. I needed it said during my teenage years, when the world weighed on me so heavily. I loved and resented her at the same time. I always wanted to hurl accusations at her and accuse her of not being there when Walt abused me, and I wanted to ask her how she could believe the lies he told her about me. That is what still hurts after all these years. I understand now that Walt wanted Mother to get rid of me. How I wish she had.

After retirement I wanted to indulge my love for animals. As a volunteer animal handler at the Indianapolis Zoo, it was a privilege to cuddle and discuss animals such as chinchillas, an opossum, a pink-toed tarantula, various snakes, blue-tongued skinks, bearded dragons, ferrets, parrots, tortoises, rabbits, guinea pigs, millipedes and giant Madagascan cockroaches, along with an array of other amazing critters.

It was a treat to take the animals to schools, nursing homes, juvenile delinquent facilities, and festivals, and to share with the public information about the marvelous creatures that share the earth with us and to let them touch these amazing ambassadors for their species.

My precious Ebony left me in October, a few weeks before her 14th birthday. I talked to her and she understood every word I said. She could communicate with me like no other dog has. She made me feel like I was her mother, and she was my special daughter. She fought so hard to live. Her vet fought so hard. We did every test known to man. I don't know what happened to her little body. I tried so hard to save her, to keep her with me, healthy and happy. It became difficult for her to walk. She barely ate. We were at the vet's every day her last week. The bills were astronomical, but I didn't care what it cost to save her life. She was my daughter and I would have paid any price to keep her alive.

Finally her vet said, "Charlene, you're done all you can and more than most. Let her go in peace."

I got a friend to drive us to the vet and I held Ebony and cried all the way. I thanked her for being a wonderful daughter and for teaching me and others of the special love of animals. I asked her to forgive my impatience at times, the times I was away longer than I meant to be, and I told her she was going to play with Granny Bertha in heaven. I loved her so much. Even now, five months later, I can't talk about Ebony without crying. She was my last present from Mother and a beautiful and special daughter. Maybe one day Ebony, Mother and I will play together again. I miss them both.

I come from a people of great humanity, people who possess a unique sense of justice and fair play. I grew up feeling that people were basically good even though the chaos in the world around me, and even in my home, told another story. The values learned many years ago both at home and in the years of interacting with those less fortunate, enable me to continue to be caring, sympathetic, and always available to help others. I belong to that great mélange of colors and cultures that make the United States the diverse nation that it is. To serve others is my calling; to serve humbly those much less fortunate; to be the voice for those with no voice; to try to right wrongs, and to tweak the consciences of others. I have been privileged to serve women in prison, animals in orphanages and zoos, the elderly in nursing homes, and children by being a Child Advocate. As Aunt Bess always said, "Thanks is not money, but it spends just the same."

My newest calling is to minister to Roman Catholic priests in prison. These are priests who have been accused of sexually abusing others. Not every priest in prison is guilty. The sex abuse scandal erupted in 2002 and when the bishops began offering money to accusers without any proof that they had been abused, more and more accusers appeared with their hands out. Many innocent priests were abruptly removed from their parishes without the benefit of counsel or trial. Victim advocate groups found "victims" and raised their voices of hate against the church.

Many accusers claimed to suddenly remember being abused 30 or 40 years ago by some priests. Without further ado, the mighty Bishops threw them out, and the state arrested them. Juries quickly sent them to prison, and the accusers walked away with considerable amounts of money from the church, as did their attorneys.

The conviction of priests became a new livelihood for the lawyers who prosecuted them. The priests usually were represented by poorly prepared public defenders. These priests were isolated and totally alone during their trials. Often their families deserted them because of embarrassment.

After one priest had been killed in prison, I wondered how others were faring, and I searched the Internet to find out where some were incarcerated. I wrote to them asking about their treatment in prison. Several replied to my letter. The research became too depressing, and I put away the article I was writing. I got it out two years later and completed it. I demanded to know why our church officials have never asked for prayers and forgiveness for those in prison. They always ask for prayers for the accusers. Bishops apparently don't visit priests in prison. What kind of shepherds are these who abandon their sheep when they make a misstep?

My article was published in the July 20, 2007, issue of the *National Catholic Reporter*, and the response was overwhelming. I received e-mails, letters and telephone calls from priests and lay people, and my article was passed around in prisons by incarcerated priests. They all said it was time for somebody to stand up and ask for forgiveness and love for priests in prison. Everyone, of course, did not support my stance, including some at my own parish, with the exception of those I love and respect. Not all of my friends supported me.

One friend said,

"I haven't exactly come around to your degree of compassion for them (priests in prison), but I support you in your convictions."

A priest wrote from prison,

"I say this from my heart, and from all the fallen priests who love you, you are more a priest and a bishop than many who call themselves such..."

A wise, loved and respected woman in Alaska says,
"Your suffering from abuse has tendered your heart and soul.
It has developed in you a profound ability to identify with the fallen and the grief-stricken."

Despite the rash of laicizations carried out by the church, imprisoned priests remain priests. Their priesthood can never be taken away, according to the vows they take: "Thou art a priest forever, after the order of Melchizedek."

I will never understand why our church has washed its hands of the ones who need the love and support of our church now more than ever. I write to a number of these priests and the only thing each one asks for is prayers for their families, for their accusers, and for themselves. I ask God daily to envelope them in a gigantic hug. May they feel His presence today and every day.

Christ Is Present

Into this world, this demented inn,
in which there is no room for him at all,
Christ has come uninvited.
But because he cannot be at home in it,
His place is with those who do not belong,
who are rejected by power
because they are regarded as weak,
those who are discredited,
who are denied the status of persons,
tortured and exterminated.
With those for whom there is no room,
Christ is present in this world.
He is mysteriously present in those
for whom there seems to be nothing
but the world at its worst.

- *Thomas Merton*

Made in the USA
Middletown, DE
24 November 2015